Research Papers

Research Papers

Fifteenth Edition

William Coyle
Late of Florida Atlantic University

Joe Law
Wright State University

WADSWORTH
CENGAGE Learning

Australia • Brazil • Japan • Korea • Mexico • Singapore • Spain • United Kingdom • United States

WADSWORTH
CENGAGE Learning

Research Papers, Fifteenth Edition
William Coyle and Joe Law

Senior Publisher: Lyn Uhl

Acquisitions Editor: Kate Derrick

Senior Assistant Editor: Kelli Strieby

Editorial Assistant: Jake Zucker

Senior Media Editor:
    Cara Douglass-Graff

Marketing Manager: Jenn Zourdos

Marketing Coordinator: Ryan Ahern

Senior Marketing Communications
    Manager: Stacey Purviance Taylor

Associate Content Project Manager:
    Anne Finley

Senior Art Director: Jill Ort

Print Buyer: Susan Carroll

Senior Rights Acquisition Account
    Manager: Katie Huha

Production Service:
    Matrix Productions Inc.

Senior Photo Editor: Jennifer Meyer Dare

Photo Researcher: Megan Lessard

Cover Designer: Wing Ngan

Cover Image: © Caro/Alamy

Compositor: Macmillan Publishing
    Solutions

For product information and technology assistance, contact us at **Cengage Learning Customer & Sales Support, 1-800-354-9706**

For permission to use material from this text or product, submit all requests online at **www.cengage.com/permissions.** Further permissions questions can be e-mailed to **permissionrequest@cengage.com.**

Library of Congress Control Number: 2009922977

ISBN-13: 978-0-547-19081-5

ISBN-10: 0-547-19081-6

Wadsworth
20 Channel Center Street
Boston, MA 02210
USA

Cengage Learning products are represented in Canada by Nelson Education, Ltd.

For your course and learning solutions, visit **www.cengage.com.**

Purchase any of our products at your local college store or at our preferred online store, **www.ichapters.com.**

Printed in the United States of America
3 4 5 6 7 8 14 13 12 11 10

Brief Contents

Detailed Contents

3   Using Basic Reference Sources   47

4   Evaluating and Recording Material Responsibly   61

5 Avoiding Plagiarism   79

6 Constructing Your Outline   93

10 Documenting a Paper APA Style   203

Appendix A

Abbreviations and Basic Terms   227

Appendix B

Chicago Manual of Style (CMS)   233

To the Instructor

Few moments are more pleasing than those in which the mind is concerting measures for a new undertaking.

The Rambler, no. 297

Much has changed in the fifty years that have passed since William Coyle's *Research Papers* first appeared in 1959, particularly the ways in which students can gather and record information. It is possible to search the card catalogs of a number of libraries simultaneously, retrieve the full text of a journal article and download it as a computer file, distribute questionnaires worldwide via e-mail, view rare manuscripts, and do any number of other things undreamed of in the mid-twentieth century. Despite such transformations in the tools and materials used in research, however, the basic tasks remain the same. Writers still must determine a topic, widen their understanding of it, develop a working hypothesis, plan and draft their work, and eventually produce a paper that presents their claim in a well-documented argument. And, along the way, they should expect to revise their thinking about the topic and return to earlier "steps" they had thought they had completed.

The fifteenth edition of *Research Papers* reflects all of these aspects of writing a research paper in a new century. That is, while it provides guidance for such things as evaluating sources on the Internet and documenting a posting to an online discussion group, it also continues to stress the importance of planning and revising in crafting a paper.

New to This Edition

Two sample papers are new to this edition—James Kebler's paper on John P. Parker and Melissa Lofts's paper on the benefits of breastfeeding—and Paul Sanchez's paper on animal hoarding has been significantly revised. All three draw more substantially on online sources than samples in earlier editions. In addition, facing-page commentary has been added to the APA paper.

Getting Started

All too often students approach a writing assignment in a haphazard manner, trusting inspiration or luck to carry them from one sentence to the next. The term *research process* and the description of a step-by-step procedure may mislead them into assuming that writing is a sequence of mechanical activities conducted like a precision drill. To be understandable and clear, a description of research writing must be sequential; but the actual writing, of course, will not follow a linear progression. Still, following a systematic procedure in writing their research papers should make them better writers and, perhaps, better students as well.

Getting a paper under way is often the most difficult phase of the writing process. Students should be urged to search for a topic that truly interests them. If they find one, they may discover, perhaps to their surprise, that research can be enjoyable. Chapter 1 suggests such preliminary techniques as a mental inventory, a research log, and brainstorming. Also discussed are two considerations often given insufficient attention by inexperienced writers—determining the purpose of a paper and identifying its potential audience.

Using the Library

Students are often bewildered by their first encounter with an academic library, and recent innovations like online catalogs and computer searching may heighten their apprehension. A single long chapter on the library might be rather intimidating, so general library search strategies (including Internet searches) are explained in Chapter 2, and specialized reference tools are described and illustrated in Chapter 3. The latter chapter emphasizes periodical indexes. The ability to use such works in print or in electronic form could be a valuable by-product of a student's research project. Chapters 2 and 3 list many more general and specialized reference works.

Finding, Evaluating, and Organizing Material

Today students often wish to rely solely on information found on the Internet, in many cases without stopping to evaluate its reliability or usefulness. *Research Papers* encourages them to balance those resources with books and periodicals—and to assess all of those sources critically. In addition, Chapter 4 suggests still other sources of information, such as interviews and direct observation. For recording notes, computerization and the use of photocopies are increasingly common strategies, perhaps even the dominant mode. No matter what medium a student uses—note cards, photocopies, downloaded computer files—the principles recommended here will still apply. Because plagiarism, either accidental or intentional, can occur during the collection of material and also in the actual writing of a paper, this subject is discussed in Chapter 5, which comes between the sections of the book dealing with collecting information and those dealing with writing the paper.

Writing the Paper

There are few subjects on which composition teachers disagree so drastically as the purpose and the value of outlining. Some feel that devising a logical outline is an effective way of ensuring unity and coherence; some insist that each essay is unique and should develop its own structure by a gradual, organic process. For proponents of outlining, Chapter 6 discusses outlines from a fairly conventional point of view and contains exercises involving outlining procedures and conventions.

To emphasize that a successful paper is usually composed in stages, not dashed off in a single sitting, the rough draft is discussed in Chapter 7 and the final copy in Chapter 8. Various methods of introducing quotations are illustrated; students are encouraged to blend quotations into their text and, in fact, to summarize borrowed material rather than overload a paper with quotations. These chapters also suggest that students learn to take advantage of the many features available in word processing packages as aids in both developing their ideas and producing the final product. Students can move large blocks of text and quickly produce multiple versions of sentences or paragraphs as they search for the best expression of their ideas. Although manual typewriters have all but disappeared, many writers use a computer as though it were one, typing a new header on each page and centering titles manually. Students should be advised to learn how their software can handle these areas as well. Students should consult handbooks for mechanics, but a summary of punctuation marks as they are used with quotations (pages 112–113) is included for quick reference.

Chapter 8 discusses the revision of a paper, including the importance of conciseness, accuracy, and gender-neutral language. Sample papers in Chapters 9 and 10 illustrate different styles of documentation, but they can also be useful examples of various types of papers. During the early stages of the research assignment, you might ask students to read all four papers to get a general impression of content, style, and manuscript form.

Documenting a Paper

The MLA style of documentation is dominant in English courses, and it receives the most detailed treatment in this book. The forms recommended are those described in the seventh edition of the *MLA Handbook for Writers of Research Papers* (2009). The citation of electronic media is covered in detail. Citing references within the text and keying the citations to a list of Works Cited is easy to master, and students quickly come to appreciate the simplicity and the efficiency of this procedure. Some students' styles improve because in-text citation facilitates the blending of quotations into their text. Because a citation in parentheses is so much easier to write than a footnote or an endnote, it is possible that the incidence of plagiarism will be reduced. The features of MLA style are illustrated in Chapter 9 in a sample paper with commentary on the facing pages. Because many instructors assign literary topics for research papers, a brief paper on Kate Chopin's "The Story of an Hour" also is included in Chapter 9.

Because the discussion of documentation takes up more space in this book than important matters like content, organization, and style, perhaps students should be reminded that bulk is not always a measure of importance. A student using MLA style should know the standard forms for books and periodicals (pages 133–134 and pages 142–143). For a source that deviates from the norm, an example can be found by consulting the checklist on page 132. A second checklist (page 132) is an index to special problems that are illustrated by bibliographic examples.

The style recommended by the American Psychological Association (APA) is described in Chapter 10 and is illustrated by a sample paper. This chapter, which deals with both print and electronic sources, follows the fifth edition of the *Publication Manual of the American Psychological Association* (2001). If your students plan to major in one of the social sciences or in education, you might want them to document their papers in APA style. Actually, MLA and APA styles are similar enough that a student who masters one can readily adapt to the other. The other documentation system your students are likely to encounter is the *Chicago Manual of Style* (15th ed., Chicago: U of Chicago P, 2003). It is described briefly in Appendix B.

Research Papers can be adapted to whatever degree of supervision you consider appropriate. Students who have written research papers in high school may need little classroom discussion of research procedures and can use the book as a "self-paced" guide supplemented by individual conferences with you. If, on the other hand, your students are not familiar with research techniques, *Research Papers* follows the preparation of a paper from the search for a topic to the final proofreading and is organized in sections that can be assigned on a day-to-day basis. The book is also suitable for group research projects, in which three or four students investigate a subject cooperatively—a teaching procedure that some instructors find effective. Collaborative research is discussed in the *Instructor's Manual*, which is available from Cengage Learning. The manual also contains notes on each chapter, some supplementary exercises, and answer keys to exercises when needed.

Like a special family dinner, *Research Papers* contains more of everything than is actually necessary. There are more exercises than most instructors will use, so you can select the ones that best meet the needs of a class or individual students. There are more reference works listed in Chapters 2 and 3 than any one student will need, but the range of reference works and the descriptions of various documentation styles should make the book useful to students when they take courses in other departments. Although many students sell or discard textbooks as soon as a course is over, they should be encouraged to retain *Research Papers* for future use.

The headnote quotations for each chapter are taken from the writings of Samuel Johnson, an exemplar of diligence and downright common sense; they may sustain both you and your students through the trials and triumphs of research.

A Farewell

I am saddened to note the passing of William Coyle. His name remains on the textbook he first published half a century ago, and I trust that it remains true to his vision.

Acknowledgments

I would like to express gratitude to the staff of the Paul Laurence Dunbar Library at Wright State University for their assistance, confirming the wisdom of this manual's advice to consult a librarian when questions arise. I am particularly grateful to the Wright State University Libraries and to the administrators of OhioLINK for permission to reproduce illustrations demonstrating features of the online card catalog and sample online databases.

I am indebted to the following reviewers for their helpful comments and suggestions: Christine Ferguson, Scottsdale Community College; Karen Herreid, Riverland Community College; Steve Holland, Muscatine Community College; Kristen Holland, Franklin University; Michael Hricik, Westmoreland County Community College; and Jeremy Venema, Mesa Community College.

JOE LAW

To the Student

> *Composition is, for the most part, an effort of slow diligence and steady perseverance, to which the mind is dragged by necessity or resolution, from which the attention is every moment starting to more delightful amusements.*
>
> The Adventurer, no. 138

Writing, as Samuel Johnson pointed out so long ago, is hard work. However, the sustained diligence it requires can also bring rewards—delight, even—if you have chosen to investigate a topic that arouses your curiosity and stirs your imagination. Developing and writing a good research paper can also have practical benefits in acquainting you with procedures and skills that you will need in future courses. In any field you can expect to be required to use the library efficiently, to interpret and organize ideas, and to document borrowed materials. Because *Research Papers* is designed to be useful to you throughout your college career, it contains far more reference works and examples of documentation than you will need for a single paper. It has been made as inclusive as possible so that it can be used as a guide in advanced courses. Even if you usually sell textbooks back to the bookstore, you would be wise to keep this one on your bookshelf.

Documentation (listing the sources used in a paper and crediting a source for each piece of borrowed language or summarized information) seems daunting to some students and distracts them from more important matters like organizing material logically and writing clearly. The system of documentation used in this manual is that of the Modern Language Association (MLA style). It is simple and easy to use. Do not be intimidated by the lengthy set of examples in Chapter 9. Once you master the basic forms for a book (pages 133–134) and a periodical (pages 142–143), you can adapt variant forms to them. Another system in widespread use is that of the American Psychological Association (APA style), which is described and illustrated in Chapter 10. If you major in education or one of the social sciences, you will need to become familiar with this style. Actually, APA and MLA styles are similar enough that if you master one, you can easily adapt to the other. The intricacies of documentation are not as important as finding effective support for a suitable topic and writing the results in a pleasing and appropriate style.

The ability to gather, interpret, and organize information is a valuable skill in college and in almost any business or profession. The purpose of this manual is to help you attain and use that skill.

JOE LAW

Research
Papers

Shaping Your Topic

It is indeed true that there is seldom any necessity of looking far or inquiring long for a proper subject.

The Rambler, no. 184

Everyone engages in some form of research almost every day, though usually without thinking of it as research. If you have a free evening and want to go to a movie, you may pick up a newspaper or go online and look through the movie reviews to help you decide what you want to see. Or you may ask your friends for their recommendations. If you're in the market for a new car, you may search the Internet for the one that best fits your needs and your budget, and you may look for the best deal on that model in the same way. Anyone who wants to decide what college to attend, predict which team will win the Super Bowl, invest in stock, buy a house, plan a vacation, or find the best price on a pair of sneakers will need to conduct some form of research to achieve those goals.

Research is just as important in people's professional lives. Farmers watch the commodities market, politicians study polls, physicians constantly learn about new drugs and medical procedures, accountants must keep up with changing tax codes each year, lawyers search out precedents to apply to new cases at hand, purchasing agents find the best source for materials, teachers learn new teaching strategies and technologies, and managers determine the effectiveness of a company's advertising campaigns. In short, in one form or another, everyone carries out some sort of research all the time.

For students, research often takes the form of research papers. Instructors in various courses may assign papers on street gangs, term limits for legislators, the Vichy government during World War II, affirmative action, the film version of a Jane Austen novel, or any of a thousand other topics.

The main difference between academic research and other types is the conditions under which it is carried out. Research undertaken in a class will probably emphasize the process itself. You will have to select and limit a topic, you probably will be asked to report on your progress along the way, and you will produce a formal document at the end of the process. Although professional and personal research also involves selecting and narrowing a topic, you are less likely to be conscious of it. Such things as knowing you need to replace a printer at work and deciding to find out what other movies a particular actor has made will automatically narrow the topic *and* scope of your research for those purposes. There is usually an end product too, whether it takes the form of an action, an informal conversation, or a short memo.

This book concentrates on the more formal sorts of research you will be asked to do for your classes, but in carrying out the activities described here you should be looking for ways to draw on this experience to do research in other courses and outside school as well.

Conducting Your Research

In conducting research, as the second syllable of the word implies, you *search* for information. As the first syllable implies, searching calls for *re*peated effort. But looking for material is only part of your task; you also analyze, interpret, evaluate, organize, and write the results of your search. The first steps in this procedure are choosing a suitable topic, finding a tentative central purpose or thesis, watching for useful books and journals, and considering aspects of the topic that might make up the basic plan of your paper.

Although you will use this book to prepare a research paper for your composition class, it will acquaint you with a basic research process applicable to future assignments in any of your courses, from brief reports to full-scale term papers. Preparing a research paper is not as systematic as the word *process* suggests, but in general you follow these steps:

1. You begin with a broad *subject* area and a general idea, a provisional conjecture about that subject (a hypothesis).
2. As you read and think about your subject and consider your purpose and prospective audience, you narrow the subject to a *topic.*
3. As you determine what you hope to accomplish in your paper, you reduce your original hypothesis into a definite idea about your topic—a *thesis.*
4. You investigate your topic by reading books and articles and by exploring other sources of information in search of material to support your thesis and then recording it on *note cards* or some other easily retrievable format.
5. You organize your notes in a sensible *plan.*
6. You write the results of your research in an organized essay, *documenting* the sources of all borrowed facts and opinions.

Laying out the research process as six discrete steps is somewhat misleading because preparing a research paper—like all writing—is not a linear procedure. You will often be engaged in two or more phases of the process at the same time. Occasionally you will need to turn back to a phase already discussed in class, and at other times you will need to look ahead to a phase not yet covered. As in most endeavors, there will be false starts, duplication of effort, changes of direction, wasted time, and outright blunders. To minimize such frustrations, this book traces the procedure from the search for a topic to the final proofreading. Following the general pattern of this process will save you time and trouble, but do not consider it a set of unalterable rules. No two people work in exactly the same way, and you should adapt the suggested procedures to your own work habits.

Making Preliminary Decisions

As you begin your research, considering some basic questions about the nature of your paper, your purpose, and your audience may help you find a workable topic.

The Nature of Your Paper

Be certain that you know whether your instructor expects a *report* or an *argument.* The first is a record of your research, and the second develops a viewpoint about that research. For example, explaining the operation of state lotteries would be a report; contending that lotteries are unfair because they are played by low-income people and, in effect, reduce taxes for nonplayers would be an argument. A description of juvenile work camps would be a report; an essay claiming that the camps are ineffective would be an argument.

A report is concerned with *who* or *what;* an argument also considers *why* or *how.* An argument not only presents information but also analyzes and interprets it in relation to a thesis—a statement of purpose, a proposition to be examined, an interpretive judgment, a central idea. To write an argument, you acquaint yourself thoroughly with a narrow topic, devise a valid thesis, and develop it with your own ideas and with material drawn from a variety of sources. A report simply conveys information and may be drawn from a single source. If you wrote a term paper in high school, it may have been a report. But research papers in college will almost certainly be arguments.

Your Purpose in Writing

As you consider possible topics, ask yourself what purpose your paper might accomplish—to explain, to analyze, or to persuade. The same paper may involve all three purposes—explanation, analysis, and argument—but one will dominate. Determining your purpose should help you focus on a narrow topic and a meaningful thesis.

An *explanatory* paper is written to inform or clarify, to acquaint the reader with a body of material. The most common fault in this type of paper is the lack of a unifying thesis. An account of the proliferation of shopping malls would be explanatory.

Analysis means dividing something into its component parts and examining their relationships. An analytical paper considers separate aspects of a topic in order to support a thesis. These aspects usually become the major steps in the plan. Incomplete analysis is probably the most common fault; it is easy to take for granted or disregard a major aspect of a topic simply because it seems so obvious. A discussion of possible reasons for the appeal of shopping malls (convenience, lower prices, greater selection of goods, etc.) would be analytical.

An *argumentative* paper attempts to persuade a reader to accept your judgment on an issue and, perhaps, to take some action. Because topics for such papers are often controversial, it is important not to be swayed by personal bias. Avoid an emotional topic like abortion or the death penalty if you cannot deal with it objectively. There is no standard plan for such a paper, but an effective strategy is to summarize ideas opposed to your own and then present your own case. An argumentative paper might concede the advantages of shopping malls but contend that they drive small merchants out of business, create traffic problems, provide meeting places for youth gangs, and destroy the commercial center of a city.

The sample papers in Chapters 9 and 10 illustrate various purposes. Paul Sanchez's paper (Chapter 9) explains what animal hoarding is and suggests some ways to deal with it. Colleen Lee's paper (Chapter 9) analyzes the language of "The Story of an Hour" and argues that the message of the story is more ambivalent than some critics recognize. James Kebler's paper (Chapter 9) examines the life of John P. Parker and argues that his achievements deserve to be better known. The paper by Melissa Lofts (Chapter 10) surveys the health benefits that accrue to mothers who breastfeed and urges that this information be made available more widely.

Your Audience

All writing is communication, and all communication is a two-way process involving a writer or a speaker and a reader or a listener. In written communication, it is easy to ignore your invisible audience. However, your audience should determine what and how you write. In describing the World Series to a British reader, you would need to supply definitions and other facts that an American reader would not require. Similarly, writing about cricket for an American audience would require much elementary information. A paper on the topic of acid rain written for an ecology class might be quite different from one written for an industrial engineering class. A paper on *Alice in Wonderland* written for a class in children's literature would differ from an analysis of the book written for a seminar in Victorian fantasy.

When choosing a topic, identify your audience and ask yourself how much prior knowledge your readers have, what opinions they may hold, and how their interest can be aroused and sustained. Writing for an audience of specialists is usually not a good idea. Assume that your readers have a general familiarity with your topic and that they are thoughtful, open-minded, and perceptive. Keep your imagined audience in mind during every phase of the research process.

Because your instructor will, in fact, be your primary audience, you probably should not choose a subject on which he or she is an expert. Students are sometimes advised to make classmates their audience, and writing for your peers is especially appropriate when papers are read in class or are circulated and read by other students. It may help to imagine a reader who is approximately as familiar with the subject as you were when you began your research. On this basis, you can determine what terms must be defined and how much factual support is needed. Adapting your style and your materials to your readers' interest and knowledge should help you maintain a consistent tone and point of view throughout your paper.

Helpful Techniques for Getting Started

A Research Log

When you begin your work, set aside a section of your notebook for a log or journal in which you jot down possible topics, sources to consult, questions to consider, possible main points, and reminders to yourself. Treat this log as an informal diary, recording what you hope to accomplish, problems you foresee, and progress you make. After you are committed to a topic and a thesis, you will probably write most of your notes on cards or type them on your computer, but in the early stages of your research, a day-by-day record can be very useful.

A Work Schedule

A research paper is always assigned several weeks in advance, but you should begin work as soon as possible. Use the Timetable on the inside front cover to establish a schedule for completing each step in the research process. Meeting or beating a deadline can be a minor triumph that will give you a psychological lift. A running record in your research log will keep your mind focused on your topic and may prod your conscience if you let several days pass with nothing accomplished.

Unfortunately, it is easy to ignore an assignment that is due several weeks in the future. Some writers procrastinate and then subject themselves to desperate all-night sessions. You probably could produce a paper by spending two days in the library and two nights at your study table, but the results would certainly be eyestrain, frazzled nerves, and a mediocre essay. A successful research paper evolves slowly through continued effort. Collecting and organizing material will take longer than you expect, and the more time you have for revision, the better. Despite temptations to postpone your research project, start looking for a topic as soon as the paper is assigned.

The human mind functions in mysterious ways. While a topic lies dormant, an incubation process can occur, and an idea or an elusive phrase may flash into your awareness like the light bulb above a character's head in an old-time comic strip. Even though you are not consciously pondering your topic, your mind may subconsciously refine it, enhance it, or narrow it so that when you begin taking notes, your ideas will fall into place more readily than you expected. Obviously you cannot rely too much on this sort of subconscious assistance, but you lose the benefits of a mental gestation period if you try to choose a topic and turn out a paper on the weekend before it is due.

A Mental Inventory

Students sometimes rush to search the Internet or the Reference Room, neglecting an important body of information—what they already know about a subject. Because you are not likely to choose a totally unfamiliar topic, you should assess what is already available in your mind. Paul Sanchez had seen a story on local television news about animal hoarding, and the term struck him as unusual. Colleen Lee had read "The Story of an Hour" and an essay about it for a class, and she was surprised that the author of the essay seemed to ignore some details in the story that did not fit with the interpretation being put forward. James Kebler's professor in an African American studies course required a paper about a figure who should be recognized as a role model, and James had recently learned about John P. Parker at the Underground Railroad Freedom Center while visiting relatives in Cincinnati. Melissa Lofts had already decided to breastfeed the child she was expecting and wondered how long she should continue to do so.

Brainstorming

Brainstorming is a discovery technique that allows the mind to cruise, activated by free association as one detail, fact, or idea suggests another.

A portion of one of Paul Sanchez's brainstorming sessions illustrates his exploration of his topic, animal hoarding:

THE WORK OF PAUL SANCHEZ

Where is the line that separates an animal lover with a lot of pets from a hoarder?

Are there any local cases I could investigate?

How common is it?

What would it take to recognize animal hoarding as a form of mental illness?

Can people be "cured" of hoarding?

If hoarding is a mental illness, would changing the laws make any difference?

What happens to repeat offenders?

What kinds of animals are hoarded most often?

What happens to the animals that are rescued?

How much does it cost to take care of them?

Free association is not the most systematic or logical mental activity, but allowing your mind to work spontaneously can be highly productive. Some items, of course, will be irrelevant, but you can easily ignore or delete them.

Brainstorming is useful during the early stages of your research because it can help you refine a topic and determine the main points that will form your basic plan. It can also be productive when you begin taking notes. After a session in the library, spend a few minutes considering what you have read and jot down useful ideas. Sometimes a fresh approach to a topic or an effective phrase will pop into your mind when you least expect it.

Narrowing Your Subject

Ex. A.1 The term *subject* designates a broad area of knowledge: cancer, Istanbul, insects, football; *topic* denotes an aspect of a subject: melanoma, the Blue Mosque, Japanese beetles, paying college athletes. A subject is narrowed to a specific part of the topic; a thesis designates an approach to the subject.

If you are assigned a general subject like "Education," you will need to find a topic like "School Uniforms" and compose a thesis such as "Although many claim that mandatory school uniforms violate students' First Amendment rights, courts have consistently ruled that they do not." If your assignment is open-ended, you will be on your own to explore a general subject, find a narrow topic, and formulate a defensible thesis.

Evaluating Possible Topics

In any research paper, no decision is as important as the choice of a topic. Devote considerable time and thought to finding one that both interests you and meets the requirements of the assignment. A topic that bores you when you choose it will grow still more boring as you do the research, and the resulting paper will probably bore the reader.

Evaluate a topic in terms of the following criteria:

- *It should be narrow enough to be developed fully.* Because a research paper seems relatively long, there is a natural tendency to look for a broad topic. But if the assignment is 2,000 words, the paper will be eight or nine pages long—about the length of a column and a half in a newspaper. It is impossible to discuss "Byzantine Architecture" or "The Life of Mozart" in that little space. Biographical papers are often unsatisfactory, in fact, because they attempt to cover the subject's entire life. If you write about an individual, focus on one aspect of that person's career, accomplishments, or character.
- *It should require research.* Personal experience or a subjective attitude that cannot be supported by facts and opinions from outside sources would be unsuitable. It would be impossible to find supporting material in the library for "My Most Embarrassing Moment" or "What I Believe."
- *It should be a topic that you can consider objectively.* A controversial question may motivate your research, but strong preconceptions may distort your judgment. Also, judging the reliability of information may be difficult; charges and countercharges may frustrate your attempts to sift the true from the false. Sexual harassment, animal rights, and right-wing talk-show hosts are viable subjects, but they may lead to topics that will be too difficult to be objective about or too complex for a short paper.
- *It should be a topic that you are curious about but not overly familiar with.* A research paper should take you into new territory. If you do decide to work with a familiar topic, your aim should be to learn something about it, not to choose something "easy" that will reduce the amount of effort required to complete the paper. Research should produce a thrill of discovery, not bored recognition of the familiar. If you have no interest in politics, a paper on a presidential campaign would probably not be interesting to you or to your reader. On the other hand, if you know a great deal about cameras, collecting information on photography might prove tedious unless you are making new discoveries as you work.
- *It should be within your scope.* Whether a topic is too technical for you to investigate depends on your background and your interests. "Mitral Stenosis" might be an appropriate topic for a premed student but possibly not for a philosophy major. "The Discovery of Neptunium" would be a difficult topic for a student with no knowledge of physics and chemistry. "Shakespeare's Women Characters" would not do for a student with little background in literature. In general, avoid topics involving totally unfamiliar concepts and baffling terminology.

Helpful Techniques for Narrowing Your Search

Surfing and Browsing

Surfing the Internet and browsing in the library are sometimes dismissed as casual activities without a direct path to a fixed goal. However, both can be very productive, especially in looking for a topic. Many Internet search engines give seemingly unlimited possibilities when you enter a general search term, such as *school uniforms.* In addition to the thousands of hits from such a search, each page you pull up usually contains a number of links to related pages. Scanning these items may suggest an aspect of a subject that leads you to a topic. You can browse books and magazines in the same way, looking at titles on the library shelves and scanning indexes for sources that look promising.

One of Paul's first online searches led him to the home page of the Hoarding of Animals Research Consortium (HARC), part of which is shown in Figure 1.1. Across the top of the page is the navigation bar with six divisions: About HARC, About Hoarding, Health Issues, Animal Welfare, Intervention, and Resources. Each of those divisions is further divided, as the drop-down menu for the Health Issues button shows.

FIGURE 1.1 Hoarding of Animals Research Consortium home page
http://www.tufts.edu/vet/cfa/hoarding/

Some Web sites also have a link to a site index (sometimes called a site map), which gives the contents in the form of a text list. Figure 1.2 comes from the home page of AnimalConcerns.org, a site that Paul discovered as he was surfing. The page provides links to additional information as well as a list of resource topics that suggest ways of thinking about the larger topic.

Continued

THE WORK OF PAUL SANCHEZ

FIGURE 1.2 *http://www.animalconcerns.org/sitemap.html*

Print resources are especially rich sources of lists to scan for additional ideas. An excellent place to begin is *Library of Congress Subject Headings,* four large volumes bound in red usually found near the catalog in a library. This publication identifies the classification numbers for a subject and also subdivides main headings.

Paul found no entry for "animal hoarding," but another heading—"Animal rescue"—looked promising:

Sample entry from *Library of Congress Subject Headings*

Animal rescue (May Subd Geog)
UF   Rescue of animals
BT   Animal welfare
NT   Dog rescue
        First aid for animals
        Pet adoption
        Wildlife rescue

Key
May Subd Geog = a place name may follow the heading
UF = Used for (a term that is not used)
BT = Broad term (class to which heading belongs)
RT = Related term (associated with the heading)
NT = Narrow term (member of class represented by heading)

Colleen consulted another excellent resource, a volume of *Twentieth-Century Literary Criticism,* which included a list of references for further reading at the end of the section on Kate Chopin. Each of the resources listed there was accompanied by a brief annotation that helped Colleen decide whether she wanted to look for those sources. Here, for example, is the description of a biography of Chopin:

Toth, Emily. *Kate Chopin.* New York: William Morrow and Company, Inc., 1990, 528 p.
> Biography that questions long-held views on Chopin's life and writing; includes appendices, photographs, and a select bibliography.

Sample annotated entry from *Twentieth-Century Literary Criticism*

While looking for books about John Parker and the Underground Railroad, James Kebler found J. Blaine Hudson's *Fugitive Slaves and the Underground Railroad in the Kentucky Borderland,* a study of Underground Railroad activity in the area where Parker lived and worked (Jefferson: McFarland, 2002). The detailed table of contents gave him a quick overview of the topics covered, including some key names and places. The index provided still another look at possible topics to pursue.

Excerpt from table of contents:
Chapter VII: Individuals and Cases of Note

> Fugitive: Eliza Harris
> Fugitives: Thornton and Lucie Blackburn
> Fugitive and Friend of the Fugitive: Henry Bibb
> Friends of the Fugitive: Delia Webster and Calvin Fairbank
> Fugitive and Friend of the Fugitive: Lewis Hayden
> Friend of the Fugitive: Edward James "Patrick" Doyle
> Friends of the Fugitive: Shelton Morris and Washington Spradling, Sr.
> Fugitive: Rosetta Armstead/Anderson
> Fugitive: Margaret Garner
> Fugitive: Rachael
> Friends of the Fugitive: Charles Bell and Oswell Wright
> Friends of the Fugitive: Elijah Anderson and Chapman Harris
> Friends of the Fugitive: John Parker and the Rev. John Rankin

Excerpt from index:
Rachael (Fugitive Slave: Escape from Louisville, 1857) 147–148
Racial Attitudes (American) 5–7; Myths of Black Inferiority 5–6; Regional Patterns 20
Rankin, the Rev. John (Friend of the Fugitive) 124; Eliza Harris escape 130; Leader of Maysville/Ripley
> Underground 153; Lewis Hayden escape 134; "Liberty Hill" 153–154

Table of contents and index

Any listing that subdivides a general subject can jog your imagination, put your mind in a reductive mode, and assist you in finding a narrow topic.

Exploratory Reading

During the preliminary stages of your research, besides scanning indexes and similar listings, you will undoubtedly read some general discussions of your subject, not looking for information but for an aspect of the subject that can serve as your topic. Encyclopedias, handbooks, and general magazines are usually best for this type of reading. Taking notes during your exploratory reading, except for a brief comment on the potential usefulness of a source, is a waste of time. Until you are firmly committed to a topic and a thesis, you cannot determine whether a fact or an opinion will be relevant.

Although your paper should not duplicate one written for another course, a class discussion, especially one in your major field, may lead you to a suitable topic. A remark in your American history class about Pickett's charge at Gettysburg might send you to the library to explore the subject. While listening to class lectures, talking with your friends, watching television, or reading the newspaper, be alert for a reference that stirs your curiosity: for example, reality TV competitions, global climate change, performance-enhancing drugs in sports, the comic techniques of Stephen Colbert, same-sex marriage, sports card collecting, the Endangered Species Act, twenty-first century theocracies, or gaming theory.

Skimming

A by-product of your research project may be improved reading skills—especially your abilities to skim a Web page or the pages of a book efficiently. Exploratory reading requires intelligent skimming—a skill that can be developed by practice. It does not mean skipping every other page or reading only the top three lines of each page. It means making a conscious effort to increase your reading rate by taking in more words each time you focus your eyes. Try to pick up an author's main ideas; concentrate on the first and final sentences of each paragraph and the opening and closing paragraphs of articles. By skimming you can judge whether you should return to a source when you begin purposeful reading and note taking.

THE WORK OF MELISSA LOFTS

While browsing the Internet for information about how long mothers should breastfeed, Melissa saw that the length of time recommended by professional healthcare groups was usually significantly longer than the actual time reported in studies. She jotted down the following potential research questions:

Is there a scientific basis for the claim that breastfeeding is better than bottle feeding?

Have any of the studies showing benefits to mother and child been challenged? Or are they really conclusive?

Why do so many women not continue to breastfeed the full recommended length of time?

Do women realize that there are health benefits for themselves as well as for their children?

Do not settle on the first topic that pops into your mind. Review your own interests, scan indexes in print or on databases, skim general articles, and explore the library stacks and the Internet to find a suitable topic. Even if you are satisfied with your choice, however, taking extensive notes would be a waste of time until you commit to a thesis.

Formulating a Thesis

Ex. A.2   Your thesis is an assumption about your topic, an approach to it, a proposition to be examined, a premise to be supported, a controlling idea that will determine what kind of material you look for. However it is defined, a thesis narrows your topic further and assures that it will be manageable. Like your topic, it is subject to revision. You may discover evidence that changes your original idea, so you should regard your thesis as tentative, at least until you have completed your rough draft.

In your outline, the thesis should be a single sentence, usually with the topic of the paper as the grammatical subject, but it will probably be expanded into several sentences in the opening of the paper. Although you are not ready to construct an outline at this stage, composing a thesis is a worthwhile test of a tentative topic. You will probably try several versions, juggling phrases and searching for more exact words until you arrive at a satisfactory statement. Keep revising until you can express your central idea clearly in that sentence. Avoid overly obvious statements like "The purpose of this paper is . . ." or "My paper will discuss . . ." Also try to avoid general terms like *important* or *interesting.* If, after conscientious effort, you cannot write a satisfactory thesis statement, you probably should look for a different topic or a new approach to the one you have.

Melissa immediately thought of two possible theses concerning breastfeeding. Note that her first attempt would result in a simple report, whereas the second tends more toward argument:

Although studies show that breastfeeding has significant health benefits for both mother and child, many women do not continue the practice as long as healthcare professionals recommend.

Women should continue to breastfeed their children the full term recommended by healthcare professionals because of the benefits not only to their children but to themselves.

THE WORK OF MELISSA LOFTS

You are on your way to a thesis statement when you begin asking *Why?* or *How?* during your exploratory reading. Asking yourself questions can be a means of arriving at a thesis. Questions like the following might be developed into thesis statements:

- How does the Red Cross determine how funds will be distributed in national disasters?
- What styles of furniture are most popular in the United States?
- Which diets and exercise programs are most effective for losing weight?
- Which names for babies were favored in the 1990s?
- Why are reality shows popular on television?
- Why does soccer appeal so strongly to sports fans in Europe and Latin America?
- Why did Paul Revere become a hero of the American Revolution?
- Why are horror movies popular with young moviegoers?
- Should airlines be regulated more closely?
- Should cigarette smoking in all public places be prohibited?

Probably the first four questions would produce explanatory papers; the second four, analytical papers; and the final two, argumentative papers.

During his exploratory reading on animal hoarding, Paul wrote the following questions in his research log:

When did this term originate?

What effect do media reports have?

How can we tell the difference between legitimate animal rescue operations and hoarders?

How would defining animal hoarding as a psychological condition affect the legal treatment of hoarders?

Although a thesis may develop from one or more questions, its final form should be a declarative statement that requires amplification. It is often derived from a cause-and-effect relationship, one of the most common and most productive modes of thinking:

Animal hoarding should be recognized as a psychological condition because . . .

Recognizing animal hoarding as a psychological condition would result in more effective legislation because . . .

Paul's first concern was being sure his readers would understand the phenomenon known as animal hoarding. His first attempt at a thesis would have resulted in a report rather than an argument:

Animal hoarding is a little-understood phenomenon.

A second attempt led to a thesis that was likelier to result in a paper that had a larger element of persuasion:

Animal hoarding is a serious problem that must be dealt with effectively.

Colleen also began with a statement that was very general and required no development:

Kate Chopin's "The Story of an Hour" is a powerful story.

As she brainstormed about what she found especially intriguing about the story, she realized that the seemingly contradictory elements in the story made it difficult for her to say that the main character's happiness when she is freed from her marriage is presented in a totally positive light. Her next attempt took that uncertainty into account:

In "The Story of an Hour" Kate Chopin gives the reader ambivalent messages about Mrs. Mallard's attitude toward freedom from her marriage.

The assignment to which James was responding was designed to provide students with a thesis-oriented starting point. That is, everyone was asked to choose an African American figure from the past and explain why he or she should be considered a role model worthy of remembrance. Even so, when James made a first attempt at a thesis, the result would have led him just to summarize the events of the life of John P. Parker:

After gaining freedom from slavery, John P. Parker became an important "conductor" on the Underground Railroad and eventually became a successful businessman and inventor.

When James realized that he was likely to write a report rather than the argument he knew his professor wanted, he wrote this version of his thesis in his research log and added the words *So why is this important?* He wasn't ready to answer that question yet, but it would guide him as he learned more about the details of Parker's life.

Melissa began with a thesis that proved to be a dead end:

Although studies show that breastfeeding has significant health benefits for both mother and child, many women do not continue the practice as long as healthcare professionals recommend.

She quickly realized that this thesis would lead only to a more detailed version of the fact she had just stated. Instead, she began to think about what might persuade women to extend the length of time they nurse their children:

Because of the positive benefits to a mother's health, women should continue to breastfeed their children for the length of time recommended by professional healthcare organizations.

Your first version of a thesis is not an ironclad commitment. Do not hesitate to change it as you continue your research.

Writing a Prospectus

When you have chosen a topic and a thesis and done some exploratory reading, your instructor may require that you submit a prospectus—a paragraph or two that identifies your topic, your thesis, the kinds of sources you plan to consult, the problems you anticipate, and any special aspects of your project. Even if a prospectus is not required, it can be a helpful way of ensuring that you chart a sensible course and follow it. Include a copy of your prospectus in your research log; it will help you determine what kinds of notes to take and what main ideas to use as the framework of your outline.

The prospectus for Paul's paper can serve as an example:

I will discuss why animal hoarding is a serious problem, what may cause it, and what can be done about it. Animal hoarding occurs all over the country, and rescuing animals costs huge amounts of money every year. It also poses a health danger and sometimes leads to the demolition of the property where the animals were kept. Animal hoarding seems to be a complex psychological problem, and officially recognizing it would make it easier to intervene in hoarding cases. Some states are beginning to consider legislation that may make it easier to deal with hoarders. There are very few print resources on this topic, but there are many Internet sources that appear to be reliable.

Recording Possible Sources

At the close of your paper, on a page headed Works Cited, you will list the sources you have used. During your exploratory reading, you will almost certainly notice some books and articles that look useful. You should, therefore, begin compiling a working bibliography—a file of potential sources. Of course, you will expand it when you begin purposeful reading and note taking.

Include all the information that belongs in Works Cited. Arranging and punctuating the items in standard bibliographical form now will reduce the possibility of omissions or transcription errors when you compile the final Works Cited page. A full array of bibliographic forms in MLA style can be found in Chapter 9; the standard form for a book is illustrated on pages 133–134 and those for periodicals on pages 142–143. Forms for APA style are found in Chapter 10. Recording the call number of a book or the location of a periodical and a brief note on how you might use the source will also prove helpful. These notes are for your guidance, of course, and do not appear in Works Cited. If a source contains nothing useful when you examine it more closely, write *Nada, Zilch,* or some other code term so that you do not waste time looking at that source again. However, do not throw away the information; it may be useful if you revise your topic or your thesis.

Compiling a preliminary bibliography is a test of your topic. Students frequently complain that there is not enough material in the library, but such complaints are seldom justified. No library contains everything ever printed, but your school library probably has information on most of the topics you are likely to investigate. If you cannot find the material, however, the result is the same as though it were not there. The sooner you find a shortage of material, the better. In that case, you must expand the topic or abandon it. More often, though, compiling a preliminary bibliography results in an embarrassment of riches; there is so much material that you must narrow your topic or your thesis.

Considering Main Points

After you narrow your topic and formulate a thesis, your brainstorming can become more purposeful.

THE WORK OF JAMES KEBLER

After reading and thinking for several days about John P. Parker, James compiled a running outline in his research log:

1. helped over 1,000 slaves escape (estimate varies)
2. recruited soldiers for African American regiment in Union army
3. patents for tobacco press, screw for tobacco press, and "soil pulverizer"
4. purchased own freedom at age 18
5. had to overcome temper
6. net worth of Parker's property more than doubled in less than 20 years
7. march from Richmond to Mobile at age 8 or 9 (800 miles)
8. Fugitive Slave Law (1850) increased danger
9. had as many as 25 employees at one time
10. wanted to establish African American clientele for products of foundry
11. a leading businessman of Ripley
12. only 77 patents issued to African Americans by 1886
13. sold from mother at age 8
14. $1,000 reward "dead or alive"
15. Ripley known as a "notorious abolitionist hole"
16. Parker's children all successful professionals

17. respected by everyone in Ripley
18. white man working for Parker challenged him to steal his father's slaves
19. only 55 African Americans held more than one patent in 1901
20. manuscript of autobiography unpublished until 1996
21. escape from Mobile to New Orleans
22. first experience helping slaves escape
23. Phoenix Foundry
24. time in Cincinnati
25. working relationship with Rev. John Rankin
26. saw success in business as more effective path to equality than political lobbying
27. during 1962 sesquicentennial celebrations, city of Ripley recognized Parker's importance to town's prosperity

As he considered this list, James saw five main topics:

Parker's early life as a slave: 4, 5, 7, 13, 21

Parker's activity with Underground Railroad: 1, 2, 8, 14, 15, 18, 22, 24, 25

Parker's business skills: 6, 9, 11, 23, 27

Parker's inventions: 3, 12, 19

Parker's greater significance: 10, 12(?), 17, 19(?), 26

Not clearly related: 16, 20

While attempting to sort out his ideas, James recognized that he was concentrating much more on Parker's life than on Parker's significance today. Because the latter was the focus of the assignment, he knew he would need to look more closely at this point. As he worked, he thought some of these topics might be treated so that they would fit into the discussion of Parker's significance. James put the numbers into two different categories, adding a question mark to one set to remind himself that he should be prepared to look closely at organization when he began to draft that portion of the paper. This early running outline had enabled him to reconsider his topic and give direction to his next efforts in gathering information.

Exploring a subject, narrowing it to a topic, formulating a viable thesis, compiling a file of sources, and listing possible main points are not separate procedures to be completed in sequence. Most or all of them are under way simultaneously during the early stage of the research process.

Checklist for Shaping Your Topic

☑ I started with a broad *subject area* and a *hypothesis*—a general idea or conjecture about that subject.

☑ I narrowed my *subject* to a *topic* by considering the *purpose of my paper* and my *prospective audience.*

☑ I explored books, articles, and other sources of information to find material about my topic and *kept organized, appropriately documented notes* so I could readily retrieve the information again.

Exercise A

Preliminary Decisions

A.1. Suitable Subjects. Write an X after any of the following subjects that seem unsuitable for a research paper. Circle three that seem promising and be prepared to suggest how each might be narrowed to a topic and narrowed further by a thesis.

1. The novels of Margaret Atwood _____
2. Comedy clubs _____
3. Biological terrorism _____
4. Serial killers _____
5. The British Royal Family _____
6. Internet censorship _____
7. Electroencephalography _____
8. The Boy Scout movement _____
9. Stay-at-home fathers _____
10. The Korean War _____
11. The American dream _____
12. Numerology _____
13. The Boston Marathon _____
14. Macho images in advertising _____
15. The tabloid press _____
16. Bacteriophages _____
17. U.S. funeral customs _____
18. Political correctness _____
19. The Unabomber _____
20. Online shopping _____

A.2. Thesis Statements. An unsuitable thesis is usually a general statement that requires little or no amplification; a satisfactory statement involves an opinion to be explained, contradicted, or defended. Write an X in front of any unsatisfactory statement listed below. Be prepared to suggest how one of the satisfactory statements might be developed.

_____ **1.** There are at least 14,000 species of mushrooms.

_____ **2.** Although the Armory Show of 1913 raised much opposition, that exhibition of European art was a major influence on American painting.

_____ **3.** My paper will discuss First Amendment rights.

_____ **4.** High schools should restore Latin as an elective for college-bound students.

_____ **5.** The bodies of Nicholas II of Russia, his wife Alexandra Fyodorovna, and three of their five children were exhumed in 1991, more than seventy years after they were executed.

_____ **6.** Although Barry Bonds holds the career home run record, his pathway to the record has been controversial.

_____ **7.** Unfortunately, the courts are reluctant to allow grandparents to adopt their grandchildren.

_____ **8.** The execution of John Brown made him a hero in the North and a martyr to the cause of abolition.

_____ **9.** Colleges should pay athletes because they bring in large amounts of revenue for the school.

_____ **10.** In _Othello,_ Iago skillfully manipulates his victims by playing on their weaknesses.

_____ **11.** School vouchers would solve many problems of modern education by allowing parents to select the most effective schools for their children.

_____ **12.** No matter how successful she may be, a woman executive will probably find her future limited by the "glass ceiling."

Exercise B

First Steps

Begin with a general subject you are considering for your research paper and reduce it in scope at least three times. Then write your tentative topic.

General Subject _____

     1. _____

     2. _____

     3. _____

Tentative Topic _____

Sometimes a title is an effective way of narrowing a topic. Devise a possible title for your topic.

Title _____

Brainstorm the topic you are considering; free-associate, allowing one idea or detail to suggest another. List some aspects of the topic suggested by this procedure.

_____

_____

_____

_____

_____

_____

_____

_____

Compose a thesis statement that would cover at least four of the items above. You would, of course, revise it as you continued your research.

Tentative Thesis _____

_____

_____

Locate in the library two books and articles that seem relevant to your topic and thesis. Using proper bibliographic form, either hard copy or electronic, create a Works Cited entry for each. Follow the basic forms illustrated on pages 133–134 and 142–143.

Learning Research Resources and Procedures

> *When we enquire into any subject, the first thing we have to do is to know what books have treated of it. This leads us to look at catalogues and the backs of books in libraries.*
>
> Boswell, *Life of Johnson*, vol. 1

Many people use Internet searches as their principal source of information, but the academic library is still at the heart of the research process. Although some of the essential resources described in the next chapters are available online for students, many can be accessed only in brick-and-mortar libraries on campus. Among the benefits of the physical library is the availability of expert librarians, who can assist you in learning how to use some of the resources in this chapter and direct you to a great many others as well. Not to be underestimated either is the concentration of so many resources in one place.

Even if you are accustomed to using a large public library, you will probably find the facilities and the procedures in your school library quite different and, at first, even baffling. A public library is designed to provide reading materials of all levels of difficulty to readers of all ages with all kinds of different interests. An academic library is designed to provide supplementary materials for courses and primary sources for scholarly research. Familiarity with your school library can be the most valuable by-product of your research project and should be useful for the rest of your college career.

Understanding the Library

Ex. C As in any new situation, curiosity and observation can help you adapt. Watch what other students are doing. Don't hesitate to ask a librarian for help. You will encounter new terms and abbreviations that relate to library procedures (see Appendix A). The sooner you feel at home in the library, the better. Perhaps as a new student you were taken on a guided tour. Follow this with your own exploration. Some libraries distribute charts that show the major facilities and the locations of various categories of books. A good way to familiarize yourself with the library is to draw a simple floor plan and keep it in your notebook. The main features will include the following:

- *Information desk.* In a large library someone is usually stationed near the main entrance to answer questions and direct visitors. You will find this person very helpful while you are becoming acquainted with the library.
- *Circulation desk.* Sometimes called the "main desk," this is the nerve center of the library where books are checked out and returned.
- *Stacks.* The shelved books are not always open to undergraduates. If not, you submit a call slip for each book you need and wait for it to be brought to your study table. Even if you can go to the stacks, a search of the shelves may be misleading because important books can be checked out, in special collections, or on reserve. Browsing in the stacks, however, can sometimes result in fortunate discoveries.
- *Catalog.* A card catalog or an online catalog is a record by author, title, and subject of all books in the library. Your school library will probably list its collection on OPAC (Online Public Access Catalog), which will also list books in some other libraries.
- *Reference books.* Reference books are collections of information intended to be consulted rather than read consecutively. General works like *Readers' Guide* or *Encyclopedia Americana*, which are more or less useful in all fields, are usually shelved in a special room or section. Specialized works such as handbooks, abstracts, and indexes to journals are available in every field. Get to know the basic reference works as well as the specialized ones in your major field.
- *Reserve books.* Books to be used in the library or withdrawn only for brief periods are placed on reserve. They may be shelved at the circulation desk or in a separate reserve section. A file or a computer printout listing reserve books is usually available.
- *Periodicals.* Current periodicals are usually shelved in a reading room or another central location. Each category will be arranged alphabetically. After they have been bound, the volumes are assigned call numbers and shelved according to their subject matter. If a journal is available electronically, that will be noted in the catalog entry.
- *Microform readers.* Readers for microfilm and other microforms are usually located in a special room.
- *Computer terminals.* Computer terminals offer access to indexes, bibliographies, abstracts, and full-text articles on CD-ROM. These terminals will also give you access to the World Wide Web, an important source of books and periodicals and an invaluable research tool. Student research projects today usually begin with a computer search.
- *Union catalog.* A computerized catalog (OPAC) lists holdings of some other libraries. You can sometimes learn that a book you need is in a nearby library.
- *Interlibrary loans.* In most academic libraries, a separate department processes requests for books and articles to be obtained from other libraries. This service, which usually takes a week or more, is not always available to undergraduates.
- *Media center.* Films, slides, videotapes, recordings, and similar materials may be housed in a special department.
- *Photocopies.* Copy machines are usually available throughout a library. Look for them first in the vicinity of the periodicals. You may need to purchase a special card for paying for copies.
- *Computer labs.* Some libraries set aside a room equipped with computers for students' use, and wireless access is often available in many parts of the facility.
- *Carrels.* Study desks can be reserved in some libraries. Books can be shelved there for a limited time. The use of carrels is frequently restricted to faculty and graduate students.

Using the Catalog

A library catalog is an enormous bibliography. It lists all of the books in the library and may also include entries for periodicals, cassettes, CDs, films, microforms, and other materials. To find materials dealing with your topic, you will need to use the catalog—whether it is a card catalog or an online catalog. Some libraries have retained a card catalog for materials acquired before the advent of OPAC in the early 1980s, but most have transferred their entire holdings to OPAC. The classification systems in both types of catalog are basically the same.

Call Numbers

In a large library of a million or more volumes, a foolproof system for locating each book is essential. A book is, therefore, assigned a specific code symbol (a call number), which will be found on the spine of a book and on all catalog entries for that book.

The first part of a call number (the top two or three lines) is the *classification number,* which is the same in all libraries using the same system. Below it is the *book number* (sometimes called the *author number* or the *Cutter number*), a combination of letters and numbers. The book number identifies different books on the same subject. The year of publication may be included to indicate an edition. The larger the library, the more symbols will be required in a book number. Two books with the same classification number are differentiated by their book numbers:

	Michael Feldman *The Unbounded Frame*	Edward K. Spann *Brotherly Tomorrows*
Classification numbers	HX 653	HX 653
Book number	.F44	.S62 1989

Classification Systems

The two classification systems in general use are the Dewey Decimal system and the Library of Congress system. You should become familiar with the one used in your school library, especially the categories related to your major field of study.

The Dewey Decimal System

Dewey Decimal classification, as its name suggests, is based on numbers divisible by ten. The various fields of knowledge are divided into ten general categories:

000–099	General Works
100–199	Philosophy
200–299	Religion
300–399	Social Sciences
400–499	Philology
500–599	Pure Science
600–699	Applied Arts and Sciences
700–799	Fine Arts, Recreation
800–899	Literature
900–999	History, Geography, Travel, Biography

Each category is subdivided by tens, as illustrated here:

500–509	Pure Science
510–519	Mathematics
520–529	Astronomy
530–539	Physics
540–549	Chemistry
550–559	Geology
560–569	Paleontology
570–579	Biology
580–589	Botany
590–599	Zoology

Each of these fields is also subdivided, as in this example:

510	Mathematics
511	Arithmetic
512	Algebra
513	Geometry
514	Trigonometry
515	Descriptive geometry
516	Analytic geometry
517	Calculus
518	Unassigned
519	Probabilities

Each category is subdivided further by adding numbers after a decimal point:

511	Arithmetic
511.1	Systems
511.2	Numeration
511.3	Prime numbers
511.4	Fractions
511.5	Analysis
511.6	Proportion
511.7	Involution, evolution
511.8	Mercantile rules
511.9	Problems and tables

A weakness of the Dewey Decimal system, which was devised in the 1870s, is that the vast expansion of knowledge has made most categories inadequate. Classification numbers are often long and cumbersome. The Dewey Decimal system is most likely to be found in relatively small libraries.

The Library of Congress System

The Library of Congress system, which is based on letters supplemented by numbers, is preferred by most large libraries. Because there are twenty-one main categories instead of only ten, classification numbers require fewer symbols. The letters I, O, W, X, and Y are not used. The major categories are as follows:

A	General Works, Polygraphy
B	Philosophy, Religion

C	History, Auxiliary Sciences
D	History, Topography (except America)
E	America (general), United States (general)
F	United States (local), America (except the United States)
G	Geography, Anthropology
H	Social Sciences (general), Statistics, Economics, Sociology
J	Political Science
K	Law
L	Education
M	Music
N	Fine Arts
P	Language and Literature
Q	Science
R	Medicine
S	Agriculture
T	Technology
U	Military Science
V	Naval Science
Z	Bibliography, Library Science

Further subdivision is made by adding a second capital letter. For example, the principal subclasses of category N (Fine Arts) are as follows:

N	Visual Arts (general)
NA	Architecture
NB	Sculpture
NC	Drawing, Design, Illustration
ND	Painting
NE	Print Media
NK	Decorative Arts, Applied Arts, Decoration, Antiques
NX	Arts in General

A subclass is subdivided by numbers from 1 to 9999, to which decimals may be added. Here, for example, are some subdivisions of ND (Painting):

1290–1460	Special Subjects (human figure, landscapes, animals, still life, flowers)
1700–2495	Watercolor Painting
2550–2888	Mural Painting
2890–3416	Illuminating of Manuscripts and Books

Classification number + book number = call number. No two books have precisely the same call number. A call number functions like your home address: the state, the city, the ZIP code, the street, and the house number are progressively more specific, and the total address designates your house and no other.

Online Catalogs

OPAC offers much more than a listing of a library's holdings. Your school's library may be linked to regional libraries so that OPAC serves as a union catalog. If so and you find that a book you need is in another library, you can request it through interlibrary loan. In many OPACs, you can

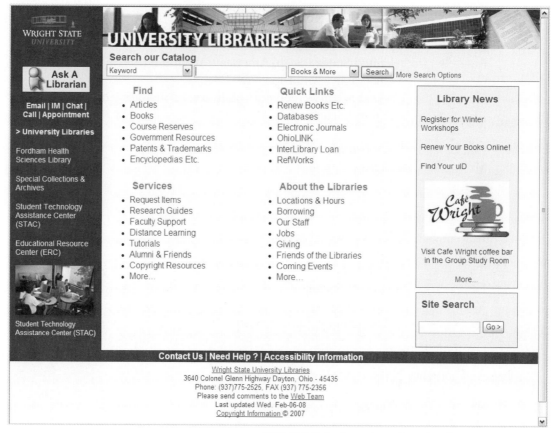

FIGURE 2.1 Sample university library home page

also conduct a subject search and find references to relevant sources. You will need to use specific search terms so that you are not confronted by hundreds of references (see page 47). In some systems, related subjects (like the tracing on a card) are included in a title entry.

The first time you use an online catalog, you may need assistance from a librarian, but when you press the Enter or Return key, relatively simple instructions will appear on the screen. The commands will vary depending on the computer and program used, but general procedures are standardized.

Figure 2.1 illustrates a typical home page of an academic library. Note the drop-down menu on the left that allows you to search by keyword, title, author, subject, and so on. A similar menu on the right allows you to narrow your search within books, music, media, online resources, and several options.

THE WORK OF
COLLEEN LEE

Colleen had seen the name Emily Toth cited in several articles about Kate Chopin. To search for books by Toth, Colleen chose Author as her search category and typed Toth, Emily. Figure 2.2 shows the resulting list of titles.

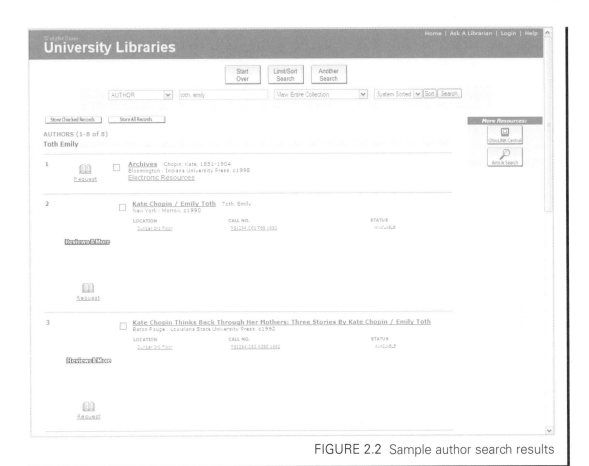

FIGURE 2.2 Sample author search results

James Kebler knew that John P. Parker's autobiography was called *His Promised Land,* but he was unsure of whether to search by editor or author. However, he knew he could locate the book by selecting a title search and entering His Promised Land. The result is shown in Figure 2.3.

As the annotations on Figure 2.3 indicate, the screen for each book provides a good deal of essential information. Especially useful is the inclusion of the Library of Congress subject headings used for this book and links to the other holdings in this library with these same subjects.

To enlarge his potential bibliography, James selected the link to Underground Railroad and found twenty-two titles (the first four appear in Figure 2.4).

THE WORK OF
JAMES KEBLER

Continued

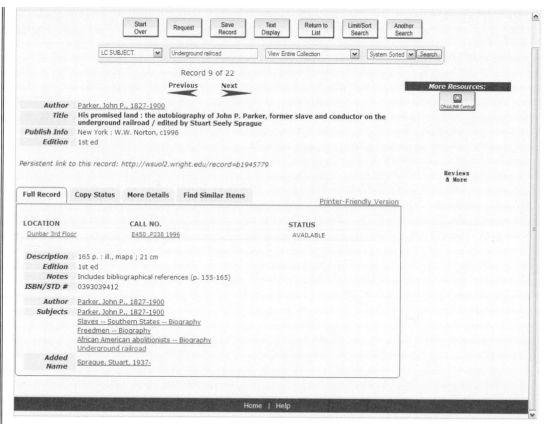

FIGURE 2.3 Sample title search results

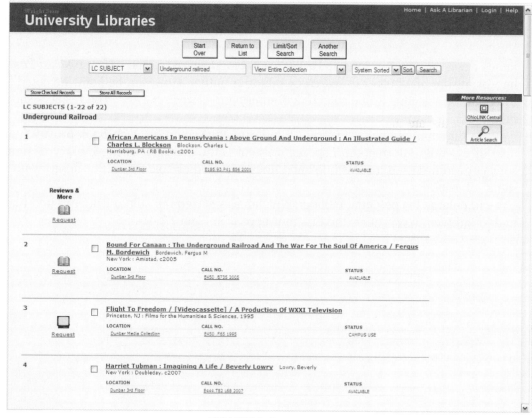

FIGURE 2.4 Results from the Underground Railroad link

Locating Books

The following suggestions may save you some time and annoyance when you search for books.

- Many libraries post charts that indicate the location of basic reference works and general categories of books.
- In a card catalog and on the shelves, works by a writer come first and works about that writer follow. This is especially important to remember if you investigate a prolific author such as Shakespeare or Dickens.
- Be alert for sources indirectly related to your topic. When you are investigating something, its importance magnifies; you feel that any book pertaining to your special interest should be cataloged under that heading. Sometimes useful discussions of a topic will be found on a single page of a book or in an article on a different, though related, subject. Use the "see also" references in the *LC Subject Headings* (see Chapter 1) and your imagination to find relevant sources. Be conscious of the periphery of your topic. For example, when James was looking at subject headings, he noted the following terms that he could use in addition to *Underground Railroad* and *Parker, John P.*:

  African American abolitionists—biography

  Freedmen—biography

  Slaves—Southern States—biography

- When you find a promising title in the online catalog, you may be able to print out the information. You may also have the option of e-mailing the information to yourself or saving it to your own disk or USB drive. If you cannot, be sure to copy the call number accurately. Omitting or changing one letter or numeral may make it impossible to find the book.
- After finding a book in the stacks, look at the books on either side. They will be related in subject matter even though you did not find them in the catalog.

Alphabetization Practices

In cataloging and, more importantly, in shelving books, most libraries follow the procedures listed here.

- Numerals are alphabetized as though spelled out; for example, *1984* by George Orwell will be found in the Ns.
- Abbreviations are usually filed as though the first letter was a word (the practice followed in most telephone books). For example, AT&T will be found near the beginning of the As. This practice is not universal, however; check all possibilities and, if necessary, consult a librarian.
- Names beginning with Mc or M' are filed as though spelled Mac.
- In authors' names and in titles, prefixes like *de* or *von* and articles (*a, an,* and *the*) are disregarded.
- Most libraries alphabetize word by word (a practice sometimes described as "short before long") as in *Encyclopedia Americana* rather than letter by letter as in *Encyclopaedia Britannica* and in telephone books. For example:

  Word by Word   bay, Bay State, bay window, bayberry, Bayonne
  Letter by Letter   bay, bayberry, Bayonne, Bay State, bay window

- If a book or an article is especially useful, check the catalog and periodical indexes for other works by the same author and with the same subject headings.

- If a book you want is listed as available but is not on the shelves, it may have been mis-shelved. Look at the shelves above and below, and look behind the books to make sure that it has not been accidentally pushed out of sight. Occasionally, the book you need will be found on a cart holding books to be reshelved or near a photocopier. Library research may give you new appreciation of the words *serendipity* and *tenacity*.

Understanding Internet Resources

The Internet has been called "a library without walls," and that metaphor aptly illustrates its strength and weakness as a research tool. While a traditional library screens, selects, and organizes information, the Internet is an extremely permissive collection, accepting text documents and graphics from virtually anyone with access to an Internet server. Although the Internet has enormous potential as a research tool, its users must critically assess what they find there.

Because the Internet contains so much information, students may assume that documents of all types and descriptions are available there, but that is not the case. Broadly speaking, the "free Internet" contains information that is in the public domain, not protected by copyright or licensing restrictions. This means that most books and articles published in the past seventy-five years will not be found on the Internet. That is why the Internet should not be the only computer resource used in your research, but it is often a good place to begin your research.

What Can You Find on the Internet?

An incredible variety of material is available on the Internet—chat groups, weather reports, batting averages, restaurant and entertainment guides, games, store catalogs, and airline schedules, as well as research reports and studies, some periodical and newspaper articles, and a variety of primary source materials. The first rule for an Internet researcher is to remain focused on the research topic and to resist the temptation to be distracted by unrelated sites. The second rule is to review the source, point of view, and completeness of all documents related to the research topic. When reviewing these documents, ask yourself the following questions:

1. Who hosts the site where you found a document? Look at the "domain" the site is in, identified by the last three letters of the home page address. Is it an academic institution (.edu), government agency (.gov), nonprofit organization (.org), or commercial organization (.com)?
2. If the host is a commercial organization (.com or .biz), has the type or quality of the information been compromised by the company's marketing motive? Review the completeness of documents and look for evidence of a marketing bias.
3. If the host is a research institute or advocacy group (.org), has the type or quality of the information been compromised by an ideological bias? Trace the URL back to the home page of the issuing source, and learn what you can about the group's political viewpoint and ideology.

    Specific Document: http://www.aclu.org/religion/gen/33210res20071213.html
    Home Page: http://www.aclu.org/
4. If the host is a college or university (.edu), is the document a stand-alone item from an unknown source or is it part of a larger research program? If part of a larger program, what type of program is it? A research program sponsored by the university and directed by a committee of professors or librarians has higher value than a class project created by students several years ago. See if the document contains a link back to a page that describes the project as a whole. If not, trace the URL back to a home page that describes the project. Keep in mind, too, that campus computing centers host many Web pages that are not officially sanctioned by the university.

5. Is the author a recognized authority in the field? Some have described the Internet as the world's largest vanity press because there are virtually no controls over self-publishing. You should generally ignore anonymous postings that lack biographical information about the author or a list of previous publications. A set of access tools discussed later in this section will help filter out many unreliable Web sites maintained by self-proclaimed experts.

6. Is the version of the document you found on the Internet the most current and comprehensive version available? Unfortunately, this is often a difficult question to answer. The introductory text will sometimes indicate if the document is a draft version circulated prior to an official release. If the document is called a "Summary" or "Executive Summary," then it is probably part of a longer report that you should try to find through a library search.

These notes of caution should not suggest that Internet resources have little or no research value. The following types of highly reliable resources are available in abundance on the Internet.

Books

Thousands of books in the public domain are now available on the Internet, where the ability to perform word searches may prove useful for some research paper topics, especially in the humanities. For example, if you were writing on light imagery in *Othello* or the concept of the poet in Plato's *Republic,* a word search of the electronic text would help to confirm that you had found and marked all relevant passages in your print version. The University of Pennsylvania currently hosts a large compilation of links to online books (http://digital.library .upenn.edu/books/), and Google Books has been working with libraries around the world to make out-of-copyright books available online (http://books.google.com/).

Government Documents

Congressional and federal agency publications contain current and authoritative information on a range of policy issues that are common research paper topics, such as abortion, affirmative action, environmental pollution, global warming, and prison conditions. In the past, when these publications were available only as print documents, libraries cataloged and stored them in separate collections, and the difficulty of access probably contributed to students' reluctance to include them as part of their research. The Internet has made these public documents much more accessible. Thousands of these publications are now available on government Web sites, and many can be accessed from two easy-to-use search sites:

"FedStats," covering statistical publications from more than seventy federal agencies (http://www.fedstats.gov/).

"Thomas: Congress at Work," covering the *Congressional Record,* the status of bills before Congress, the text of recently passed laws, and the transcripts of many congressional committee hearings (http://thomas.loc.gov/).

Magazines and Newspapers

The Internet availability of magazine and newspaper articles depends on business decisions made by commercial publishers. Some provide the full text of a current issue on their Web sites; others provide only abstracts or condensed versions of the current issue; still others provide access only to back issues. When using one of these sites, you should try to ascertain the completeness of what you find on a particular Web site; if the text of an article on the Internet seems incomplete, you should locate the print version in the library or obtain an electronic version through a commercial database.

Magazines and journals that originated as electronic publications, the so-called e-zines and e-journals, present a different set of problems. When using one of these publications, you should consider the reliability of the source, the professional qualifications of the authors, and, for scholarly, scientific, and technical journals, the presence of a *peer review* process, indicating that academic experts in that field have reviewed and approved an article for publication. Two publishers currently maintain lists of links to online magazines and newspapers: *NewsLink* (http://newslink.org/) and *Editor and Publisher* (http://editorandpublisher.com/eandp/index.jsp).

Public Policy Reports

Advocacy groups and some research organizations seek to influence government policy and public opinion and often make a wide range of material available. Organizations like the American Civil Liberties Union (ACLU), the Heritage Foundation, the Cato Institute, and the Sierra Club maintain Web sites containing the full texts of their publications. If you already know the name of an organization, you can easily locate its Web site. You can find a number of these groups listed in the Yahoo! directory for public policy institutes (http://dir.yahoo.com/Social_Science/political_science/public_policy/institutes/), which provides a very brief description of the groups as well as links to their sites.

Rare Prints and Manuscripts

Most large research libraries have separate departments that collect, catalog, and preserve rare print materials and unpublished manuscripts from organizations and famous persons. Many have recognized the Internet as a means of reaching a broad audience and have begun to digitize selections from some of their most popular collections. The result is a rich array of primary source material suitable for a research paper. SunSITE Digital Collections at the University of California, Berkeley, maintains an extensive list of links to other online collections of manuscripts and images (http://sunsite3.berkeley.edu/Collections/).

Browse and Search Strategies

In its early stages, the research process requires that you browse and search for potentially useful sources. While browsing, the mind is exploratory and curious; while searching, it is focused and purposeful. A combination of browsing and searching helps you recognize if your research topic is too broad and needs narrowing, and it uncovers a more complete set of relevant sources than could be found by either strategy alone.

A dual browse-search strategy is critical to the Internet researcher because no single access tool is precise enough or comprehensive enough to find all the relevant, high-quality sources on a given topic. The emergence of Web search engines in recent years (e.g., Lycos, Google, Excite, AltaVista) has improved access tremendously, but these powerful tools have two weaknesses: they often return irrelevant search results, and they cannot keep pace with the growth of the Internet.

Internet researchers can turn this apparent weakness to their advantage if they browse and search in combination, particularly during the early exploratory stages of their research project. Here's how such an approach might work:

1. Enter your research topic in the search box of one of the major search engines.
2. Review your search results, ignoring obvious false hits but investigating those that sound promising.
3. Review the source of each site accessed and the relevance, timeliness, and completeness of each document accessed. If the site still looks promising, bookmark it (using the bookmark tool in your browser) and print or save all relevant documents. If you are at a public terminal in a library or computer lab, you will need to e-mail the information to yourself or save it to your own disk or flash drive.

4. Web sites often have links to related sources. Explore these links. Your search engine might not have found these materials.

5. As you review these sites and learn more about your topic, you will come upon secondary topics that sound interesting. New searches using these additional topics might yield a fresh batch of documents with still more links to explore.

6. Run those same searches using at least one other search engine. You will doubtless uncover more related materials.

Though far from ideal, this process increases the likelihood that you will find high-value content on the Internet, helps in refining your search strategy, and aids in your thinking about your topic.

Advanced Searching and Subject Directories

To improve their efficiency and accuracy, some of the major search engines have added "advanced searching" capabilities that enable users to search for words in a title or search for documents in a particular domain (e.g., .gov). The home page of each search engine typically has a link to a page explaining its advanced searching capability. Another option is to use a "subject directory," a database of Internet materials selected by librarians and other subject specialists. A subject directory typically is organized as a hierarchy of links: Users navigate from broad to narrow subject areas and then perform a search on a set of Web sites assigned to that narrow area.

Yahoo! provides one of the best-known subject directories on the Internet (http://dir .yahoo.com/), but it is less selective than directories tailored for academic research purposes. Figure 2.5, from *Librarians' Internet Index* (http://lii.org/), shows a subject directory for the topic of breastfeeding. Note the amount of information provided about the sites.

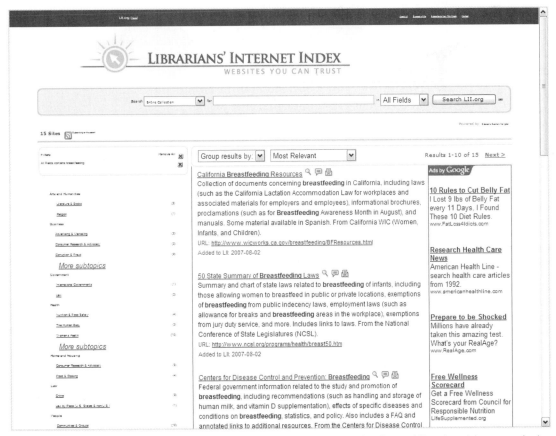

FIGURE 2.5 Sample of search results from *Librarians' Internet Index*

After unsuccessfully searching the card catalog for books dealing with animal hoarding, Paul decided to search the Internet from home. Selecting Google as his search engine, he entered the question, "What is animal hoarding?" in the search box (most search engines will process such natural language queries). The result was approximately 121,000 hits. Paul then went to Google Scholar (http://scholar.google.com), which restricts the search to scholarly sources. His first attempt returned 11,900 hits, but when he searched by enclosing the words *animal hoarding* in quotation marks, he found 74 results. He began to review these much more manageable results, looking for serious public policy analyses or research studies from respected sources, and he soon found several that looked promising. The first link took Paul to a site sponsored by the Hoarding of Animals Research Consortium (HARC), a collaborative effort by specialists in the fields of psychology, sociology, social work, psychiatry, veterinary medicine, epidemiology, and animal protection. The page is hosted by the Center for Animals and Public Policy, which is affiliated with the Tufts University School of Veterinary Medicine. Another link led to an article in the online version of the *Journal of the American Veterinary Medical Association.* Still others took him to animal advocacy sites that were linked to information about pending legislation in the home state of the organization, and some led to newspaper articles about individual incidents of hoarding (many of those links were no longer active).

Paul's experience suggests some guidelines for using the Internet as a research tool:

1. Use Internet materials critically. Filter and evaluate them based on document source and type.
2. Search and browse in combination. No search engine is powerful enough to cover all the material available on the Internet. Paul found some valuable sources simply by linking from one site to another.
3. Use your Internet experience to refine your search strategy. Paul read that the term *animal hoarding* is a recent one and that the behavior had sometimes been called "animal collecting," a phrase that might help him locate earlier materials. He also saw the names of several authorities and organizations that were frequently cited and made a note to look for books or articles by them.
4. Print or save valuable documents. Although the Internet is a rich source of information, documents do not have the permanence of print materials. Some Internet experts estimate that the average life span of a Web page is only seventy-five days. If you print a document, be sure the preferences are set so that the printout includes the URL of the site and the date you accessed it. If you save the document to a disk, a flash drive, or your hard drive, be sure to make a note of the full URL and the date. You will need this information if you cite the document in your paper.

Searching Commercial Databases

If you explored the Internet during the first phase of your research, then a search of CD-ROM and online databases of newspaper and periodical articles is the logical next step. These databases have two distinct advantages over the Internet. They cover copyrighted materials that are usually not found on the free Internet, and they support a more controlled and focused search of their contents. You will find these databases in the library, which sometimes allows students offsite access as well.

Types of Databases

The first time you use a database you should assess its scope of coverage. Is it a general database covering a broad range of newspaper and magazine articles? Or is it a specialized collection of articles that apply to a single academic discipline, such as literary studies, psychology, or history? While you will find relevant information on most research topics in a general database, you will often find more in-depth coverage in a specialized database, including journal articles, essays in books, and conference papers. Examples of general and specialized databases are described in Chapter 3.

You should also assess the contents of a particular database. Is it a bibliographic database containing author and title information, publication facts, subject indexing, and abstracts? Is it a full-text database containing the complete text of the articles? Or is it a hybrid—a bibliographic database with some full text? You should resist the temptation to limit your sources to the full texts that are available electronically. Good research still requires some legwork—a willingness to find the print version and retrieve it from the stacks.

Basic and Advanced Searching

Companies that design databases and sell them to libraries invest a great deal of time and money in studying how students use computers and perform searches, and they design their products accordingly. Because many people prefer to perform free-text searches—to enter a word or phrase in the search box and hope for the best—most commercial databases offer a "basic" search feature that looks much the same from product to product. The basic search screen in Figure 2.6 comes from *Academic Search Complete,* a database that provides bibliographic citations, abstracts, and full texts of scholarly publications in a number of areas. The

FIGURE 2.6 Basic search from *Academic Search Complete*

basic search is extremely simple. Enter the term or terms you are looking for, and click on the search button. The search locates all instances of those terms in the records in the database, and the results are often so extensive as to be unusable. In that case, it would be better to turn to an advanced search.

The phrase "advanced search" should not suggest that such a search is so difficult that only an expert can perform it. Although an advanced search requires more strategic thinking and data selection than a basic search does, it yields more precise results because it exploits the detailed content tagging found in the database. As Figure 2.7 shows, the advanced search allows the reader to use several search terms. The drop-down menus to the right of the search term (here labeled "Select a Field") allow the user to select the field to be searched. In this particular database, there are seventeen options. Probably the most useful of the options are author, title, subject terms, abstract, and all text. The drop-down menus to the left of the second and third search boxes enable the user to include additional search terms. It is possible to search for those terms in either the same field as the first term or in a different field. In addition, the bottom portion of the search screen makes it possible to target the search by selecting such things as the type of document, the language of publication, and even the type of illustration.

A particularly important consideration is whether to carry out the search using *Boolean* operators to expand or narrow the relationship between two or more search terms. In Figure 2.7 that choice would be made by selecting "Boolean/Phrase" in the box labeled "Search modes." The standard operators are OR, AND, and NOT (sometimes expressed as AND NOT).

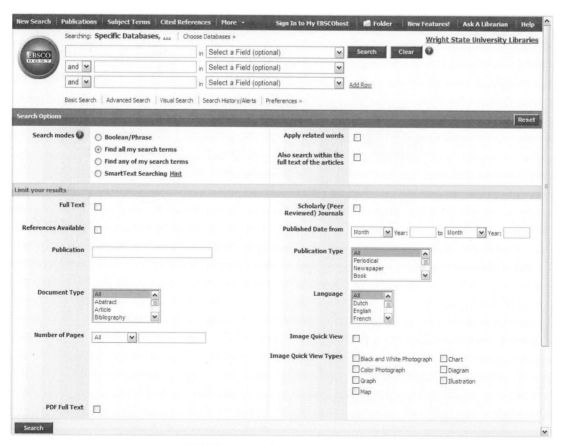

FIGURE 2.7 Advanced search from *Academic Search Complete*

In a Boolean search, joining two terms with OR broadens the search:

or

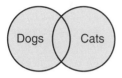

Dogs OR Cats

If terms are joined by AND, both of them must be in the record. This strategy obviously narrows a search.

and

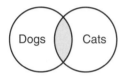

Dogs AND Cats

Using NOT or AND NOT will narrow a search and retrieve fewer sources. Only the first term must appear in a record; if both terms appear, the record will be disregarded.

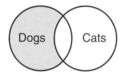

Dogs NOT Cats

Many databases offer a WITHIN or NEAR operator for finding records in which the two terms occur in relative proximity to one another.

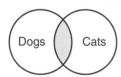

Dogs W/3 Cats

Proximity searching is best used as a means of finding passages in a full-text database in which two topics are discussed in relation to one another.

Boolean searching, it so happens, is an unadvertised feature on most basic search screens—in commercial databases and even on the World Wide Web. To conduct such a search, you merely need to use Boolean operators to connect topics within the search box:

    comedy AND television AND prime time
    comedy OR humor OR slapstick

These searches become a bit more complex when you want to mix AND and OR operators within one search statement. Because search engines will process an AND expression before an OR expression, the following statement will return confusing results:

> comedy OR humor AND television

The solution is to enclose the OR expression in parentheses, which instructs the search engine to perform this operation first:

> (comedy OR humor) AND television

A better solution is to use the advanced search screen for such complex searches because you can select Boolean operators from drop-down menus and rely on the search engine to build your search statement. This is the appeal of an advanced search—it makes complex searching easier.

THE WORK OF
PAUL SANCHEZ

Paul wondered if any instances of animal hoarding had occurred recently near where he lived. To find out, he went to *LexisNexis Academic,* which provides access to over 5,600 sources, including national, regional, and international newspapers, magazines, wire services, and broadcast transcripts. Using the Boolean term "animal W/1 hoarding," Paul selected U.S. Newspapers and Wires as a source and specified the previous year for the date (Figure 2.8). The results can then be sorted geographically. Paul skimmed through a number of the resulting stories and, whenever he found a promising reference or a powerful detail, e-mailed a copy of the story to himself.

FIGURE 2.8 Sample *LexisNexis Academic* search screen

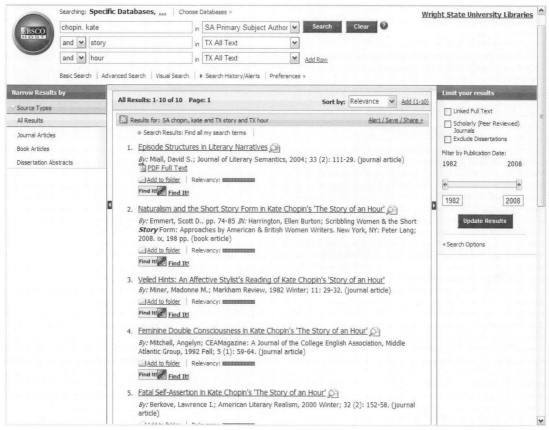

FIGURE 2.9 Sample results from *MLA International Bibliography*

Colleen wanted to find critical essays about Kate Chopin's short story "The Story of an Hour." She went to *MLA International Bibliography,* a specialized database that draws bibliographic information for literature and related fields from over 3,500 journals, monographs, dissertations, and other materials. Coverage for the database begins with 1963. When she searched for Kate Chopin as a subject, she found 576 records. A quick look showed her that most of the entries were about Chopin's novel *The Awakening.* When she used the Boolean strategy of narrowing the search by looking for Kate Chopin as the Primary Subject Author field AND Story AND Hour in the All Text fields, she found nine articles (Figure 2.9). Colleen downloaded copies of the full texts available, and when she checked the "find a copy" links on the others, she learned that her library had two of them. She printed out the citations and went to look at the additional ones available.

Using the Reference Room

In the early stages of your research, the most useful library facilities will probably be the catalog, databases, and general reference works like those listed at the close of this chapter. Some you will use chiefly during your exploratory reading as you search for a topic; others, such as dictionaries, you will use throughout your research to verify information. Probably the most useful research tools will be indexes to periodicals, which enable you to find articles just as the catalog enables you to find books. Many of the general indexes listed in this chapter are available online and on CD-ROM.

The Reference Librarian

Librarians in the Reference Room are specially trained to answer questions and to direct researchers to sources of information. Take a moment to prepare your questions before asking for help. It is difficult for a busy librarian to give a helpful response to a vague, general question. Don't just ask where you can find *Readers' Guide;* instead, ask what periodical index is most suitable for your topic.

> **Vague:** I need some information about Hawaii.
> **Improved:** I need a map (or a history, or the population, or the principal exports) of Hawaii.
> **Vague:** Where are the art books?
> **Improved:** Where can I find out where the term *Impressionism* came from?

Even if your school library remains open until midnight, reference librarians may be on duty only in the daytime. Plan your library visits accordingly.

General Reference Works

General reference works are more or less useful in all fields. They are usually shelved in a separate room and must be used there. Specialized reference works may be found in the Reference Room, or they may be shelved in the general collection according to their call numbers. In the lists in the following subsections, a dash after a year (e.g., 1976–) indicates continuing publication, usually on an annual basis. Whenever possible, a U.S. publisher or distributor is cited. Titles of edited works rather than editors' names are cited first because you are more likely to recognize a book by its title and because the editor may change when a new edition is published, but the title will remain the same. Brief comments in parentheses describe special features of some works. Indexes are discussed in Chapter 3.

Atlases and Gazetteers

For geographical information, consult an atlas (a collection of maps) or a gazetteer (a dictionary of places). Check the copyright year of any of these works to be certain that you will get up-to-date information; for example, any discussion of the Soviet Union will be inaccurate in an atlas published before 1992.

> *Encyclopedic Atlas of the World.* 6th ed. New York: Oxford, 2002.
> *Hammond Atlas of the World.* 4th ed. Union: Hammond, 2003.
> *National Geographic Atlas of the World.* 8th rev. ed. Washington: Natl. Geographic, 2005.
> *The Times Atlas of the World.* 3rd ed. London: Times, 2006.

Biographical Dictionaries

For a complete account of a person's life, consult full-length biographies, but for checking biographical facts, reference works like those listed here would be more convenient to use. There are hundreds of specialized works such as *Who's Who in Opera* or *Who's Who in Health Care.*

American Men and Women of Science. 21st ed. 8 vols. New Providence: Bowker, 2003.
Biography Index. New York: Wilson, 1947–. (Quarterly; cumulated annually and every five years. An index to books and articles about living and nonliving persons.) Database coverage from 1984.
Current Biography. New York: Wilson, 1940–. (Monthly except August; annual cumulations. Articles about living persons. Especially useful for current celebrities. Index in each volume covers preceding years of the decade.)
Dictionary of American Biography. 20 vols. New York: Scribner's, 1928–. (DAB. Reissued in 11 vols. in 1974. Supplements. Authoritative articles on nonliving Americans who made significant contributions to American life.)

Dictionary of National Biography. 22 vols. London: Smith, 1908–1909–. (*DNB.* Rpt. 1985. Supplements. The basic source of information on nonliving British notables.)

Who's Who. London: Black, 1849–. (Annually. *Who Was Who* reprints discontinued entries.)

Who's Who Among African Americans. Ed. Shirelle Phelps. Detroit: Gale, 1996–.

Who's Who in America. New Providence: Marquis, 1899–. (Biennially; annually since 1994. *Who Was Who in America* reprints discontinued entries.)

Dictionaries

For spelling, capitalization, and similar information, use any standard dictionary. For a listing of related words that can serve as a word finder, use a thesaurus. For precise shades of meaning and a wide range of synonyms, use an unabridged dictionary. For the semantic history of a word with dated quotations illustrating changes in meaning, use a historical dictionary (*OED* or *DAE*).

A Dictionary of American English on Historical Principles. Ed. William A. Craigie and James R. Hulbert. 4 vols. Chicago: U of Chicago P, 1936–44. (*DAE.* A historical dictionary of American words and meanings modeled after the *OED.*)

Dictionary of American Regional English. Ed. Frederic G. Cassidy and Joan H. Hall. 4 vols. to date. Cambridge: Harvard UP, 1985–2002. (One more volume will complete this authoritative record of American usage. Maps show the distribution of many terms.)

McGraw-Hill Dictionary of Scientific and Technical Terms. Ed. Sybil P. Parker. 6th ed. New York: McGraw, 2003.

Oxford English Dictionary. 20 vols. Oxford: Clarendon, 1989. (*OED.* Originally published as *A New English Dictionary on History Principles* [*NED*], 1884–; retitled in 1933. Four-volume supplement, 1972–86. Dated quotations trace the history of a word's meanings.)

Random House Webster's Unabridged Dictionary. 2nd ed., rev. New York: Random, 2005.

Roget's International Thesaurus. Ed. Barbara Ann Kipfer. 6th ed. New York: HarperResources, 2001. (Several other editions of this work, first published 1852, are available.)

Webster's Third New International Dictionary of the English Language. Springfield: Merriam, 1961. (Often referred to as *W3.* Later printings contain revisions and lists of new words. Supplements.)

Dictionaries of Quotations

Works like those listed here are useful if you want to find a quotation (sometimes an effective way of opening a paper), learn the source of a quotation, or verify its exact wording. Because methods of organization vary, examine the preface before using one of these books.

Bartlett's Familiar Quotations. Ed. Justin Kaplan. 17th ed. Boston: Little, 2002. (Arranged chronologically by author. Key-word index.)

Oxford Dictionary of Quotations. Ed. Elizabeth Knowles. 6th ed. New York: Oxford UP, 2004. (Arranged alphabetically by author. Key-word index.)

What They Said. Beverly Hills: Monitor, 1969–. (Annually. Collections of statements by prominent persons.)

Encyclopedias

These and other encyclopedias are available in a variety of electronic forms.

Academic American Encyclopedia. 21 vols. Danbury: Grolier, 1997.

Collier's Encyclopedia. 24 vols. New York: Macmillan, 1997. (Designed for high school and college use. Annual supplement, *Collier's Encyclopedia Yearbook.*)

The Columbia Encyclopedia. Ed. Barbara A. Chernow and George A. Vallasi. 6th ed. Detroit: Gale, 2000.

Encyclopedia Americana. International ed. 30 vols. Danbury: Grolier, 2006. (Supplement, *Americana Annual.*)

The New Encyclopaedia Britannica. 15th ed. 32 vols. Chicago: Encyclopaedia Britannica, 2002. (In 1974 the *Britannica* was completely restructured into three parts: *Micropaedia,* 12 vols., containing short factual articles; *Macropaedia,* 17 vols., containing more than 4,000 in-depth articles; and *Propaedia,* an outline of knowledge and an index to the other 30 vols. Supplement, *Britannica Book of the Year.*)

Wikipedia, one of the most popular online encyclopedias, should be used with caution: entries may be posted by anyone and accuracy is not guaranteed.

Government Publications

The vast number and the great variety of materials published by national, state, and local government agencies make reference works like the following indispensable. Some libraries maintain a separate catalog and filing system for government documents, in which case you may need assistance from a reference librarian to locate what you need (see pages 64–65). Many of these publications are now available online or on CD-ROM; they are often easier to work with in those formats (see page 31).

American Statistics Index. Washington: CIS, 1973–. (Annually; monthly supplements. Index and abstracts of all federal government publications that contain statistical data.)

Congressional Information Service Index to Publications of the United States Congress. Washington: CIS, 1970–. (Monthly; annual cumulations. Brief abstracts. Useful for hearings and other activities of Congressional committees. Usually referred to as *CIS/Index.*)

Guide to U.S. Government Publications. Ed. John L. Andriot. McLean: Documents Index, 1973–. (Annually. Quarterly supplements.)

Monthly Catalog of U.S. Government Publications. Washington: GPO, 1895–. (Monthly; semi-annual and annual cumulations. Indexes.)

Statistical Abstract of the United States. Washington: GPO, 1879–. (Annually. Summary of statistical information of all kinds.)

Yearbooks

Yearbooks and almanacs are useful sources of statistics and other factual data.

Countries of the World and Their Leaders Yearbook. Detroit: Gale, 1980–. (Annually.)

Europa World Year Book. 2 vols. London: Europa, 1946–. (Factual data on European countries in vol. 1; on other countries in vol. 2. Now published in the United States by Gale.)

Facts on File. New York: Facts on File, 1940–. (Weekly news digests. Annual cumulations.)

Guinness Book of Records. New York: Facts on File, 1962–.

Information Please Almanac. Boston: Houghton, 1947–.

Statesman's Yearbook. New York: St. Martin's, 1864–. (A British handbook. Useful for information on governmental and international organizations.)

The World Almanac and Book of Facts. New York: St Martin's, 1868–.

Checklist for Learning Research Resources and Procedures

☑ I have become familiar with the layout of the library (or libraries) I will use in doing my research.

☑ I have searched the library catalog for books about my topic.

☑ I have searched commercial databases for information related to my topic.

☑ I have determined the source of each Web site I plan to use for my paper.

Exercise C

Exploring the Library

C.1 In your school's library:

1. Are there separate libraries for undergraduate and graduate students? _____

2. Are there any specialized libraries, e.g., medical, legal, engineering? _____

3. What are the opening and closing hours on weekdays? _____

4. What are the weekend hours? _____

5. How long can books be checked out? _____

6. What is the fine for overdue books? _____

7. What classification system is used? _____

8. Is there a card catalog as well as an online catalog? _____

9. If there is a card catalog, are the cards filed in one alphabetization (a dictionary catalog) or in separate author, title, and subject alphabetizations (a divided catalog)? _____

10. Does the online catalog include holdings from other libraries? _____

11. Are the stacks open or closed? _____

12. Where can you learn what periodicals the library holds? _____

13. Are bound periodicals shelved in alphabetical order or according to their call numbers? _____

14. Is there a browsing shelf? Where is it? _____

15. Is there a recorded music collection? Where is it? _____

16. Is there a rare book room? Where is it? _____

17. How can you learn what books are on reserve? _____

18. Where are reserve books located? _____

19. What reference works are available online? _____

20. Are CD-ROM computers available? _____

21. Is there a photocopying service? Is a special copy card required to operate copiers? _____

22. Do undergraduates have interlibrary loan privileges? _____

23. Are study carrels available? _____

24. What microforms (microfilm, microfiche, ultrafiche) are available? Where are the readers? _____

25. Is there a computer lab? What hours is it open? Are printers available there? If so, is there a charge for printing? _____

26. Is there a viewing room for films? _____

C.2 Where can you find each of the following library resources? (Provide a room name or number or a quick sketch.)

1. Catalog (card or online) _____

2. *Dictionary of American Biography* _____

3. *Readers' Guide to Periodical Literature* _____

4. *Library of Congress Subject Heading* _____

5. Maps and charts _____

6. Current magazines _____

7. Government documents _____

8. Encyclopedias _____

9. *Who's Who* _____

10. Microform readers _____

11. *Book Review Digest* _____

12. *Oxford English Dictionary* _____

13. *New York Times Index* _____

14. Photocopiers _____

15. Computer lab _____

Exercise D

Searching Reference Works

Under each item write the information requested and the reference source where you found it.

1. Source of "Hope springs eternal."

   Information: _____

   Source: _____

2. Event in Jewish history commemorated by Pesach

   Information: _____

   Source: _____

3. Title of one novel by winner of the 2007 Nobel Prize for Literature

   Information: _____

   Source: _____

4. Date and significance of Saint Cecilia's Day

   Information: _____

   Source: _____

5. Grandfather of the author of *The Education of Henry Adams*

   Information: _____

   Source: _____

6. Names of children of George W. Bush

   Information: _____

   Source: _____

7. Mother of Dionysus

   Information: _____

   Source: _____

8. Capital of South Carolina

   Information: _____

   Source: _____

9. Atomic number and symbol of iron

Information: _____

Source: _____

10. Medical function of Ephedrine

Information: _____

Source: _____

11. Birth name of Malcolm X

Information: _____

Source: _____

12. Painter of *Les Demoiselles d'Avignon*

Information: _____

Source: _____

13. Birthplace of Warren G. Harding

Information: _____

Source: _____

14. Village described in "The Deserted Village" by Oliver Goldsmith

Information: _____

Source: _____

15. Winner of the Heisman Memorial Trophy award in 1968

Information: _____

Source: _____

16. City where *Oedipus Rex* by Sophocles takes place

Information: _____

Source: _____

17. Birth name of film star Angelina Jolie

Information: _____

Source: _____

18. Distribution of votes cast in President Andrew Johnson's impeachment

Information: _____

Source: _____

Using Basic Reference Sources

The first task is to search books.

The Rambler, no. 154

Besides learning your way around the library, you should become familiar with basic tools of research, such as CD-ROM databases, Internet resources, indexes, and bibliographies. You can discover some books and articles related to your topic by searching a catalog, by browsing in the stacks, or by paging through journals, but you will miss useful material if you do not consult research tools such as those described in this chapter. Unless you have spent considerable time in a large library, you will be amazed at the vast amount of information available and at the various methods of locating it. Most of the reference sources described in this chapter can be accessed in databases found online or on CD-ROM. Print versions usually will be shelved in the Reference Room, but some may be at the reference librarian's desk or in the stacks. The library you are using may have one of these resources exclusively in one form or the other, but many will have some of both. In some, for example, bound copies of *MLA International Bibliography* may be available only up to 1963, the point at which electronic coverage of this important resource begins.

Each medium has its advantages and drawbacks. A database allows you to search all available years at once, whereas the print version of an index or bibliography requires looking in every individual volume for every term you search. Most electronic sources will allow the user to print, save, or e-mail records, so the time required to transcribe information accurately is greatly reduced. Print versions, however, make certain kinds of browsing possible. For example, the *see* and *see also* cross-references found in print sources may lead you to some search terms you had not thought of—terms you may have to generate independently to search a database. Likewise, subdivisions visible in print may suggest new ways of thinking about your topic. Print versions of some indexes also have features not available in other formats (see, for instance, the discussion of *Book Review Digest,* page 57). While you are still exploring your topic, it might be to your advantage to look at a few print sources first, then use the information you gain when you work with databases.

One more word of advice: Be prepared to spend some time refining your search terms, especially when you work with databases. Initially you may find no entries for your topic—or thousands. If you're having difficulty determining the terms to use, several strategies may help. First, look at a print version of one of these sources to see what subject headings are used. The volumes of *Library of Congress Subject Headings* mentioned in Chapter 1 may also be useful. In a database, you can also check for subject headings when you do locate a reference that looks promising. Finally, a reference librarian can be extremely helpful in refining search terms.

Because articles are parts of larger units, they are sometimes more difficult to locate than books, but they are indispensable. For many topics, articles contain the most relevant and up-to-date information. The resources described here are more or less useful in all fields. Librarians can help you locate indexes and databases that are appropriate for particular disciplines.

General Listings of Books and Articles

Ex. E

Books In Print

If you have difficulty finding books for your topic, you should consult *Books In Print*, which provides bibliographic descriptions and publication status information for approximately 3.5 million books from over 165,000 U.S. publishers, distributors, wholesalers, and book agents. It includes data concerning out-of-print books, forthcoming books, children's books, and audio and video recordings. You can include or eliminate these categories as you search the database, and you may browse by general subject categories or by specialized index categories (author, publisher, series, and so on).

THE WORK OF JAMES KEBLER

After narrowing his topic to the Underground Railroad, James did a quick online search in *Books In Print* using "Underground Railroad" as a keyword. Figure 3.1 is the opening portion of his results, which included books that are in print, out of print, or pending publication, as well as other media (video, audio). The search resulted in fourteen titles, sorted by date, each with links to further information. Figure 3.2 illustrates the bibliographic record attached to the fourth title (*Front Line of Freedom: African Americans and the Forging of the*

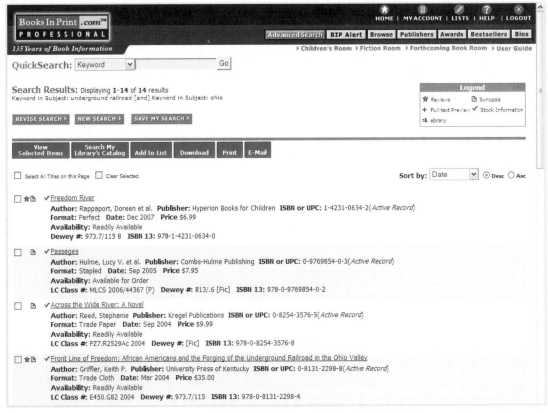

FIGURE 3.1 Sample *Books In Print* keyword search results

Bowker Subjects:	FUGITIVE SLAVES UNITED STATES
	OHIO RIVER AND VALLEY HISTORY
	UNDERGROUND RAILROAD
	AFRICAN AMERICANS HISTORY
	ANTISLAVERY MOVEMENTS UNITED STATES
General Subjects (BISAC):	HISTORY / United States / Civil War Period (1850-1877)
	HISTORY / United States / General
	HISTORY / United States / State & Local / Midwest (IA, IL, IN, KS, MI, MN, MO, ND, NE, OH, SD, WI)
	SOCIAL SCIENCE / Ethnic Studies / African-American Studies
LCCN:	2003-024588
LC Class #:	E450.G82 2004
Dewey #:	973.7/115
Physical Dimensions (W x L x H):	6 x 9 in.
	.899 lbs.
Synopsis/Annotation:	While most books on the underground railroad focus on the white "conductors" and black "passengers," Front Line of Freedom looks at the primarily black-led frontline struggle along the Ohio River, which made the underground railroad American first successful interracial freedom movement.
	While most books on the underground railroad focus on the white "conductors" and black "passengers," Front Line of Freedom looks at the primarily black-led frontline struggle along the Ohio River, which made the underground railroad American first successful interracial freedom movement.
	The Underground Railroad, an often misunderstood antebellum institution, has been viewed as a simple combination of mainly white "conductors" and black "passengers." Keith P. Griffler takes a completely new battlefield-level view of the war against American slavery as he reevaluates one of its front lines -- the Ohio River, the longest commercial dividing line between slavery and freedom. In shifting the focus from the much discussed white-led "stations" along routes conducting fugitives through free states to the primarily black-led frontline struggle along the Ohio, Griffler reveals for the first time the history and crucial importance of the freedom movement in the river's port cities and towns. Front Line of Freedom examines the full context of America's first successful interracial freedom movement, which proved to be as much a struggle to transform the states north of the Ohio as those to its south. In a climate of racial proscription, mob violence, and white hostility, the efforts of Ohio Valley African Americans to establish and maintain viable communities became inextricably linked to the steady stream of fugitives crossing the region. By revealing the pivotal role of African Americans, Front Line of Freedom sketches the contours of what became a truly interracial struggle against slavery, demonstrating collaboration at every level of the enterprise. As Griffler traces the efforts of African Americans to free themselves, he provides a window into the process by which this clandestine network took shape and grew into a powerful force in antebellum America.
Author Info:	Keith R. Griffler is assistant professor of African American Studies at the University of Cincinnati. (Blackwell)

FIGURE 3.2 Sample synopsis and subject links from *Books In Print* entry

Underground Railroad in the Ohio Valley). Note that the bibliographic record includes a substantial synopsis as well as additional links, which identify additional subject headings that James might use for further exploration of the topic.

The print version of *Books In Print* consists of separate volumes in which books are listed by author, by title, and by subject, with another separate volume for publisher information. Although searching these volumes may seem somewhat unwieldy, using them during an early stage of your research may be productive. The subject volume contains cross-references and subdivisions that may be valuable in helping you think about ways to approach your topic. Once you have that information, you can search the online version using those terms.

Vertical File Index

Vertical File Index is a subject index to pamphlets and other inexpensive materials, such as charts and maps. Each entry contains a brief abstract and directions for ordering the item. This reference is especially useful for students in education and for classroom teachers. The monthly issues are cumulated quarterly and semiannually.

Essay & General Literature Index

An author-subject index to anthologies, collections of essays, and other composite volumes, *Essay & General Literature Index* covers all fields in the humanities and social sciences, but its emphasis is on literary subjects. Database coverage begins with 1985.

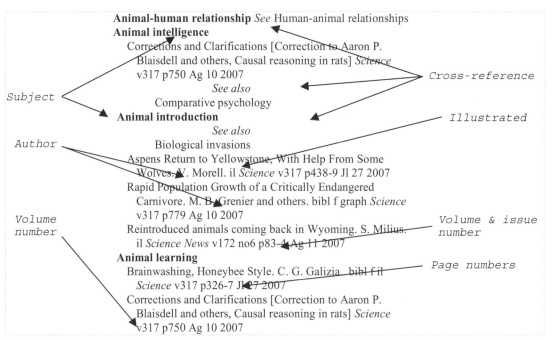

FIGURE 3.3 Sample entries from *Readers' Guide*

Readers' Guide

Readers' Guide to Periodical Literature indexes over 400 periodicals, ranging from *AARP: Modern Maturity* to *Zion's Herald*. Although it is useful for popular or nonacademic subjects, many instructors prefer that students use scholarly journals. Many students learn to use *Readers' Guide* in high school and feel comfortable with its listing of author and subject entries in a single alphabetization. An article will be listed under the author's name and under at least one subject heading. Titles of articles are seldom main entries, but short stories and plays are listed by title. Reviews of films, dance recitals, musicals, operas, radio and television programs, and plays are listed collectively under generic headings. Cross-references are liberally used in the print version, and they may suggest useful ways for continuing to think about your topic. Figure 3.3 suggests the extent of these cross-references. Book reviews, however, are listed in an appendix. Database coverage begins with 1983.

Humanities International Complete

Humanities International Complete provides full text of hundreds of journals, books, and other published sources from around the world. It includes all data from *Humanities International Index* (over two thousand titles and two million records), plus full text for more than 770 journals. Database coverage begins in 1975.

Figure 3.4 shows the first screen of an author search that Colleen did for Kate Chopin. The fourth item is a detailed analysis of the story that Colleen has chosen for her paper, and the fact that Chopin's name does not occur in the title of the book points to the value of such a search.

THE WORK OF COLLEEN LEE

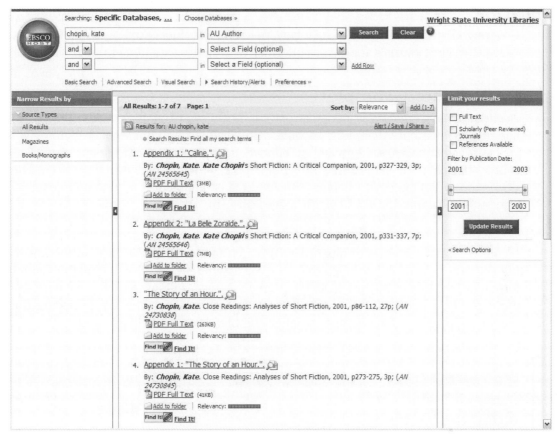

FIGURE 3.4 Sample entries from *Humanities International Complete*

Education Abstracts

Education Abstracts, which covers over 500 periodicals relating to education, contains some full-text articles as well as abstracts and citations. Indexing begins with 1983, abstracts with 1994. In its print form, under the title *Education Index*, it is published ten times a year and cumulated annually.

ERIC

Educational Resources Information Center (ERIC) is a federally funded project that indexes both published articles and unpublished papers, reports, and other documents. Students may overlook this research tool because they assume (understandably) that it is intended only for research in education; actually, it covers a broad range of topics. Since it is in the public domain, it is available on an unusually large number of electronic sources, including direct online access (http://www.eric.ed.gov).

As with the other databases, the descriptors you find on individual records can be used to refine further searching. There is no charge for using *ERIC* to retrieve citations and abstracts; on the basis of this information, you can often retrieve full texts from other databases in your library without any cost. For a fee, it is also possible to obtain a copy of the text (available in paper, microfiche, and electronic form). Of course, if the record is a book or journal article, you can obtain it through your library or interlibrary loan.

SocINDEX

Covering all the subdivisions of sociology, *SocINDEX* includes well over a million records. For over 620 "core" journals, it provides informative abstracts extending from 1895 to the present.

Academic Search Complete

Academic Search Complete is a popular place to begin searching for articles. It contains citations and abstracts of more than 4,500 scholarly publications and full-text access to over 3,500. It covers social sciences, the humanities, education, engineering, and science. Coverage of most sources begins in the mid-1990s, though for some sources it begins in the 1970s. The general discussion of databases in Chapter 2 included illustrations of the basic and advanced search screens for *Academic Search Complete* (pages 35–36).

THE WORK OF
PAUL SANCHEZ

Figure 3.5 represents the results of Paul's search for "animal hoarding" in the abstracts of full-text articles available through the database. Each item includes the full bibliographic information: the title of the article, the author(s), the magazine or journal in which it appears, the date, the volume and issue numbers, the page on which the article begins, the total number of pages, and the number of color and black-and-white illustrations.

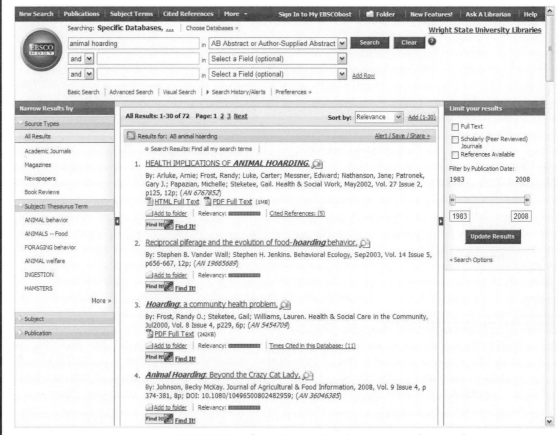

FIGURE 3.5 Sample results of *Academic Search Complete* search

The text documents that you find can be viewed in one (or both) of two formats—hypertext markup language (HTML) or Portable Document Format (PDF), a file format developed by Adobe requiring a special reader (if it is not already installed on the computer you are using, you will be prompted to download a free version of the reader). Each format has its advantages. The HTML version will highlight the search terms you used (usually in italics or boldface), which may speed up your preliminary reading. A PDF file reproduces an article just as it appears in the magazine or journal, which allows you to cite specific page numbers from that source if you use it in your paper.

Newspaper Indexes

Thanks to computerization, many major U.S. newspapers are now indexed in print, online, or both. You may be able to use an index to a newspaper in the city where the event you are investigating occurred. The most widely available index, however, is the *New York Times Index*, which began publication in 1913. Paperbound issues come out every two weeks and are cumulated quarterly. Annual cumulations are hardbound. News items are listed by subject and are arranged chronologically. There are numerous cross-references. This index can be useful for dating events even if the newspaper itself is unavailable.

If individual people are particularly important to the subject you are researching, two other sets of reference works, prepared by Byron A. Falk, Jr., and Valerie R. Falk, may be especially useful in working with the *New York Times:*

Personal Name Index to "The New York Times Index" 1851–1974. 22 vols. Verdi: Roxbury Data Interface, 1983.
Personal Name Index to "The New York Times Index" 1975–2001 Supplement. 9 vols. Sparks: Roxbury Data Interface, 2004.

Newspaper Source

Newspaper Source includes full text for over 200 sources, including 170 regional U.S. newspapers and twenty international newspapers, as well as transcripts from television and radio news sources. This database also contains abstracts for the *New York Times* and the *Wall Street Journal–Eastern Edition.*

LexisNexis Academic

LexisNexis Academic draws on over 5,600 sources to provide full-text coverage of a wide variety of fields. News articles are updated daily, making it especially useful for coverage of national and regional newspapers, wire services, and broadcast transcripts. It is also a good source of information for law-related issues, including court decisions, statutes, regulations, and legal opinions. Chapter 2 includes an illustration of a *LexisNexis* search screen (page 38).

General Indexes

Bibliographic Index

A good way to begin compiling your list of Works Cited is to consult *Bibliographic Index,* an author-subject listing of both books and articles that contain bibliographies. It is published quarterly and cumulated once a year. Online it can be accessed from a variety of providers.

Biography Index

Biography Index cites biographical articles appearing in more than 3,000 periodicals, 2,000 current books of individual and collective biography, and biographical material in other books. Database coverage for this index begins in 1984.

MLA International Bibliography

For literary topics, the most useful reference is *MLA International Bibliography,* published annually by the Modern Language Association. Database coverage begins with 1963. The database version of the *MLA International Bibliography* was introduced in Chapter 2 (page 39). Figure 3.6 shows the individual record for one of the articles retrieved by the search illustrated there.

In the print version, the arrangement proceeds from the geographical (American), to the chronological (1880–99), to individual writers (Kate Chopin), to individual works ("The Story of an Hour"). If no year is cited in an entry, you can assume it was published in the year covered by the bibliography. Abbreviations like *StWF* (*Studies in Weird Fiction*) are identified at the beginning of a volume.

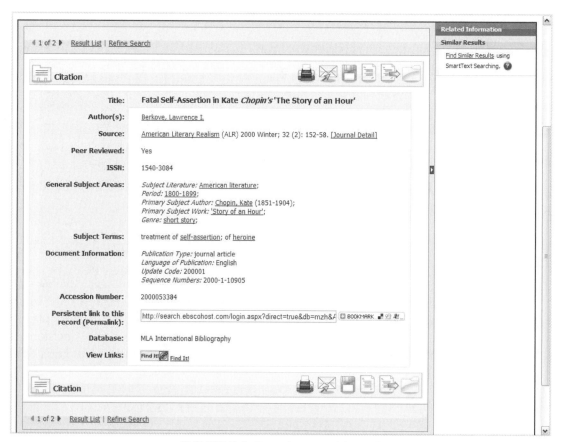

FIGURE 3.6 Sample record from *MLA International Bibliography*

Citation Indexes

Most periodical indexes are organized by author and subject—and sometimes by title—but a citation index allows you to locate articles that cite a particular writer. The three best known citation indexes are produced by Thomson Reuters: the *Arts & Humanities Citation Index* (covering nearly 1,400 journals), *Sciences Citation Index Expanded* (covering over 7,700 journals), and *Social Sciences Citation Index* (covering over 2,400 journals). Selecting the cited references search will take you to a screen that allows you to specify the author being cited, a particular work being cited, and even the year the cited work was published.

Figure 3.7 shows the search Colleen created to locate articles that cite "The Story of an Hour," the Kate Chopin story she wants to write about. She left the box for the year of publication open because she knew the story had been reprinted a number of times and she did not want to exclude an article simply because it used a different edition of the story.

The search resulted in nine records (Figure 3.8), four of them duplicating references Colleen had already found. Two of the others were references to articles she had not located at all in her *MLA International Bibliography* search, and the remaining two were titles that she had seen but that had not been identified as dealing with "The Story of an Hour."

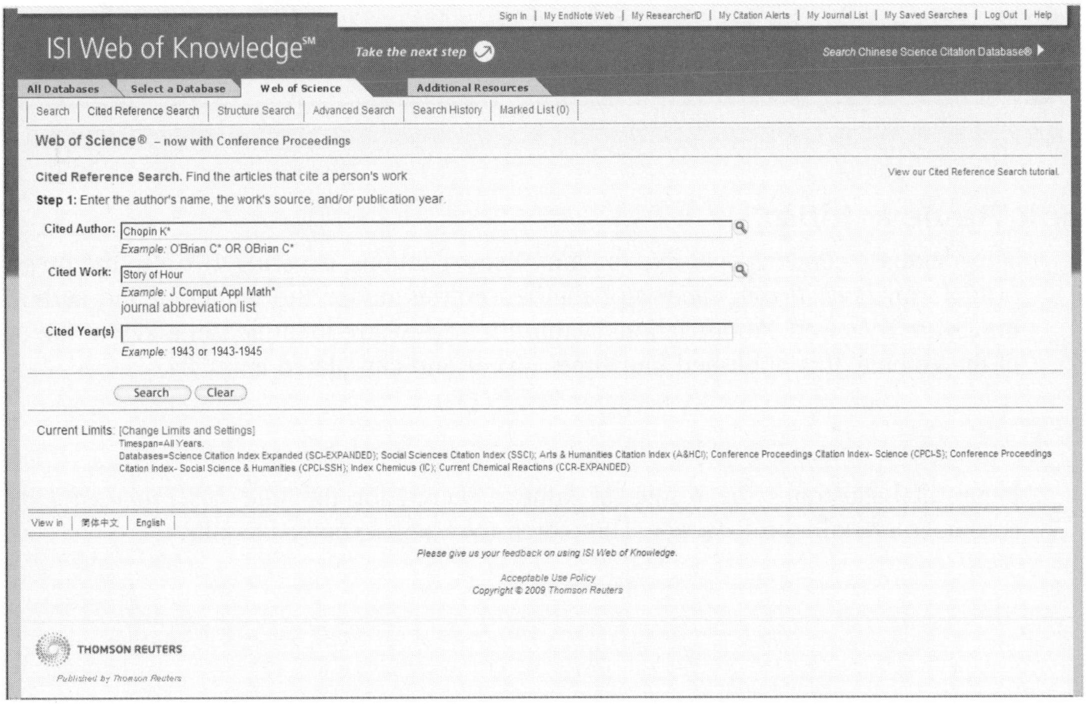

FIGURE 3.7 Sample of a Cited Reference Search in the *Arts & Humanities Citation Index*

Continued

FIGURE 3.8 Results of a Cited Reference Search in the *Arts & Humanities Citation Index*

Book Review Index

This database contains over five million review citations, covering 1965 to the present. In its print form, *Book Review Index* alphabetizes entries under the names of the authors whose books are reviewed. Abbreviations within the review are identified in a key at the beginning of the volume. It is published four times a year and cumulated annually.

THE WORK OF
JAMES KEBLER

Figure 3.9 illustrates the results of James's search for the title *His Promised Land*, the autobiography of John P. Parker. The search returned seventeen results.

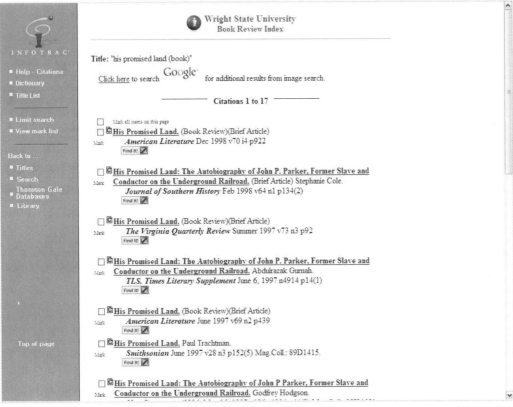

FIGURE 3.9 Sample results of *Book Review Index* search

Book Review Digest

Book Review Digest indexes book reviews found in nearly 100 periodicals published in the United States and Canada. The print version provides a description of the book, a brief summary of its content, and excerpts from reviews. The database version condenses this information into an abstract that gives an overview of the book and summarizes the reviewer's reaction, usually in the reviewer's own words.

Checklist for Using Basic Reference Sources

☑ I have searched for information about my topic using the following resources discussed in this chapter:

_____ *Academic Search Complete*

_____ *LexisNexis Academic*

_____ *Books In Print*

_____ *Other*

☑ I have searched for information about my topic using the following additional resources that were *not* discussed in this chapter:

_____

_____

_____

Exercise E

Searching for Books and Articles

Under each item write the information requested and the reference source where you found it.

1. Author and title of an article about Kate Chopin's "Fedora"

   Information: _____

   Source: _____

2. Location of review of John Lauritsen's *The Man Who Wrote Frankenstein*

   Information: _____

   Source: _____

3. Title of a newspaper editorial dealing with performance-enhancing drugs and professional athletics

   Information: _____

   Source: _____

4. Author and title of an article dealing with Posttraumatic Stress Disorder (PTSD)

   Information: _____

   Source: _____

5. Title and author of an article that cites Harriet Martineau's *Autobiography*

   Information: _____

   Source: _____

6. Title and author of a multivolume biography of Johann Wolfgang von Goethe

   Information: _____

   Source: _____

7. Title and author of an article about high-stakes testing in schools

   Information: _____

   Source: _____

8. Title and author of an annotated bibliography dealing with the Civil War

   Information: _____

   Source: _____

9. Title and author of a book about the brewing industry in the United States

Information: _____

Source: _____

10. Title and author of a book chapter about Charlotte Perkins Gilman's "The Yellow Wallpaper"

Information: _____

Source: _____

Evaluating and Recording Material Responsibly

> *Everyone finds that many of the ideas which he desired to retain have slipped irretrievably away.*
>
> *The Idler,* No. 72

The ability to find information is a useful skill, but it will not guarantee a successful research paper. It is only a first step. You must also be able to evaluate your sources, read efficiently, select material supporting your thesis, and take usable notes.

Evaluating Sources

You will need to evaluate your sources on two levels. First, is the information reliable? Second, how useful will a source be for your own paper? Be sure to think seriously about both questions. Information may be accurate without being especially useful, and unreliable information may be useful for showing problems associated with certain points of view.

For many students the first question may be especially daunting if they have never been asked to question what they read. Perhaps because they have been taught to rely so heavily on textbooks, some students feel excessive reverence for everything they see in print. Yet publication does not make something reported as a fact true or an opinion valid. Composing a research paper provides a good opportunity to learn how to judge the reliability of sources and to extract relevant material from them. Only a specialist can judge the reliability of a source authoritatively, but considering the following points can help you determine whether a source is likely to be (1) trustworthy and (2) relevant to your research project.

Criteria for Evaluating Internet Sources

Evaluating information you find on the Internet is crucial, but you can follow the same principles you would use to assess information in any other area of your life. You probably would not buy a car from a stranger without making some investigations, and the same should be true of "buying" what you find on the Internet (or any other source).

1. Author. If an author is named, that is the place to begin. Remember that anyone with access to the technology can become an Internet author. Consequently, determining the author's credentials may be more difficult and less conclusive than when you are working with a print source. However, you may follow the same strategies you would use when working with a book or article. That is, if you're just beginning to learn about a topic, you might consult a faculty member, librarian, or some specialist in that field. You may also consult reference works like *Who's Who*. The number of times an author is cited in *Citation Index* (see pages 55–56) is a good indication or his or her significance.

2. Domain. A second means of evaluating information is to identify the host of the site where the document appears by looking at the domain of the site, identified by the last three letters of the home page address. It might be a postsecondary educational institution (.edu), a U.S. government agency (.gov), a nonprofit organization (.org), or a commercial organization (.com or .biz). Recognizing the domain can help you identify the purpose of the site and the nature of the organization sponsoring it.

3. Purpose. Probably the single most important factor to consider in evaluating an Internet document is its purpose. Broadly speaking, most Internet sites are intended to sell, to persuade, or to inform. While a site is likely to include elements of all three approaches, one purpose usually outweighs the others. That purpose will, of course, have a profound effect on the kind of information presented and the way it is presented. Keep the purpose of the site in mind as you consider the remaining criteria.

4. Sponsoring organization. While recognizing the publisher of a book or journal can be helpful in evaluating that source, it is crucial in evaluating sources you find on the Internet. For example, if you are researching the topic of abortion, knowing whether a page you have found has been posted by the National Abortion and Reproductive Rights Action League or by the National Right to Life Committee is essential in evaluating the information you find. Likewise, if you are investigating automobile safety, you would probably find significant differences in the way the Web site of the National Highway Traffic Safety Administration reports on a particular vehicle and the way the manufacturer's site describes it.

It is not always obvious just what organization is sponsoring a page, especially if you have landed on that page as part of a search for a term. If that is the case, look for a link that will take you to the main page of the document, where you are likeliest to find information about the sponsoring organization. Does the site provide information that will allow you to find out more about the sponsoring organization? If you are not familiar with that organization, take a few minutes to investigate it.

Remember, too, that working back to the domain name in the URL of a specific document will take you to the organization's home page:

Specific Document: http://www.nrlc.org/abortion/pba/PBAall110403.html
Home Page: http://www.nrlc.org/

In this illustration, the National Right to Life Committee is the organization posting the specific document, and the home page provides a good deal of information about the organization.

5. Tone. Does the site advocate a particular point of view? Does it mention opposing views? How fairly does it represent those views? Is the tone of the source fair, balanced, and objective?

6. Accuracy. Is the information provided accurate? Can you verify information in a second source? Does the site document the information it provides?

7. Timeliness. Is the information up to date? When was it first posted? When was it updated? Some Web pages will provide this information very clearly, but it is often not the case. In many browsers, you can find this information by pulling down the View menu and looking for information about the page.

8. Links to other resources. Just as bibliographies and notes in print sources can provide useful leads for further research, Web pages can often take you to additional valuable resources. Be careful, though, to keep track of your "location" on the Internet. It is easy to go to a completely different Web site without being aware of it. Each change of site requires that you evaluate the new site just as carefully as you did the previous one.

9. Index. Just as you can use an index or table of contents to see if a book is relevant to your topic, you can use the search function to locate key terms in a long document. For instance, an Internet search for information about connections between Eugene O'Neill's play *The Emperor Jones* and the historical figure Marcus Garvey will probably lead you to an essay called "Marcus Garvey: Life & Lessons" in *The Marcus Garvey and Universal Negro Improvement Association Papers Project* at UCLA (http://www.international.ucla.edu/africa/mgpp/lifeintr.asp). Using the "search" or "find" function will let you find the words *Emperor Jones* and determine quickly whether this site will be useful for your project.

Criteria for Evaluating Print Sources

In evaluating information you find in books and articles, follow the same principles just discussed, although some features will differ for print sources.

1. Author. Because books and journal articles usually undergo some sort of review before they are published, some screening has been done already. However, appearance in print does not guarantee a writer's reliability. Writers and their views are sometimes described in reviews, so you should investigate all authors, whether their work is in print or online.

2. Publisher. As you carry out your research, you will come to recognize names of respected publishers. Generally, you can assume that the books they publish are trustworthy. In the same way, the reputation of a periodical may attest to the reliability of an article. Most scholarly associations and most universities publish at least one journal. Brief evaluations of many journals can be found in *Magazines for Libraries*, 16th ed. (New York: Bowker, 2007), edited by Cheryl LaGuardia, Bill Katz, and Linda Sternberg Katz. This reference work lists periodicals by subject and evaluates each one. If you are in doubt regarding a journal, consult a faculty member or a librarian. Needless to say, you should avoid or use with caution information from a tabloid purchased in a supermarket.

3. Publication date. The copyright year on the reverse of the title page will tell you how recent a book is. This is especially important with social and scientific subjects. An article on computer technology or a book on the British royal family written before 1995 would not be very useful. A biography of Woodrow Wilson or a description of the Brooklyn Bridge, on the other hand, probably would not suffer so much from the passage of time.

4. Documentation. An author's notes and bibliography are an indication but not proof of reliability. In addition, the bibliography and the notes may direct you to other sources.

5. Reviews. It may be helpful to examine reviews of a book. Consult *Book Review Digest* or *Book Review Index* (see page 56) to locate reviews. Sometimes a review itself can be a valuable source.

6. Title. The full title of a book or an article usually indicates its content and purpose and thus its relevance. Someone doing research on medical treatment during the Civil War might well overlook *Microbes and Minie Balls* by Frank R. Freemon if he or she did not take note of the subtitle: *An Annotated Bibliography of Civil War Medicine.*

7. Preface. Some readers automatically skip over introductory material, but an author's preface may be a valuable overview of the content and purpose of the book.

8. Table of Contents. The chapter titles indicate the major topics treated in a book.

9. Index. The alphabetical listing of topics covered in a book can help you determine whether that source will be useful. You could make an alphabetical list of relevant persons, places, and events (inverting proper names as they would appear in an index), then quickly check the indexes in biographies and histories, looking for any of your key items. If you are writing about a literary work, be sure to determine the indexing system being used. Some indexes list each work separately, and some list all works under the author's name.

10. Abstract. Many scholarly journals preface each article with a brief summary of its content. Collections of abstracts are also available in print and electronic form.

11. Illustrations. Paging through a book will show you whether there are maps, diagrams, or graphs that might be useful.

12. Glossary. A technical book may include a useful list of terms with brief definitions.

Fact vs. Opinion

Ex. F

In your reading, you will find two kinds of material: facts and opinions.

A fact denotes something that actually exists; it can be verified or proved. The annual snowfall, the signs of the zodiac, and the price of gasoline are verifiable facts. A thesis statement cannot be wholly factual, for it would not require development. You use facts to support your opinions.

An opinion is abstract; it is an idea about a fact or about another opinion. It is an interpretation, a deduction, a supposition, a conjecture. Statements that winters are becoming more severe, that persons born under the sign of Capricorn have certain personality traits, and that gasoline is expensive because of a conspiracy among oil companies are opinions. The nucleus of your thesis statement should be an opinion of your own. Opinions taken from your sources can be used as supplemental support but not as absolute proof of your ideas.

A fact can be confirmed; an opinion can be explained or defended but not proved definitively. That the Edsel was a commercial disaster is a fact; reasons for its failure are opinions. That "The Star-Spangled Banner" is the national anthem is a fact; that it is seldom sung well is an opinion. That Jack Ruby killed Lee Harvey Oswald is a fact, witnessed by millions of people on television; possible reasons for his action are opinions.

Any research paper will contain both facts and opinions taken from outside sources. Beware of authors who present opinions as if they were facts. Unfortunately, some students record opinions from their reading but do not venture enough opinions of their own. They are so intent on climbing the tree that they never go out on a limb. Taking notes from printed sources can benumb the mind, but stay alert and infer conclusions from what you read. You may need to qualify your inferences with words like *perhaps, may,* or *probably,* but do not hesitate to express opinions when they can be supported by evidence. Differentiate between facts and opinions when you take notes from a source and when you incorporate them into your paper.

Other Sources of Information

Most of the supporting material for your paper will come from books and periodicals in your school library, but you should not overlook other possibilities such as those described here.

Government Publications

The federal government is a prolific publisher of pamphlets and reports on all kinds of subjects. The Government Printing Office (GPO) produces more than a million copies of various publications each year, most of which are distributed by the Superintendent of Documents. There are many papers on scientific subjects and many reports by congressional committees. Government documents are most likely to be helpful if you are investigating a current topic; you would find nothing on the Children's Crusade but a considerable amount on child abuse.

To learn what is available, consult *Monthly Catalog of U.S. Government Publications.* Monthly issues of the print version are cumulated twice a year. The semiannual volumes list publications in several ways, including author, title, subject, and title keyword indexes. The monthly catalogs use the same indexes plus descriptive entries. The subject index is arranged alphabetically so that it lends itself to browsing for a topic. A document is assigned an entry number that enables you to find a description in the monthly catalog, where documents are listed in numerical order.

After finding one or more promising titles, you have two options for obtaining print versions of the documents:

1. Look for them in your school library or in nearby libraries. You may need a librarian's assistance because most libraries file government publications by their entry numbers rather than by Library of Congress or Dewey Decimal classification numbers.

2. Order them from the Superintendent of Documents (GPO, Washington, DC, 21401) or from the agencies that issued them. Include the classification numbers. Congressional committees are listed in *Congressional Directory;* agencies of the executive branch are listed in *United States Government Organization Manual.* If you are going to use this method, begin your search for government publications as soon as possible because the process will probably take several weeks.

The GPO now makes many of its publications available online via USASearch.gov (http://usasearch.gov/). This site contains links to a wealth of information. As Figure 4.1 shows, many links are provided for online versions of government documents.

FIGURE 4.1 Sample results of a USASearch.gov search for government publications

Corporate Publications

Most companies publish pamphlets and brochures of various kinds in addition to their annual reports. Some of this information may be posted on the Internet. A clear, courteous request will often result in whatever printed materials are available. Remember, though, that those publications will be basically corporate advertising.

Organizations

The *Encyclopedia of Associations* (Detroit: Gale, 1956–), which is revised annually, classifies organizations in eighteen categories—such as religious organizations, cultural organizations, and fan clubs. The variety of entries suggests that Americans are joiners, with a remarkable range of interests. You will find, for instance, organizations for surfers, Elvis Presley fan clubs, associations related to sports for people with disabilities, and automotive groups. Each entry provides essential information, including Web site and e-mail addresses, and at least one officer. A sample entry appears below.

10918 ■ National Humane Education Society (NHES)
PO Box 340
Charles Town, WV 25414-0340
Ph: (304)725-0506
Fax: (304)725-1523
E-mail: nhesinformation@nhes.org
URL: http://www.nhes.org
Contact: Michael Mahrer, Dir. of Development and Marketing
Founded: 1948. **Members:** 350,000. **Staff:** 40. **Regional Groups:** 2. **Description:** Works for animal welfare. Conducts humane education program and rescue and relief services. Educates the public about all aspects of humane issues. **Libraries: Type:** open to the public. **Holdings:** 45; video recordings. **Subjects:** humane topics. **Publications:** *NHES Journal*, quarterly. Newsletter. Features information on humane education. **Price:** free. Alternate formats: online. **Conventions/Meetings:** quarterly board meeting.

Sample entry from *Encyclopedia of Associations*

Additional Library Sources

- **Special collections.** The latest edition of *American Library Directory* (Medford: Information Today, 2007) will direct you to special collections. Because it is arranged alphabetically by state, you can easily check listings for nearby libraries as well as your school library. A sample entry follows.

TEXAS RANGER HALL OF FAME & MUSEUM, Texas Ranger Research Center, 100 Texas Ranger Trail, 76706. (Mail add: PO Box 2570, 76702-2570), SAN 362-3971. Tel: 254-750-8631. Reference Tel: 254-750-8639. Toll Free Tel: 877-750-8631. Fax: 254-750-8629. E-Mail: trhf@eramp.net. Web Site: www.texasranger.org. *Dep Dir*, Christina Stopka; *Librn*, Judy Shofner; Staff 2 (MLS 1, Non-MLS 1) Founded 1976
Library Holdings: Bk Vols 2,200
Special Collections: Ex-Texas Ranger Association Papers; Frank Hamer Papers (Bonnie & Clyde); M D "Kelly" Rogers Coll; M T "Lone Wolf" Gonzaullas Papers; Texarkana Phantom Killer, Oral History
Subject Interests: Law enforcement
Automation Activity & Vendor Info: (Cataloging) TLC (The Library Corporation)
Function: Res libr
Restriction: Non-circulating. Open by appointment only

Sample entry from *American Library Directory*

- **Clippings.** Many libraries maintain a file of newspaper and magazine clippings, especially on subjects of local interest. Such files are not always listed in the catalog and can be located only by consulting a librarian.
- **Microforms.** Many books and periodicals have been reproduced on microforms (microcard, microfiche, microfilm). Because such materials are often located in a special file, you may overlook a wealth of material unless you ask a librarian.
- **Interlibrary loans.** Sometimes a book or a copy of a journal article not in your library can be obtained from another library. This service, which usually takes a week or more, is not always available to undergraduates. When you submit a request, you will probably be asked to indicate where you found the reference. Make a brief note on your source card—e.g., *MLA International Bibliography.*

Personal Research Sources

- **Interviews.** A specialist in the field you are investigating can sometimes supply useful information. Paul Sanchez learned a good deal by talking with a local animal control officer and with a coworker who was part of an animal rescue group. Do not invade the office of a stranger without an appointment. Dress appropriately and arrive on time. A tape recorder will be very useful if your informant does not object. Use a battery-operated recorder to avoid having to fumble with the cord and search for an outlet. Familiarize yourself with the subject and prepare thoughtful, specific questions in advance. Don't argue with your informant even if you disagree with what you hear; an interview is a conversation, not a debate. As a courtesy to your informant, send a thank-you note or, if it seems appropriate, a copy of your paper.
- **Lectures.** Watch the calendar of events being offered at your school. If you are fortunate, a visiting lecturer may be speaking on a topic related to your research. With some topics you might find it helpful to sit in on a class even though you are not registered for the course. Ask the professor for permission.
- **Correspondence.** Sometimes you can obtain valuable facts and opinions by writing to a knowledgeable expert. However, you should refrain from requesting information that could be obtained from a reference book. Also, avoid vague requests for "all the information about" a subject. Make your letter courteous and concise. If your topic involves a foreign country, you might write to the United Nations delegation (see a Manhattan telephone directory) or to the embassy (see a Washington, DC, directory). Some countries maintain tourist bureaus in major cities. Consult a telephone directory and address your request to the director of the bureau. If you are using an Internet source, you may find a link for e-mailing the author of the site or its sponsoring organization. Likewise, more and more journals include the e-mail address of the authors of articles. If you use e-mail to correspond with an expert, use the same kind of approach as in a written letter. Don't be misled by the ease of sending e-mail into being inappropriately informal. The reader's response to your request for information will be shaped by his or her reaction to the message you send.
- **Telephone call.** Sometimes information can be obtained by a telephone call in lieu of a letter or a personal interview. Identify yourself as a student, state the information you need, and ask to speak to someone who can supply it.
- **Observation.** Some topics require that you visit a hospital, a laboratory, a battlefield, an archaeological dig, a courtroom, or some other site. Take notes on the spot or as soon as possible after leaving. Consider using a camera; a few pictures may help you recall important features.
- **Poll.** For some topics, especially those related to current events, you could devise a set of brief questions and tabulate responses from twenty-five to fifty randomly selected

persons. You could also select a specific group of respondents. If you plan to argue that students need more instruction in geography, giving college seniors ten place-names to identify might produce evidence supporting your argument. No matter whom you poll, take time to formulate your questions carefully before you begin. Using slanted or loaded questions that might skew the results is a major hazard of polling.

- **Questionnaire.** A questionnaire is essentially a written poll. As with a poll, you should be careful to formulate your questions to avoid prejudicing your respondents' answers.

Ingenuity and imagination in seeking material to supplement library research will often make a paper more interesting to you and to your reader.

Using Sources Efficiently

Try to develop an efficient method of using sources, whether electronic or print. When browsing on the Internet, you can bookmark a useful-looking passage by clicking on the appropriate menu option ("Add Bookmark" or "Add Favorites" on most systems). The URL of the page will be saved so that you can retrieve the passage later and examine it more closely. If you cannot bookmark the site because you are using a public access terminal in a library or computer lab, you should be able to save the whole document to your own disk or flash drive or e-mail it to yourself. If you save the document in this way, be sure that you record the URL, which you will need when you document your sources in the final version of the paper.

Do not consider yourself fortunate if you find several books devoted solely to your subject. It may indicate that you are trying to cover too much in a short paper. Fairly brief passages in books and journals may be more useful than entire works. To use a print source, skim it first and then return to passages that seem pertinent. It is difficult, if not impossible, to follow an author's train of thought if you interrupt your reading every few minutes to write down a note. Devise a system for recording passages that look useful and then take notes after you have examined the work as a whole.

If you own a book or a periodical, the simplest procedure is to star or highlight a passage to which you expect to return. Do not mark a passage unless you are fairly certain that it is relevant to your thesis. Any marking is unsuitable, of course, when you are using library sources. In many school libraries, vandalism is a scandal and hampers student research assignments.

Other procedures are to insert cards in the work as you read or to attach a gummed note to the edge of each page where useful material appears. After completing your reading, you can turn back to your starting point, examine the pages where you put your bookmarks, and write your note cards. Another method is to keep track of usable passages on a piece of scratch paper.

No matter how systematic your purposeful reading and note taking have been, after you start writing you are almost certain to discover gaps that must be filled and citations that must be checked. One reason for starting your research early and setting aside several days for writing the paper is the likelihood of your having to return to the library for additional research.

Downloading and Photocopying Information

If you are looking at an article you retrieved from a full-text database, you may be able to print the article, e-mail it to yourself, or save it to your own disk or flash drive. Using a credit card or roll of coins, you can easily photocopy pages from a book or journal.

These approaches save time and reduce the possibility of transcription errors, and you should take full advantage of them. At the same time, however, you should be aware of some accompanying challenges. First, it is easy to omit key bibliographic information, so be sure you have all the data you will need when you cite these works in your final paper. More important, though, is the danger that you will think you have accomplished more than you actually have. That is, even though you have copied or downloaded forty pages, you must still decide what to quote, what to summarize or paraphrase, and what to omit.

With a photocopy or printout of an article from a database, you can mark useful passages and write comments in the margins to begin selecting what you want to use.

Figure 4.2 shows some annotations Colleen Lee made on the photocopy of a page from Emily Toth's *Unveiling Kate Chopin.*

Toth Unveiling Chopin 182

Chopin's most obvious use of the women in her family is, of course, "The Story of an Hour." Like Eliza O'Flaherty, the character Louise learns that her husband has been killed in a train crash. She is sad, and then happy to be free, and then, once her husband walks through the door alive, she is dead of a sudden heart attack. "The joy that kills," the doctors call it.

compares Louise to C's own mother

In all three stories, Kate Chopin is thinking back through her mother and criticizing the institution of marriage. But she also criticizes men, for not understanding what women really want, and for disappointing the women they say they love. Only the husband in "Athénaïse" even has an inkling of the need to change. As she grew older, Chopin understood more and more why the widows of her family chose not to remarry.

good title?

criticism of marriage

FIGURE 4.2 Sample notes on a photocopy

If you have downloaded an article or other source, you can copy and paste passages into a new document. You might create a new file that contains the most relevant passages from a single source or perhaps create one that gathers information on a single topic from different sources. No matter how you set up these files, be sure to clearly identify the source of information for each passage you include. You should also be very careful to distinguish any of your own commentary from the exact words of your source.

Figure 4.3 shows a note sheet created by Colleen as she consolidated information she had downloaded about the "Cult of True Womanhood," a phrase she had seen associated with Kate Chopin's writing. She copied and pasted relevant passages, adding a short heading that will help her locate each passage later. She highlighted quotable passages and added some comments of her own in brackets. Note that she has page references for some of the articles, which preserve the format of the original print publication, but not for others.

Continued

Welter, "Cult of True Womanhood," page 152:

The attributes of True Womanhood, by which a woman judged herself and was judged by her husband, her neighbors and society, could be divided into four cardinal virtues—piety, purity, submissiveness and domesticity. Put them all together and they spelled mother, daughter, sister, wife—woman. Without them, no matter whether there was fame, achievement or wealth, all was ashes. With them she was promised happiness and power.

Boydston, "Cult of True Womanhood" (PBS website):

As the film suggests, the lives of nineteenth-century women were deeply shaped by the so-called "cult of true womanhood," a collection of attitudes that associated "true" womanhood with the home and family. In their homes, presumably safely guarded from the sullying influences of business and public affairs, women effortlessly directed their households and exerted a serene moral influence over their husbands and children. By both temperament and ability, so custom had it, women were ill-suited to hard labor, to the rough-and-tumble of political life, or to the competitive individualism of the industrial economy. [Use to explain why Louise is so frail?]

Roberts, "True Womanhood Revisited," page 150:

Historians continue to agree that "true womanhood" was the centerpiece of nineteenth-century female identity (although in Europe, the cult was more likely to go under the name of "real womanhood" or "the domestic ideal"). In addition, cultural historians now draw widely upon the same innovative sources—magazines, fiction, advice stories—that Welter mustered up to make her case. [This could be good if I need to justify using Welter's article, which is 20 years old.]

FIGURE 4.3 Sample note sheet created by copying and pasting quotations from downloaded files

Taking Notes

From the time you begin taking notes, you should realize that you are obligated to acknowledge the sources of all borrowed facts and opinions whether you quote an author's exact words or summarize them. Of course, facts that are common knowledge and are found in several sources need not be cited. You would not cite an author who wrote that Amelia Earhart's airplane disappeared in 1937, but you would cite an author who wrote that Earhart was spying for the United States or that she was still alive in 1945. Usually, your obligation will be clear-cut. Occasionally, however, you will be confronted with an ethical question: "Is this idea general knowledge or is it a product of my own thinking?" Careful note taking and an honest attempt to give credit for borrowed material will help you provide adequate documentation and avoid any suggestion of plagiarism (see Chapter 5).

As explained in Chapter 1 (pages 13–14), when you find a source that looks useful, you should record that source with the full bibliographic information: the author's name, the title, and the publication facts. Be sure you have *all* the information that you need and that you have the *correct* information. If you find a book or an article in a database, where authors' names, article titles, and journal names are often shortened, be sure to use the actual source for the information for your final bibliographic entry. Likewise, take bibliographic information for books from the title page, not from the cover or the spine. If you are using an Internet source, be sure to record the complete URL and the date you accessed the site.

Once you have recorded your source, be sure your notes include a short reference to it, usually the author's last name and the page number. If you have more than one work by the same author, include a short version of the title as well. Be alert: it is dangerously easy to forget to record this information when you are taking notes. Few activities are as depressing as searching through several 500-page volumes to locate a passage you failed to identify when you made a note of it.

Types of Notes

The notes that you take will be quotations, various kinds of summaries, combinations of quotation and summary, and reminders to yourself.

- **Quotation note.** If you are not sure whether you will use an author's actual language, take down the quotation. When you write your first draft, you can convert a quotation to a summary, but you cannot replace a summary with a quotation except by returning to the original source. There are four general reasons for using a direct quotation:

  1. *Accuracy:* when the precise language of the original is essential (e.g., in a legal document)
  2. *Authority:* when a writer's exact words carry more weight than a summary of them
  3. *Conciseness:* when a quotation states an idea in fewer words than a summary would
  4. *Vividness:* when the language of a quotation is more colorful or more descriptive than a summary

Unless you have a good reason for quoting a passage, summarize or paraphrase it. As a general rule, there is less quotation in an excellent paper than in a mediocre one.

- **Paraphrase/summary note.** A *paraphrase* restates an author's ideas in different words. Its purpose is to clarify or interpret a passage, and it may be almost as long as the original. A *summary* is a more extreme reduction of a passage. In any type of condensation, it is essential that you double-check your note to make certain that you have not echoed the language and style of the original. Unintentional plagiarism can easily occur in summary notes. After summarizing material from a source, compare your note with the original to be certain that you have not inadvertently included phrasing that should be in quotation marks.
- **Outline note.** When only factual information is taken from a source, rough notes in outline form—the most extreme form of summary—may be sufficient.
- **Combination note.** A combination note containing both quotation and summary is especially useful because it encourages the blending of quoted material with your own words. In a sense, when you write a combination note, you are beginning your rough draft. Be meticulous in the use of quotation marks, especially in closing each quotation. Try to quote brief passages rather than long blocks of material. Merge quoted material with your own sentences.
- **Personal note.** If your memory is sometimes untrustworthy, it may be prudent to write reminders to yourself. Such a note is simply a safeguard against memory lapses and requires no citation.

The Art and Science of Quoting

Reproduce a quotation *exactly* as it appears in the source. If you copy it yourself, compare your note with the printed text to be certain that you copied it accurately. Doing this habitually will prevent transcription errors, which are easy to make. Be certain that you write all words (especially proper names) legibly; recopy any that you might misread when you write your first draft. If a quotation contains anything out of the ordinary—for example, using an ampersand (&) or omitting an accent mark—write a note to yourself at the bottom of the card so that you will reproduce the original accurately. Should there be an obvious error in the source, follow it with *sic* ("thus") in brackets. Although *sic* is a Latin word, it is used so frequently that it is generally not italicized. Do not use "[sic]" after a British spelling like *colour, analyse*, or *centre* or after an alternative spelling like *judgement*. Students are sometimes eager to use "[sic]," but the occasion seldom arises. If a passage contains an obvious error, you are not likely to quote it. You should know what "[sic]" means when you encounter it in your reading. Do not use it sarcastically to denote disagreement, and do not follow it with an exclamation point.

If you are working with electronic sources, you may be able to copy the passage you want to quote and paste it into a computer file of your own. While this ensures that you will have quoted the exact words from a source, you will still need to check it carefully since special markings (such as italics or accents in a foreign language) are likely to disappear in the process. You will almost certainly have to reformat the passage you incorporate into your paper, and you should be careful not to introduce any accidental changes at that point.

Although you cannot change the wording of a quoted passage, you can omit words as long as you do not change the meaning or the emphasis. The omission is indicated by an ellipsis (. . .), three periods with a space before, between, and after—a legitimate, though often misused, punctuation mark. If the text that you are quoting already contains ellipses, however, you must enclose your own ellipses in brackets to distinguish them from those already there. To facilitate the blending of quoted material with your own sentence (one characteristic of a skillfully written paper), you can omit the ellipsis from the beginning or from the close of a short quotation that is clearly not a complete sentence (see pages 111–112 for examples). An ellipsis is always needed, of course, when words are deleted *within* a quotation. It is even possible to combine quotations from two paragraphs; four spaced periods indicate where words have been omitted, and complete sentences should precede and follow the omitted passage. Such extensive elision seldom occurs in student papers. It is dangerously easy to distort the original context, and, in addition, students are not encouraged to quote lengthy passages. Frequently, judicious pruning of a quotation will enable you to combine it more smoothly with your text. Also, a word or phrase within brackets may clarify a passage. For example:

"El Greco [Doménikos Theotokópoulos] is admired today for his paintings that express religious

ecstasy" (Mason 46).

"In 1935 the REA [Rural Electrification Administration] was created by executive order to improve

electrification and telephone service in rural areas" (Thurman 178).

"William Harnett is best known for his trompe l'oeil [literally, trick of the eye] still-life paintings

such as *After the Hunt*" (Lawson 82).

Note Cards

With new developments in technology, many people bypass handwritten cards in favor of computer-assisted strategies for taking notes and organizing information. Because your class emphasizes the research process, your teacher may ask that you write and submit note cards as a way of demonstrating your progress.

To record pertinent information from a book by Barbara C. Ewell, Colleen created the note cards shown in Figures 4.4–4.6. They illustrate a source card, a direct quotation, and a note combining quotation and paraphrase.

Ewell, Barbara C. Kate Chopin. New York: Ungar, 1986.

PS 1294

C63Z64

1986

FIGURE 4.4 Source card

Ewell   women & self-sacrifice

"her submission to his 'blind persistence has been the guise of Love,
that self-sacrificing Victorian Ideal."

FIGURE 4.5 Quotation note card

Ewell 88   selfhood

The "nature and cost of self-assertion" is one of Chopin's
recurring themes.

FIGURE 4.6 Combination note card

Checklist for Evaluating and Recording Material Responsibly

☑ For each Web site from which I plan to use information, I have identified the author, the purpose of the site, the sponsoring organization, and the timeliness of the material.

☑ In every source that I plan to use, I can distinguish between factual information and the writer's viewpoint about that information.

☑ I have investigated other sources of information in addition to what I found in the library and online.

☑ In taking notes, whenever I recorded the exact words, I quoted them exactly and enclosed them in quotation marks, and I recorded the page number.

☑ I have verified that all photocopied and downloaded material includes all the information I need for writing an entry in the list of Works Cited (including the URL and date of access).

Exercise F

Differentiating Fact and Opinion

Classify each of the statements below as predominantly fact (F), opinion (O), or a combination of the two (C). Base your judgment on the substance of each statement rather than on your agreement or disagreement with it.

1. Oscar Wilde is the best-known Irish-born British writer of the 1890s. _____
2. He was born 16 October 1854 in Dublin. _____
3. His mother, Jane Francesca Wilde, published poetry under the name Speranza. _____
4. In 1844 his father, Sir William Wilde, established St. Mark's Hospital in Dublin, the first in Ireland to treat afflictions of the eye and ear. _____
5. The marriage of Sir William and Jane Wilde was a happy one, despite a number of difficulties. _____
6. Between 1864 and 1871, Wilde attended Portata Royal School, Enniskillen, where he was an outstanding student. _____
7. He next attended Trinity College, Dublin, and he won a Demyship (scholarship) to study classics at Magdalen College, Oxford. _____
8. In his final year at Oxford he won the Newdigate Prize for poetry and a Double First in his examinations. _____
9. He subsequently moved to London, where he struggled to make a name for himself, not only publishing essays and poems but also seeking to draw attention to himself in the press. _____
10. The year 1881 was significant for two reasons: his first book (*Poems*) was published, and he met Constance Mary Lloyd, whom he would eventually marry. _____
11. His real breakthrough came at the end of 1881, when he embarked on a year-long lecture tour of America, where he visited more than 130 cities. _____
12. In 1883 he returned briefly to America, where his play *Vera* was a failure, running only a week. _____
13. In 1884 he married Constance Lloyd, and they honeymooned happily in Paris, moving into a beautiful home at 16 Tite Street on their return to London. _____
14. Their first son (Cyril) was born in June 1885; their second son (Vyvyan) was born in November of the following year. _____
15. In 1887 and 1888 his success as a writer seemed assured with the publication of several stories (including a collection of children's stories called *The Happy Prince and Other Tales*) and his assumption of the editorship of *Woman's World*. _____
16. When *The Picture of Dorian Gray* appeared in *Lippincott's Magazine* in 1890, it was sharply criticized as immoral, thus bringing Wilde some of the notoriety he had been seeking. _____
17. When *Dorian Gray* was published in book form the next year, Wilde revised it to remove passages that he thought might be taken as references to homosexual activity and added other material to make its moral message clearer. _____

75

18. That same year his play *The Duchess of Padua* ran for three weeks in New York, and he also published *Intentions* and *A House of Pomegranates*. _____

19. The most significant event of 1891, however, was his introduction to Lord Alfred Douglas. _____

20. *Lady Windermere's Fan* had its premiere in London in February 1892, but the censor refused to license *Salomé*, a play written in French for Sarah Bernhardt. _____

21. Although Wilde was able to gain some publicity from the censor's decision, he should have realized that the standing ban on biblical subjects on stage would be enforced even though his play was in French. _____

22. Despite that setback, Wilde's career as a dramatist was soon back on track with the opening of *A Woman of No Importance* in April 1893. _____

23. *A Woman of No Importance* is regarded by many critics as the weakest of Wilde's plays of the 1890s, but it nevertheless contains sharp criticism of social conditions. _____

24. When the English version of *Salomé* was published, it was illustrated by Aubrey Beardsley, whose drawings embody the decadence of the play. _____

25. Wilde reached the pinnacle of his career in early 1895, when he had two new plays—*An Ideal Husband* and *The Importance of Being Earnest*—running simultaneously in London. _____

Exercise G

Taking Notes

The following passage is taken from *Kate Chopin* by Emily Toth, published in 1990 by William Morrow and Company, New York City. It appears on pages 252–253. The page break is shown by the slash in brackets in the second paragraph.

Kate also asked moral questions in her best-known story from 1894, "The Story of an Hour," a criticism of the ideal of self-sacrifice that still haunted women at the end of the century. In it, a wife who learns that her husband has been killed in a railroad accident rejoices in her freedom—until he returns after all, and her weak heart cannot take the shock.

The story was one of Kate's shortest, only one thousand words, but one of her most radical. Mrs. Mallard was a good wife, and Mr. Mallard a good husband, and "The Story of an Hour" was an attack on marriage, on one person's dominance over another in "that blind persistence with which men [/] and women believe they have a right to impose a private will upon a fellow-creature. A kind intention or a cruel intention made the act seem no less a crime." The demand for self-sacrifice was the crime.

1. Using the information in the heading, write a source card for this book.
2. Write the first sentence of the second paragraph as a quotation note.
3. Write a summary note that explains how Toth sees the story as an attack on marriage.
4. Write a combination note using the words "the ideal of self-sacrifice that still haunted women at the end of the century" from the first paragraph.
5. Use the second sentence of the second paragraph to create a quotation note that is a full sentence, beginning with the title of the story and ending before the quotation.

Avoiding Plagiarism

> *PLAGIARY. n. s. [from plagium, Lat.] 1. A thief in literature; one who steals the thoughts or writings of another.*
>
> A Dictionary of the English Language, vol. 2

Plagiarism is the act of using another person's language or ideas without acknowledgment. (The word *plagiarism* is derived from a Latin word for kidnapper.) A dictionary defines it as "the use or imitation of words and ideas of another person and the representation of them as one's original work." In the plainest English possible, plagiarism is theft. A serious act of dishonesty, it always carries a heavy penalty—failure of the paper, failure in the course, or even expulsion from school. It is regarded just as seriously in professional life; every few weeks, it seems, newspapers report that a public official, a corporate executive, or even a professional writer has been accused of presenting as original work something written by someone else. Even when the offense occurred twenty or more years before, the result is often disgrace and personal tragedy.

This type of plagiarism is a deliberate act, an intentional misrepresentation meant to deceive the reader. A paper lifted from a fraternity or sorority file is a blatant form of academic dishonesty, as is the purchase of a ready-made paper from a "research service" or an Internet site. Such attempts often fail to deceive the reader as intended. Experienced readers usually recognize such papers because of the marked difference between student prose and professional writing. As the Internet trade in research papers has grown, a number of plagiarism-detection services have been introduced, and many schools and individual faculty members subscribe to them. Even without those services, a teacher can locate a text posted on the Internet in only seconds.

Not all plagiarism is deliberate. It is fatally easy to omit a citation, fail to use quotation marks, or thoughtlessly echo the language of a source. Unintentional or careless plagiarism is especially likely to occur at two stages of the writing process—during note taking or during drafting. Especially if you are pressed for time, it is very easy to neglect to record a source or to borrow language without using quotation marks. As a final step in taking notes from a source, stop to verify that you have used quotation marks appropriately and recorded the source accurately. Plagiarism that occurs during the writing phase is usually the result of carelessness. While writing your rough draft, meticulously check your text against each source. Be certain that you have not used phrasing from a source without putting it into quotation marks and that you have cited the sources of all borrowed material, whether it is a quotation, a paraphrase, or a summary. If you have not used quotation marks, you have still committed plagiarism, even though you have not deliberately tried to deceive a reader. The penalty for unintentional plagiarism can be as severe as for flagrant cribbing from a book, journal article, or Internet site.

Defining Common Knowledge

Students are understandably puzzled by the statement that they need not cite a source for facts that are common knowledge or for opinions that are generally known and accepted. As a novice dealing with a new topic, you may feel overwhelmed because *everything* seems new to you. Often you can use your sources as models. When your sources provide documentation for ideas, you certainly will need to as well. However, as some facts appear without citations over and over in discussions of your topic, you will begin to recognize them as some of the generally accepted facts of that field. If you express them in your own words, you ordinarily do not need to cite them. But a fact or an opinion derived from a single source requires citation. For example, there is no need to document that John F. Kennedy was elected president in 1960 or that he was assassinated on 22 November 1963—even if you were unaware of those facts before you began your research. However, any analysis of how he came to be elected or any theory of how the assassination took place needs to be credited to the originator of that idea. If you are uncertain whether an item requires documentation, the best course of action would be to talk with your instructor, or simply to document the information as if it were not common knowledge.

Avoiding Unintentional Plagiarism: Paraphrase, Summary, and Quotation

Ex. H

Perhaps the most frequent cause of unintentional plagiarism is the careless handling of borrowed material. Quotation, paraphrase, and summary were discussed in the previous chapter in connection with taking notes, and ways of incorporating that information into your paper will be covered in Chapter 7. No matter which stage of the process you have reached, it is crucial that you treat your sources with scrupulous accuracy. If you are quoting, the words you record must match exactly the words in your source. If you are putting the ideas in your own words, then they must be your own words, not those of the source. If you combine your own words with those of the source, those of the source must be enclosed in quotation marks. You should follow these rules when you are taking notes and when you are using those notes to write your paper. Doing so should reduce—if not eliminate entirely—the problem of accidental plagiarism.

Read through the following passage, taken from page 127 of *His Promised Land: The Autobiography of John P. Parker, Former Slave and Conductor on the Underground Railroad* (New York: Norton, 1996):

> When the Fugitive Slave Law agitation was at its highest, and active prosecutions began its enforcement, everyone engaged with the work destroyed all existing evidence of his connection with it. My little memorandum book I dropped quietly in the cupola of my own iron foundry, so no one knew its existence, especially its damaging contents. But the work went on just the same, in fact, more aggressively than ever, which speaks well for the conscience and courage of the Ripley group.

In the following example, the writer has made legitimate use of information from this passage, mixing summary and clearly identified direct quotation:

> John P. Parker praised the "conscience and courage" of the Abolitionists of Ripley, Ohio, who
>
> continued their work after the passage of the Fugitive Slave Law (127).

Compare that with the following unsatisfactory example:

> The Ripley Abolitionists' work went on just the same, or more aggressively than ever, after the
>
> Fugitive Slave Law was passed (Parks 127).

This version uses language directly from the source without enclosing it in quotation marks. Thus, even though the writer includes a parenthetical citation for the book from which the information was taken, the writer has still committed plagiarism. The misspelling of Parker's name represents the kind of sloppiness that often accompanies plagiarism. In this case, the writer's carelessness looks especially suspicious, as if the writer is trying to hide the actual source being used.

Using Internet Sources

Internet sources seem to be especially problematic, perhaps because it is so easy to copy and paste material without taking the time to document it properly or perhaps because the material seldom has page numbers that can be used in parenthetical citations. Internet sources must be treated with the same scrupulous care as print sources. The following passage comes from Margaret Atwood's "Spotty-Handed Villainesses: Problems of Female Bad Behaviour in the Creation of Literature," a 1994 lecture posted on *The Margaret Atwood Information Site* (http://www.owtoad.com/spotty.pdf):

> The story of Medea, whose husband Jason married a new princess, and who then poisoned the bride and murdered her own two children, has been interpreted in various ways. In some versions Medea is a witch and commits infanticide out of revenge; but the play by Euripides is surprisingly neo-feminist. There's quite a lot about how tough it is to be a woman, and Medea's motivation is commendable—she doesn't want her children to fall into hostile hands and be cruelly abused—which is also the situation of the child-killing mother in Toni Morrison's *Beloved.* A good woman, then, who does a bad thing for a good reason.

Citing material from this source requires exactly the same approach as quoting from a printed text. It would be perfectly acceptable to incorporate a phrase from Atwood's lecture in this way:

> In "Spotty-Handed Villainesses," Margaret Atwood points to Medea's "commendable" motives,
>
> calling her a "good woman . . . who does a bad thing for a good reason."

In this illustration, the writer has identified not only the author but the title as well. When the writer quotes Atwood, the exact words are enclosed in quotation marks. Since the Internet site has no page numbers, the writer has provided all the information possible to identify the source of this particular idea. It is also possible to identify the source entirely in the parenthetical citation:

> One writer even points to Medea's "commendable" motives, calling her a "good woman . . . who
>
> does a bad thing for a good reason" (Atwood).

Atwood's name in the parenthetical citation is sufficient if the writer is citing only a single work by her (see Chapter 9 for a more detailed discussion on this point). In the following illustration, however, the writer uses some of Atwood's exact words but fails to enclose them in quotation marks:

> Medea's motives are commendable because she doesn't want her children to fall into hostile hands
>
> and be abused (Atwood).

When you use quotation marks, be sure that anything you put inside them matches the source exactly. In the first two examples from Atwood's lecture, the ellipses (three spaced periods) indicate that some words have been omitted. In the next illustration, the writer has slightly misquoted Atwood, subtly distorting the meaning of the statement:

> In "Spotty-Handed Villainesses," Margaret Atwood characterizes Euripides's Medea as "a good
>
> woman who does bad things."

While this version is technically not plagiarism, it is still unacceptable because it misrepresents the source.

Some additional illustrations from the experience of Paul Sanchez and Melissa Lofts may be helpful in demonstrating how to incorporate sources without unintentionally committing plagiarism.

THE WORK OF PAUL SANCHEZ

In the opening section of his paper about animal hoarding, Paul wanted to show the prevalence of the problem. One of his sources, Randy Lockwood's "The Psychology of Animal Collectors" (*Trends* 9.6 [1994]: 18–21), began with the following information:

> The Humane Society of the United States (HSUS) receives two to three calls a week from local agencies requesting information or assistance in dealing with collectors, and each of our 10 regional offices has become actively involved in two to three interventions involving collectors in the last year. Our experience has been that any animal care or control agency large enough to have a cruelty investigator or humane officer is enmeshed in at least one collector case at any given time. This would suggest that there are at least several thousand such individuals in the U.S. and the numbers appear to be growing. (18)

Paul's first attempt to incorporate this information reproduces almost all of the ideas—and much of the language—from Lockwood's statement. The underlining shows the words and phrases repeated verbatim (including some instances where he has changed only the verb tense) without using quotation marks:

> A decade ago, in 1994, Randy Lockwood stated that <u>the Humane Society of the United States</u>
>
> <u>(HSUS) received two</u> or <u>three calls a week from local agencies</u> needing <u>information or assistance</u>
>
> with animal hoarding cases and that <u>each of</u> the <u>ten regional offices</u> of the HSUS <u>had</u> been
>
> <u>involved in two</u> or <u>three</u> cases <u>in the</u> previous <u>year.</u> On that basis, he calculated that "at least
>
> several thousand" people in this country were involved in hoarding animals (18).

When Paul compared his summary with Lockwood's original statement, he saw that he was using too much of Lockwood's wording and then realized that he could actually express the idea much more economically by summarizing:

> On the basis of the number of calls received by the Humane Society of the United States (HSUS) and its ten regional offices, Randy Lockwood calculated in 1994 that "at least several thousand" people in the country were involved in hoarding animals (18).

For her paper about the benefits of breastfeeding, Melissa went through a similar process. She found some potentially useful information in "A Well-Kept Secret: Breastfeeding's Benefits to Mothers," written by Alicia Dermer. It was originally published in a magazine called *New Beginnings,* but Melissa retrieved the article from the Web site of La Leche League (www.lalecheleague.org/NB/NBJulAug01p124.html):

> There is much more to breastfeeding than the provision of optimal nutrition and protection from disease through mother's milk. Breastfeeding provides a unique inter-action between mother and child, an automatic, skin-to-skin closeness and nurturing that bottle-feeding mothers have to work to replicate. The child's suckling at the breast produces a special hormonal milieu for the mother. Prolactin, the milk-making hormone, appears to produce a special calmness in mothers. Breastfeeding mothers have been shown to have a less intense response to adrenaline (Altemus 1995).

The reference list at the end of the article identifies the source of the information about the reduced response to adrenaline (a point of particular interest to Melissa): Altemus, M. et al. "Suppression of hypothalmic-pituitary-adrenal axis responses to stress in lactating women." *J Clin Endocrinal Metab* 1995;80:2954.

Melissa's first attempt at incorporating this material into a draft retains far too much of the wording of the source, as the underlined phrases again indicate:

> Besides providing <u>optimal nutrition and protection from disease,</u> nursing <u>provides a unique</u> bond that mothers who do not breastfeed <u>have to work to replicate.</u> In addition, <u>Prolactin, the milk-making hormone,</u> seems to have a calming effect, and mothers who breastfeed <u>have been shown to have a less</u> powerful reaction to adrenaline (Altemus et al., 1995; Dermer, 2001).

This first version consists almost entirely of the language found in the source, with a few words omitted between some of the phrases. It also follows much the same arrangement as the original passage. In addition, Melissa faces a common dilemma with this passage, which contains a reference to another source. Uncertain how to treat the embedded reference, she has tried to include both in a parenthetical citation in APA style. In doing so, however, she has created the impression that she has gone to both sources. When readers look for Altemus et al. in the list of references, they will believe that Melissa has carelessly omitted one of her sources there. If she were to convert the reference entry from Dermer's article for her own list of references, she would create an even more serious error in that she would be misrepresenting her own work. That is, by listing the Altemus et al. article among her sources, Melissa would be representing herself as having gone to that source and drawn information from it, even though she had not done so. As a result, she would be open to charges of academic dishonesty.

Continued

THE WORK OF
MELISSA LOFTS

Fortunately, as Melissa compared her version with the original, she recognized that much of the information was not related to the health benefits of breastfeeding and that most of it should be omitted. However, the reduced response to adrenaline was a health benefit she wanted to include. She also thought she might be able to find additional information in that article, but she could not locate *The Journal of Clinical Endocrinology & Metabolism* in her library or one of its full-text databases. Melissa would be using American Psychological Association (APA) style to document her paper (see Chapter 10), so she turned to the publication manual of the organization. There she found that she should use the phrase "as cited in" to identify the secondary source in which she found the idea she wanted to cite. Thus, in her final paper, the borrowed material might be identified like this:

According to one study, mothers who are nursing respond less strongly to adrenaline (Altemus

et al., 1995, as cited in Dermer, 2001).

Her list of references would include only Dermer's article. (For additional guidance on how to document the source of a quotation that you find in a source you are using, see the discussion of Colleen Lee's paper in this chapter, as well as the section on indirect citation in Chapter 9, page 161.)

Melissa's and Paul's experiences are very typical of writers researching and writing about a topic new to them. To grasp new information, it is often necessary to restate it in your own words, and there is generally an intermediate stage in which writers go from simply repeating the information to taking real control of it. In those early stages, as you move from paraphrasing to summarizing, you are particularly susceptible to unintentional plagiarism.

THE WORK OF COLLEEN LEE

Colleen Lee faced many of the same issues as she worked on her paper about Kate Chopin's "The Story of an Hour." She knew that she needed to provide some background about the roles of women in marriage in nineteenth-century America, and she found an especially helpful source in Barbara Welter's "The Cult of True Womanhood: 1820–1860" (*American Quarterly* 18 [1966]: 151–74). This is one of the passages she marked in her printout:

> The attributes of True Womanhood, by which a woman judged herself and was judged by her husband, her neighbors and society could be divided into four cardinal virtues—piety, purity, submissiveness and domesticity. Put them all together and they spelled mother, daughter, sister, wife—woman. Without them, no matter whether there was fame, achievement or wealth, all was ashes. With them she was promised happiness and power. (152)

Colleen saw that she could easily use Welter's "cardinal virtues" to discuss the portrayal of the main character in Chopin's story. In addition, Colleen thought that some of the old-fashioned pronouncements Welter quoted from conduct manuals written for women in the first half of the nineteenth century would be both amusing and appropriate when applied to the situation Chopin describes:

> Woman understood her position if she was the right kind of woman, a true woman. "She feels herself weak and timid. She needs a protector," declared George Burnap, in his lectures on *The Sphere and Duties of Woman.* "She is in a measure dependent. She asks for wisdom, constancy, firmness, perseverance, and she is willing to repay it all by

the surrender of the full treasure of her affections. Woman despises in man every thing like herself except a tender heart. It is enough that she is effeminate and weak; she does not want another like herself." (159)

Colleen wanted to use Burnap's language but had no access to his book, which was (she learned from Welter's footnote) published in 1854. To represent her own work honestly, Colleen needed to give credit to Welter for locating Burnap's long-forgotten work. Here is the way she introduced Welter and then Burnap:

> Chopin presents Louise Mallard as an admirable woman who meets or even surpasses the ideals of the time. Those ideals can be summed up as what Barbara Welter calls the "four cardinal virtues—piety, purity, submissiveness and domesticity" (152). Welter, who uses women's conduct manuals written in the first half of the nineteenth century to show how these ideals were spread, suggests that of these virtues submission was "perhaps the most feminine" (158).
>
> As George Burnap put it in *The Sphere and Duties of Woman* (1854), a woman "feels herself weak and timid. She needs a protector." In exchange for this protection, he added, a woman willingly gives up "the full treasure of her affections" (qtd. in Welter 159).

In this passage—the result of several revisions—Colleen mixed summary and paraphrase with a limited amount of direct quotation. She has carefully identified her sources and used those identifications to help her readers see how the sources support her argument.

A research paper can be marred by various imperfections—a vague thesis, an illogical plan, monotonous sentences, inaccurate or inappropriate diction, careless documentation, and mechanical errors. Plagiarism, however—whether deliberate or unintentional—is the most serious mistake that can damage a paper. Fortunately, the simplicity of citing sources in MLA style should help reduce the incidence of careless plagiarism. From the time you start taking notes, you should recognize your obligation to acknowledge borrowed material. Careful note taking and an understanding of how to document sources (see Chapter 9) will keep you from the reality and the appearance of plagiarism.

Checklist for Avoiding Plagiarism

☑ I can determine whether a piece of information is common knowledge or requires documentation and explain why.

☑ I understand the concept of plagiarism well enough that I could use the exercises at the end of this chapter to explain plagiarism to a fellow student.

☑ I have checked my notes against the original source to determine that all language taken directly from the source has been enclosed in quotation marks.

☑ I have checked my notes against the original to determine that anything that is *not* in quotation marks would not constitute plagiarism if it were put into my paper in that form.

Exercise H

Avoiding Plagiarism

Plagiarism ranges from careless omission of quotation marks or a citation to downright theft of another's person's ideas or language. Evaluate the statements following each quoted passage and mark them S (Satisfactory) or U (Unsatisfactory). Be prepared to explain what is wrong with those marked U.

Passage 1. "Hoarding is a dark side to the human–animal bond that is vastly undiscovered," [Gary] Patronek says. "While most people may find hoarders' living conditions unbearable, the hoarders themselves see no problem, seeing their home as a safe-haven for the animals."

> Source: Tremayne, Jessica. "Can You Identify Animal Hoarders? New Legislative Push Binds Practitioners to Report Cases," *DVM Newsmagazine* Feb. 2005: 12–13. Print. (Passage appears on page 12.)

_____ **a.** Most animal hoarders believe they are providing a "safe haven" for their animals, even

though others see the situation as "unbearable" (Tremayne 12).

_____ **b.** Gary Patronek calls animal hoarding the "dark side to the human–animal bond"

(Tremayne 12).

_____ **c.** Animal hoarders are often unable to recognize the terrible conditions in which they and

their animals are living (Tremayne 12).

Passage 2. Many hoarders claimed to love their animals as their children and stated that "they all had names," as evidence of proper care towards them. Thus, to justify their behavior, hoarders identify animals as family members and profess to love them. For instance, one hoarder claimed: "My dogs are my children, to be quite honest. They are the things that give me the most joy." The hoarder was described by his roommate and business partner, saying: "He is very conscientious in his day to day care for animals. He is in love with the dogs. He knows every name, he knows their birth dates." The humane society intervening in the case claimed that the 44 dogs discovered in the house lived in horrendous conditions.

> Source: Vaca-Guzman, Maria, and Arnold Arluke. "Normalizing Passive Cruelty: The Excuses and Justifications of Animal Hoarders," *Anthrozoös* 18 (2005): 338–57. Print. (Passage appears on page 344.)

_____ **a.** To justify their behavior, hoarders identify animals as family members, give them names,

and profess to love them (Vaca-Buzman and Arluke 344).

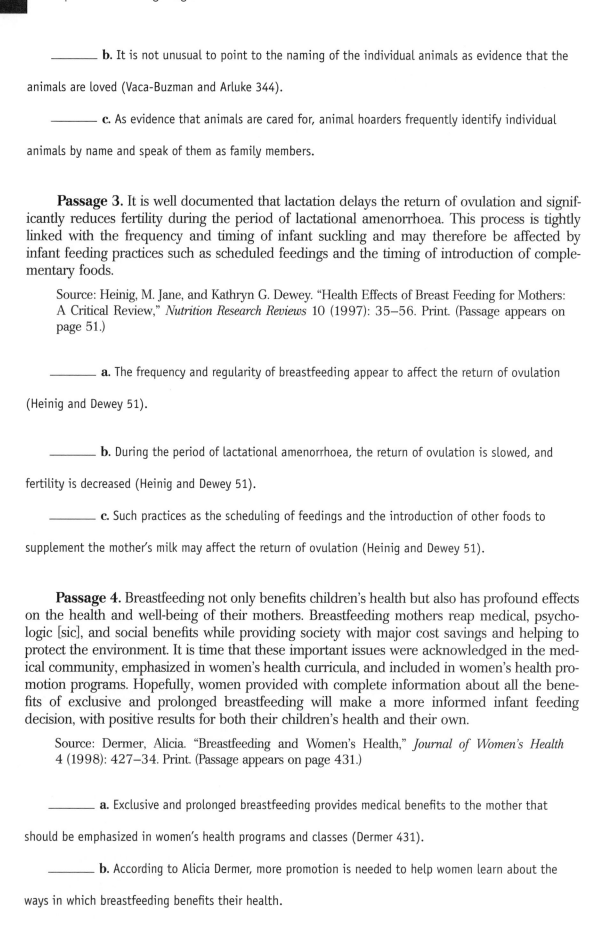

_____ **b.** It is not unusual to point to the naming of the individual animals as evidence that the animals are loved (Vaca-Buzman and Arluke 344).

_____ **c.** As evidence that animals are cared for, animal hoarders frequently identify individual animals by name and speak of them as family members.

Passage 3. It is well documented that lactation delays the return of ovulation and significantly reduces fertility during the period of lactational amenorrhoea. This process is tightly linked with the frequency and timing of infant suckling and may therefore be affected by infant feeding practices such as scheduled feedings and the timing of introduction of complementary foods.

> Source: Heinig, M. Jane, and Kathryn G. Dewey. "Health Effects of Breast Feeding for Mothers: A Critical Review," *Nutrition Research Reviews* 10 (1997): 35–56. Print. (Passage appears on page 51.)

_____ **a.** The frequency and regularity of breastfeeding appear to affect the return of ovulation (Heinig and Dewey 51).

_____ **b.** During the period of lactational amenorrhoea, the return of ovulation is slowed, and fertility is decreased (Heinig and Dewey 51).

_____ **c.** Such practices as the scheduling of feedings and the introduction of other foods to supplement the mother's milk may affect the return of ovulation (Heinig and Dewey 51).

Passage 4. Breastfeeding not only benefits children's health but also has profound effects on the health and well-being of their mothers. Breastfeeding mothers reap medical, psychologic [sic], and social benefits while providing society with major cost savings and helping to protect the environment. It is time that these important issues were acknowledged in the medical community, emphasized in women's health curricula, and included in women's health promotion programs. Hopefully, women provided with complete information about all the benefits of exclusive and prolonged breastfeeding will make a more informed infant feeding decision, with positive results for both their children's health and their own.

> Source: Dermer, Alicia. "Breastfeeding and Women's Health," *Journal of Women's Health* 4 (1998): 427–34. Print. (Passage appears on page 431.)

_____ **a.** Exclusive and prolonged breastfeeding provides medical benefits to the mother that should be emphasized in women's health programs and classes (Dermer 431).

_____ **b.** According to Alicia Dermer, more promotion is needed to help women learn about the ways in which breastfeeding benefits their health.

_____ **c.** The benefits to the health and well-being of women who breastfeed should be publicized more widely (Dermer 431).

Passage 5. Historically, what we today call the Underground Railroad was the process—sometimes organized in a network but more often not—by which slaves escaped northward to the free states, to Canada, or to points south, west, and out to sea. Broadly, it consisted of the individual and collective actions of thousands of enslaved people who were trying to achieve liberty and a new beginning to their lives.

Source: Blight, David W. "The Underground Railroad in History and Memory," Introduction, *Passages to Freedom: The Underground Railroad in History and Memory,* Ed. David W. Blight. Washington: Smithsonian, 2004: 1–10. Print. (Passage appears on page 3.)

_____ **a.** David W. Blight broadly defines the Underground Railroad as the efforts made by slaves to escape to freedom and by those who helped them (3).

_____ **b.** Broadly speaking, the Underground Railroad was the process by which slaves attempted to escape to freedom.

_____ **c.** Although movies dealing with the Underground Railroad suggest that it was an elaborate, highly organized movement, David W. Blight emphasizes that it often was not (3).

Passage 6. He was a slave who overcame the institution of chattel slavery. He was likewise an important, yet unheralded, participant in the Underground Railroad. He was, against all odds, a successful inventor and businessman in the southernmost regions of Ohio. He functioned for many years as an independent, militant black man in an essentially white power structure of trade and finance.

Source: Weeks, Louis. "John P. Parker: Black Abolitionist Entrepreneur, 1827–1900," *Ohio History* 80 (1971): 155–62. Web. 30 Apr. 2009. (Passage appears on page 161.)

_____ **a.** Louis Weeks praises the accomplishments of Parker as an African American who succeeded as an inventor and entrepreneur in an essentially white power structure of trade and finance (161).

_____ **b.** Parker's achievements include not only his own personal triumph over slavery and extensive work in the Underground Railroad but also his business successes in a white-dominated society (Weeks 161).

_____ **c.** Weeks describes Parker as an "independent, militant black man" who succeeded in a time and place where the odds were against him.

Passage 7. Somehow through this mixture of challenge and acceptance, of change and continuity, the True Woman evolved into the New Woman—a transformation as startling in its way as the abolition of slavery or the coming of the machine age. And yet the stereotype, the "mystique" if you will, of what woman was and ought to be persisted, bringing guilt and confusion in the midst of opportunity.

The women's magazines and related literature had feared this very dislocation of values and blurring of roles. By careful manipulation and interpretation they sought to convince woman that she had the best of both worlds—power and virtue—and that a stable order of society depended upon her maintaining her traditional place in it. To that end she was identified with everything that was beautiful and holy.

Source: Welter, Barbara. "The Cult of True Womanhood: 1820–1860," *American Quarterly* 18 (1966): 151–74. Print. (Passage appears on page 174.)

_____ **a.** Barbara Welter argues that magazines for women supported the traditional order by trying to persuade women to retain their traditional roles by associating "everything that was beautiful and holy" with those roles (174).

_____ **b.** As new opportunities for women were emerging at the end of the nineteenth century, the old stereotypes persisted, causing some women to feel guilt and confusion (Weller 174).

_____ **c.** Magazines for women tried to convince women that their traditional roles were necessary for maintaining society.

Passage 8. If immediately after learning of the death of her husband Louise had gone through a rapid logical process leading to a celebration of her total freedom, she might have seemed to be a hard, calculating, and therefore unsympathetic woman. Or to put the point in another way: since she has neither the physical nor moral strength to "beat [. . .] back" her attacker, which she begins to recognize but sadly never names, her responsibility is abrogated.

Source: Deneau, Daniel P. "Chopin's 'The Story of an Hour,'" *Explicator* 61 (2003): 210–13. Print. (Passage appears on page 211.)

_____ **a.** Deneau notes that a conscious analysis of her new freedom might have made Louise a less sympathetic character.

_____ **b.** According to Deneau, the absence of calculation on Louise's part, along with her inability to fight off her attacker, keep her from becoming an unsympathetic character (211).

_____ **c.** Louise Mallard would probably have seemed hard and calculating—and thus unsympathetic—if she had gone through a rapid logical analysis of her situation (Deneau 211).

Passage 9. Nonetheless, "the real" in reality programming is a highly flexible concept. Rather than solely relying upon the use of actual documentary or "live" footage for its credibility, reality programming often draws upon a mix of acting, news footage, interviews and re-creations in a highly simulated pretense towards the "real." Admittedly, mainstream television news is also involved in the recreation of reality, rather than simply recording actual events. And yet, "reality" is dramatized on reality programming to an extent quite unlike conventional television news, and this dramatization is often geared towards more promotional, rather than informational, ends.

Source: Seaton, Beth. "Reality Programming," *Museum of Broadcast Communications* (2005). 12 Jan. 2008. Web.

_____ **a.** According to Beth Seaton, "reality" must be considered a "highly flexible concept" in programs that combine actual documentary footage with acting and other forms of re-creation in a highly simulated version of reality.

_____ **b.** Reality TV programs combine film of actual events with reenactments of those events in ways that treat "reality" as a "highly flexible concept" (Seaton).

_____ **c.** Conceding that television news does not simply record events as they occur, Seaton argues that reality television goes much farther in simulating reality.

Passage 10. The right to practice one's own religion was deemed "essential" or "important" by nearly all Americans (97%); as was the right to "speak freely about whatever you want" (98%) and to "assemble, march, protest or petition the government (94%)," [Gene] Policinski [executive director of the First Amendment Center] said. "Still, Americans are hard pressed to name the five freedoms included in the First Amendment," he said. Speech is the only one named by a majority of respondents (64%), followed by religion (19%), press and assembly (each 16%) and petition (3%).

Source: "'07 Survey Shows Americans' Views Mixed on Basic Freedoms," *First Amendment Center.* 24 Sept. 2007. Web. 10 Jan. 2008.

_____ **a.** The First Amendment guarantees freedom of religion, freedom of speech, freedom of the press, freedom to assemble, and freedom to petition the government for redress.

_____ **b.** Only 16% of Americans can name freedom of the press as one of the basic freedoms guaranteed in the First Amendment.

_____ **c.** The 2007 State of the First Amendment survey revealed that many Americans are unable to name the five freedoms guaranteed in the First Amendment ("'**07 Survey**").

Constructing Your Outline

> *A plan formed by mature consideration and diligent selection out of all the schemes which might be offered, and all the information which can be procured.*
>
> The Idler, no. 8

Some students profess a deep-seated dislike of outlining, convinced perhaps that an outline serves no useful purpose. Outlining is not just mechanical busywork; it is a way of thinking. The procedure involved in outlining is basic in both written and oral communication: formulation of an overall idea (a thesis), division of material into main points, and sensible organization of supporting material for each main point. In the writing of a research paper, an outline-oriented frame of mind should influence every decision from the choice of a topic to revision of the final draft. Thinking in terms of an outline enables you to judge the relevance of facts and opinions, to organize your ideas in paragraphs, and to determine their most effective order. An informal outline could help you move from a prospectus to a first draft. Then a follow-up outline may be useful after you have written that first draft because it allows you to determine whether you have adhered to your purpose and have arranged your ideas in a logical sequence.

Types of Outlines

Outlines, which reduce a body of material to its essential parts, are of two general types: the running outline, which is a listing of facts and ideas in no particular order, and the formal outline, which shows the order, the relationships, and the relative importance of its parts. A *running outline* is most useful during the early stages of the research process when you are searching for a topic and collecting material. Phrases that you jot down in your research log as you brainstorm a topic are a running outline. Note cards before they have been evaluated and organized also are a running outline. A running outline will help you consolidate your preliminary ideas as you write a prospectus. A *formal outline* is a diagram of a paper's design, a bird's-eye view of its structure. Types of formal outlines are illustrated on pages 97–100.

Running Outlines

A running outline simply tabulates facts and opinions in the random order in which they pop into your mind. Keep a page or two in your research log for such a list. After a session in the library, devote a few minutes to brainstorming and jot down topics as they occur to you. As shown in Chapter 1 (pages 14–15), a running outline can lead a student to the choice of a topic and supporting points.

Paul wrote down a list of ideas after he had been reading and thinking about animal hoarding.

1. majority of hoarders female
2. hoarding as public health problem
3. relationship to obsessive-compulsive disorder
4. cats and dogs most common
5. Gary Patronek
6. 62 cats and 6 dogs in New Jersey mansion, plus another 26 dead animals
7. Hoarding of Animals Research Consortium (HARC)
8. 663 cats rescued in Nevada
9. nearly half of hoarders over age 60
10. costs to shelters receiving rescued animals
11. hoarding and need to control
12. Randy Frost
13. condition of houses
14. removal of 160 cats, 105 dogs, 35 birds from Illinois home
15. Pet Animal Care and Facilities Act (Colorado)
16. animal collecting
17. Connecticut couple with 20 beavers flown in from Montana

18. hoarders unable to perceive animals not well cared for
19. link between animal abuse and child abuse and domestic violence
20. hoarders' belief in special empathy with their animals
21. Act Concerning Cruelty to Animals (Illinois)
22. connection of hoarding and other medical problems
23. Louisiana home with 88 small dogs
24. infiltration of legitimate rescue groups
25. self-neglect
26. some hoarders from abusive households where animals represent stability
27. cost for Illinois rescue estimated to be $127,500
28. necessity of euthanizing many rescued animals
29. Companion Animal Hoarding Act (New Mexico)
30. inability to care for animals more important than number of animals

As he considered this list, Paul saw seven main topics:

Illustrations of animal hoarding: 6, 8, 14, 17, 23

Characteristics or definition of animal hoarding: 4, 16, 30

Characteristics of animal hoarders: 1, 9, 18, 20, 24, 25

Causes of animal hoarding: 3, 11, 19, 22, 26

Consequences of animal hoarding: 2, 10, 13, 27, 28

Legislation involving animal hoarding: 15, 21, 29

Frequently cited authorities on animal hoarding: 5, 7, 12

As he looked at grouped items, Paul saw that the first six general topics gave him a working outline for developing his paper. At the same time he realized he should probably try to develop a concluding section that recommended some course of action for dealing with animal hoarding.

Topical Maps

A more sophisticated form of running outline is a topical map (sometimes called a conceptual map or an idea cluster). It might be described as controlled brainstorming. Put your main topic in the center of a page and let free association take over. Write related ideas around the main topic, then connect them with lines. The advantage of a topical map is that it encourages you to see relationships among ideas. A topical map for a long paper would probably be too extensive for one sheet of paper and too elaborate to be useful, so this technique is more appropriate for one idea or one section of a paper.

Many people are visual thinkers and find it helpful to express ideas in the form of a picture or diagram. Try making an orbital diagram like the topical map, or think of a major idea as a tree trunk with related ideas branching from it or as a clothesline on which related ideas are suspended. Use any visual device that helps you see relationships among your ideas.

Having decided he wanted to conclude his paper offering some solutions to the problem of animal hoarding, Paul created a topical map to sort out some of the possible approaches that might be taken. As he kept adding details, he saw that this part of the topic was much more complicated than he had realized at first (Figure 6.1).

THE WORK OF PAUL SANCHEZ

Working Outlines

As shown on pages 14–15, a running outline is a kind of mental inventory that can help you determine your main points. Before you begin your rough draft, analyzing your running outline will help you arrange your main points in a logical order—a *working outline*, which is a tentative organizational strategy, a game plan. A working outline can range in extent from three or four phrases jotted in an examination booklet before you begin to write a test answer, to a detailed plan for a twenty-page paper. Whatever its length, it should be flexible. An outline is a tool, not a shackle.

A good outline evolves; it is not composed in a single operation. The writer who makes an outline and then blindly adheres to it works under a handicap almost as great as the writer who trusts to luck and writes without any advance planning. A working outline is tentative until the paper is completed. You will make revisions of three general kinds:

1. You will add some topics and delete others.
2. You will reevaluate topics. What seemed worth a main topic may be worth only a subtopic, and a subtopic may expand into a main topic.
3. You will rearrange the order of topics and subtopics to facilitate transitions and improve coherence.

Formal Outlines

If you are required to submit an outline as part of your research paper, it should conform to outlining conventions. A *formal outline* should portray clearly the design of a paper. Because it includes only the steps in the development, it will be less detailed than your working outline. It resembles the blueprint for a house; a blueprint shows the location of a wall but does not show the number of nails required or the color it will be painted. A formal outline may be composed of nouns and noun phrases (topics) or sentences or a combination of the two. For examples of each type, see pages 97–100.

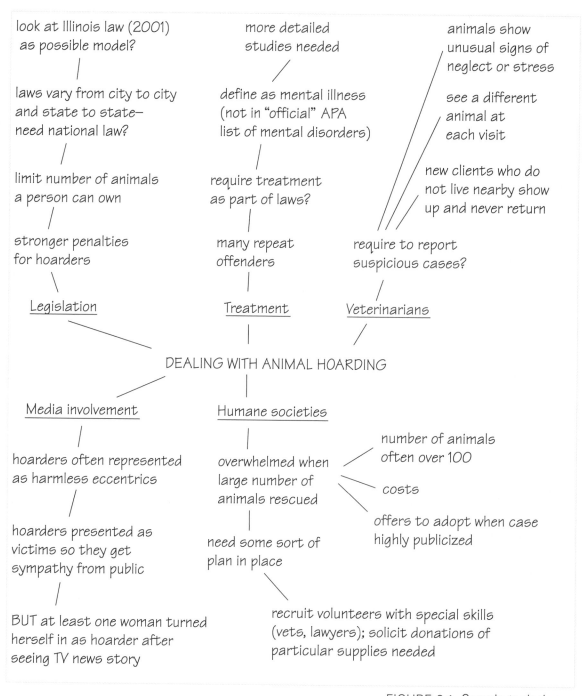

look at Illinois law (2001) as possible model?

laws vary from city to city and state to state— need national law?

limit number of animals a person can own

stronger penalties for hoarders

Legislation

more detailed studies needed

define as mental illness (not in "official" APA list of mental disorders)

require treatment as part of laws?

many repeat offenders

Treatment

animals show unusual signs of neglect or stress

see a different animal at each visit

new clients who do not live nearby show up and never return

require to report suspicious cases?

Veterinarians

DEALING WITH ANIMAL HOARDING

Media involvement

hoarders often represented as harmless eccentrics

hoarders presented as victims so they get sympathy from public

BUT at least one woman turned herself in as hoarder after seeing TV news story

Humane societies

overwhelmed when large number of animals rescued

need some sort of plan in place

number of animals often over 100

costs

offers to adopt when case highly publicized

recruit volunteers with special skills (vets, lawyers); solicit donations of particular supplies needed

FIGURE 6.1 Sample topical map

Conventions of Outlining

The purpose of a formal outline is to show graphically the order, the unity, and the relative importance of the various parts of an essay. To do this, certain conventional practices are in general use to represent the hierarchy of values.

- **SYMBOLS.** The most common system is very simple; it uses Roman and Arabic numerals and upper- and lowercase letters (Figure 6.2). To subdivide further, you would merely alternate Arabic numerals and lowercase letters. But if you subdivide to that extent, you are probably including too many details or have omitted a necessary main heading. You seldom deal with a set of ideas on four or five levels of importance.

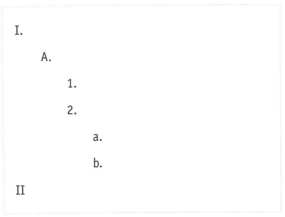

FIGURE 6.2 The hierarchy of outline symbols

All items with the same type of symbol are assumed to be of the same importance. Something is wrong with an outline in which A represents a paragraph and B represents only a single sentence.

- **INDENTATION.** All headings on the same margin are assumed to be of approximately the same importance.
- **PARALLELISM.** Ideas of equal importance are given equal or like expression. In a sentence outline, every heading should be a sentence; in a topic outline, every heading should be in the same grammatical form. For a simple example of parallelism, look at the chapter headings in this book: Shaping, Learning, Using, Evaluating, etc.
- **CONSISTENCY.** The extent to which topics are subdivided should be consistent. If one Roman numeral is subdivided into capital letters and the next one is subdivided as far as lowercase letters, the outline probably is faulty.
- **SINGLE DIVISIONS.** When you indent and begin a set of subordinate symbols, you are dividing ideas. Because nothing can be divided into one part, you should have at least two subtopics or none. A single symbol, therefore, is a danger signal.
- **CONTENT-RICH HEADINGS.** Avoid the use of general terms like *Introduction, Conclusion, Example, Description,* and *Summary*. A heading should signify the content of a portion of an essay, not its purpose or the method used.

To conform to the last two conventions (no single divisions and no omnibus headings), write your thesis at the top of the outline page and do not assign it a symbol. Writing the thesis separately is also a test of your mastery of the material. If you cannot formulate a thesis sentence, you probably need to narrow your topic or find a new approach to it. The conclusion that will appear in the paper need not be represented in the outline because it is substantially the same as the thesis.

Examples of Formal Outlines

Three kinds of formal outlines are illustrated in this section. Comparing each with the sample paper it represents will demonstrate some outlining problems and how to deal with them.

Sample Sentence Outline

(See Paul's paper on pp. 168–185.)

A sentence outline is obviously the most informative type, but it often seems verbose. The example illustrates another possible weakness of sentence outlines: They encourage the writing of similar short sentences—a common fault of mediocre prose.

Understanding and Dealing with Animal Hoarding

Thesis: Animal hoarding is a widespread, serious problem that must be understood so that it can be dealt with effectively.

I.   Animal hoarding is a widespread phenomenon, though the exact extent is unknown.

   A.   Incidents are reported all over the country.

   B.   Estimates of the number of cases vary at the local, state, and national levels.

II.   Animal hoarding is a costly problem.

   A.   Caring for rescued animals is expensive.

   B.   Confined animals destroy property.

   C.   Animal hoarding poses a health threat to hoarders and others.

III.   Animal hoarders share a number of characteristics that suggest that animal hoarding is a psychological condition.

   A.   The majority of hoarders are women who live alone.

   B.   Hoarders show signs of delusion, sometimes even paranoia.

   C.   Animal hoarders tend to collect other items.

   D.   The onset of hoarding behavior often coincides with the early loss of a loved one.

   E.   Although researchers believe animal hoarding is a psychological condition, it is not yet recognized as one.

IV.   Dealing with animal hoarders is a complex task.

   A.   It is often necessary to involve a number of social service agencies to deal with the varied aspects of the problem.

   B.   Laws vary greatly from one locale to another.

   C.   Legal action is often unsuccessful because it is often difficult to get a conviction.

   D.   When offenders are convicted, they are rarely required to have counseling, and the recidivism rate is high.

V.   Recent legislation addresses some of these problems and should make it less difficult to deal effectively with animal hoarders.

Sample Topic Outline

(*See Melissa's paper on pp. 212–225.*)
A topic outline is concise but often seems uninformative because it includes very little of the substance of an essay. A topic outline is the skeleton of an essay—all bones and no flesh.

The Benefits of Breastfeeding for Mothers

Thesis: Breastfeeding provides many health benefits for mothers, who should be encouraged to continue to breastfeed during the first six months of a child's life.

I. Need for breastfeeding

    A. Recommendations of physicians and health agencies

    B. Data showing recommendations not followed

II. Health benefits for mothers

    A. Quicker recovery of pre-baby body size

    B. Decreased risk of post-partum hemorrhage

    C. Increased spacing between children

    D. Reduced risk of breast, uterine, and ovarian cancer

    E. Decreased risk of osteoporosis

    F. Decreased risk of diabetes and heart disease

    G. Reduced stress levels

THE WORK OF MELISSA LOFTS

Combination Outline

(*See James's paper on pp. 193–198.*)
In a combination outline, the main topics are sentences, and the subtopics are phrases. Writing a sentence for each main topic may help you identify and adhere to the central idea unifying that portion of your paper. Similarly, writing the subtopics as phrases enables you to determine their most logical relationship.

John P. Parker: Freeman, Underground Railroad Conductor, Businessman, Inventor

Thesis: John P. Parker should be remembered for his achievements in gaining his own freedom from slavery, helping nearly a thousand others escape slavery, and succeeding as both a businessman and an inventor.

THE WORK OF JAMES KEBLER

Continued

I. Through his own determination and initiative, Parker was able to secure his release from slavery.

    A. Born into slavery and sold into a slave caravan at eight

    B. Attempted escape

    C. Determined on plan to purchase freedom

    D. Achieved freedom by exercising self-control not previously evident

II. Parker became a "conductor" on the Underground Railroad, helping hundreds of escaping slaves.

    A. Reluctantly became involved in helping fugitive slaves

    B. Relocated in Ripley, Ohio

    C. Displayed great bravery and resourcefulness in assisting fugitives

    D. Varied estimates of how many slaves Parker helped to free

III. Parker was a successful businessman.

    A. Built a foundry and machine shop that produced a variety of products

    B. Doubled net worth in short period

    C. Recognized by white residents of Ripley as an important part of local economy

IV. Parker was a successful inventor, holding at least three patents.

    A. Parker's patents

    B. Number of African Americans holding patents at the time

Checklist for Constructing Your Outline

☑ I have made a running outline to help me explore and organize my ideas about my topic.

☑ I have made a topical map or used some other brainstorming activity to help me explore and organize my ideas about my topic.

☑ I have tried several arrangements of ideas to see what seems most appropriate for my topic and approach.

☑ After I completed the first draft of my paper, I wrote an outline of it to evaluate the logic and effectiveness of my organization.

Exercise I

Analyzing a Faulty Outline

What's wrong with this outline? Identify at least eight errors in logic or violations of outlining conventions.

General Robert E. Lee's Civil War

Thesis: Robert E. Lee, one of America's greatest generals, faced enormous problems during the Civil War.

  I.   Divided loyalty

      A.   Disapproved of slavery and secession

      B.   Love for the Union

      C.   Loyal to Virginia

  II.   Problems with Jefferson Davis

      A.   Different social classes

         1.   Lee an aristocrat

      B.   Davis preferred a defensive war.

      C.   Refused to make Lee commander-in-chief

  III.   Lee's weaknesses

      A.   He sometimes gave vague verbal orders.

      B.   Neglected the supply services

      C.   Obsession with the defense of Virginia

  IV.   Shortages

      A.   No maps during Peninsula campaign

      B.   Less manpower than the North

         a.   Deserters

         b.   Draft evaders

  C. Lack of wagons

  D. Shortage of artillery

 V. Failures of subordinates

  A. Longstreet's delay at Gettysburg

 VI. Loss of key officers

  A. Stonewall Jackson

  B. J. E. B. Stuart

  C. Albert Sidney Johnston

   1. Killed at Shiloh

  D. Inexperienced lieutenants

 VII. Conclusion

Writing Your First Draft

A man may write at any time if he will set himself doggedly to it.

Boswell, *Life of Johnson*, vol. 1

After you have spent days or weeks compiling a list of sources, taking notes, and projecting an outline, the actual writing of your paper may seem like an anticlimax; but it is the most important phase of your research project: your work will be judged on the basis of the finished product—what you set down on paper. This chapter and the next suggest some procedures to follow, but writing is an individualistic activity that cannot be reduced to a series of lockstep operations. The suggested procedures are not mechanical steps in a formula. Try them all, but adopt those that work for you.

Putting Words on Paper

Although typewriters have become almost as obsolete as quill pens, many people compose at the computer as though they were simply using a typewriter without a ribbon, failing to take advantage of the features available to them in most word processing programs. A spell-checker identifies spelling errors, often highlighting them as you type. (Remember, though, that it cannot distinguish among homonyms—such as *cite, site,* and *sight*—and will often identify correct spellings of proper names as incorrect.) A thesaurus provides a choice of synonyms for a general word, and some programs flag possible errors in capitalization, spacing, hyphenation, and so on. A separate style-checker identifies passive verbs and overworked phrases, determines the ratio of monosyllabic to polysyllabic words, shows the frequency of subordinate clauses, and computes the average length of sentences. You can view several pages at once to check the layout of your manuscript, and you can easily shift between typefaces and fonts, which may be helpful in keeping track of ideas or sources as you plan. Some programs also include an encyclopedia that will allow you to check factual information as you compose.

Some features are especially useful for producing a research paper. MLA style calls for a header on every page (your last name and the page number), and you can set up a header that will appear automatically when you print your paper. You can also create hanging indentations for your Works Cited page, so that for each new entry the first line will be flush left and the others indented. (If you create the Works Cited entries by adding spaces or tabs to force a line break and indentations, you are likely to have problems whenever you revise or even when you change printers.) If your instructor requires you to use footnotes or endnotes, you can create them as you compose, and they will automatically be renumbered if you relocate the passage as you revise later. Time spent learning how to use these features is time well spent.

The most efficient method of producing the paper is to type the rough draft, print it, revise the printout, and then revise the computer file. Although printing the draft may seem like an unnecessary step, it is easier to judge organization and flow accurately when you can see the whole paper. Being able to make side-by-side comparisons in a print copy makes this process much more reliable. You can easily mark repetition that needs to be eliminated and identify passages that need to be relocated, devise smoother transitions and better blending of borrowed material—and then make all those changes in the computer file.

Few mishaps are as disheartening as the loss of your text because of a power failure, a faulty disk or USB flash drive, or some other unexpected occurrence. As a safeguard, save your text every few pages. At the end of each writing session, print what you have composed. Save the printout and your notes until you have completed your paper. Another safeguard is to copy your file to a backup disk or flash drive at the end of each session and store it in a safe place in case something befalls the original. Keep the backup copy containing your final draft until the paper has been graded and returned. If your paper is lost or if you are asked to rewrite it, the backup will make rewriting easier.

Getting Started

Judging your material when it exists only in your mind and in note form is impossible. When you have set it down in a rough draft, you will have something tangible that you can evaluate and revise. The number of drafts you write will depend on your work habits. Writing is not a simple task, and serious students may turn out a half-dozen drafts before producing a finished essay. Typically, a student who is writing a paper should expect to produce at least a rough draft, an intermediate copy that is carefully and thoroughly revised, and a final copy.

Finding a Time and a Place to Write

When you are ready to begin your rough draft, find a quiet place where you can work without distraction. If carrels are available in the library, look for one that is secluded and quiet. If there are no carrels, look for some other quiet area. If you work in your room, try to find a time when noise and interruptions are at a minimum. Resist the temptation—which will present itself more than once—to postpone writing to another day. Allot blocks of several hours on three or four days for composing the rough draft. Plan to work on identifiable blocks of text during each session so that you can complete one or more sections of your outline in that session. However, you should also be aware that a paper written at intervals over a period of days is more likely to be repetitious and disorganized. For that reason, read over all the previously composed material before you begin again.

Freewriting

Before actually starting to write, read through your research log to recall any notations made during the early stages of your reading that may have faded from your memory. A note may jog your imagination and suggest a relevant idea or an effective phrase. Reading and note taking can become rather mechanical tasks during which your creativity is put on hold. Freewriting at this stage can jump-start your imagination and also give you an overview of your material.

Freewriting, a first cousin of brainstorming (see page 5), simply means automatic writing with no concern for logic, spelling, commas, and other niceties. It is a discovery technique intended to generate ideas. You allow your mind to hover around a topic and set down whatever occurs to you. The result will be an indiscriminate listing of words, phrases, and brief questions. Abbreviations and other shortcuts are acceptable, even advisable, because free association, the basis of freewriting, is a fast-moving process. After spending a few minutes in a freewheeling survey of your topic, look over what you have written and evaluate it in relation to your thesis, your audience, and your purpose.

After reading and taking notes from discussions of "The Story of an Hour" in several books and articles, Colleen Lee felt she was ready to start writing. She began by jotting down phrases and questions as they popped into her mind. They served to get her rough draft under way.

Start with summary of story?

Story first published as "The Dream of an Hour" — mention that?

Vogue magazine pretty new when story published and known for publishing "daring" things.

Lots of critics mention similarities of Chopin and "daring" French writers of the time.

Role of setting (beautiful spring day after storm — patches of blue sky, singing birds, etc.).

Chopin's mother widowed at fairly early age and never remarried so she could be independent. Connect her with Louise Mallard?

L. M.'s grief is real, not faked. Chopin doesn't suggest that L. and Brently weren't happy until about 2/3 of the way through the story. Does L. not realize it herself until just now?

She tries to fight off the recognition that she will be happy — happier? — now that Brently is dead. Why? It looks like she really does love him (she knows she will cry when she sees the body) but a paragraph or two later, it's "she had loved him — sometimes"!

"Feverish triumph" in L's eyes. Is she being criticized too? Or does that just stress that it's an illusion?

Seemingly simple, very short story really very complex — a lot going on beneath the surface!

As Colleen looked over these notes, she could see that she would need to eliminate some of the first ideas she had written down so that she would have enough room in the paper to concentrate on discussing the story itself. Perhaps the final idea—the surprising complexity of the story—would make a good starting point for her discussion.

Organizing Your Notes

If you have used photocopies or note sheets, you may find you need to cut them into slips so that you can arrange them in order. If you cut them up, be sure that the source information (author and page number) is included on each slip. Spread them out on a tabletop or on the floor, if necessary, and sort them into piles. Note cards can be easily sorted in this same way, of course. Once you have determined your main points and sorted out the supporting information, you can copy and paste them into a new document, transferring each note to the appropriate position. (Again, be sure you keep track of the source information for each item.) You will now have a detailed working outline—one step away from a rough draft. It might be advisable to print this outline and post it above your desk. As you sort and classify your notes, you must be reconciled to two unavoidable facts:

1. *Some notes will be eliminated.* Anyone writing a research paper takes some notes on speculation. You should discard those that clearly are not related to your topic and put doubtful ones in a special pile for future consideration; if you change your thesis, they may be usable. In any construction, some waste is inevitable, and a research paper is no exception. Trying to squeeze in all your notes to justify the time and energy spent in recording them will destroy the unity of your paper.

2. *Some additional research may be necessary.* As you work out the detailed structure of your paper, you will probably notice weak spots that need to be reinforced. You may have to return to some of your sources for additional information or for missing publication data. You may also need to look for new sources. Try to discover gaps in your material before starting to write. Interrupting your writing to visit the library or to search online might be another form of disguised procrastination.

Fine-Tuning Your Outline

When you have organized your notes, make certain that each main point is related to your thesis and that each has sufficient support. Look over your research log to see if any ideas recorded there have slipped your mind. Even if an outline is not required with your final paper, the process of outlining will be helpful as you plan your paper. Examine the notes related to each main point to determine the best way of classifying them. Try to avoid using the same basis in a series of paragraphs. Outlines of the sample papers (pages 97–100) illustrate various systems of classification. Also consider the arrangement of subtopics within each paragraph. Sometimes you can improve coherence by shifting a subtopic so that it looks ahead to the next main point. Outlining helps you anticipate transitions.

Keep your outline in view as you write your rough draft, but do not regard it as an unbreakable contract. Revise your plan as you write, keep track of the changes, and make a final outline only after you have completed your final draft.

Getting Your Draft on Paper

When you have double-checked your outline and done whatever supplementary research is necessary, you are ready to begin your rough draft. As suggested earlier, your draft will probably be more unified in tone and in substance if you write it in a limited number of focused sessions. Do not lose your momentum by lingering over the choice of words. If you find an idea difficult to express, leave space for it and go on. As you write, keep looking ahead in your notes, trying to anticipate transitions that will connect your ideas effectively.

Keep your list of Works Cited nearby so that you can identify sources readily while you are writing. The simplest procedure is to cite the author's name and the page reference (Toth 10) immediately after the borrowed material. You can then transfer such parenthetical citations to the final copy with little or no change—one of the time-saving features of MLA style.

Opening Gambits

You will not really need a title until you prepare the final version of your paper, but making at least a tentative choice may bring your topic and thesis into sharper focus. Make your title specific and clear; use a subtitle if necessary.

Paul's original title was much too broad, so he added a phrase indicating the major directions of his paper:

> Animal Hoarding

> Understanding and Dealing with Animal Hoarding

Colleen had been struck by the phrase "monstrous joy" in Chopin's story, but she realized that an explanatory subtitle would give her readers a clearer sense of direction:

> "A Monstrous Joy"

> "A Monstrous Joy": Ambivalent Messages in "The Story of an Hour"

The recognition that breastfeeding benefits mothers as well as infants was uppermost in Melissa's mind when she titled her paper:

> The Benefits of Breastfeeding for Mothers

James added a list to suggest the diversity of John Parker's accomplishments:

> John P. Parker

> John P. Parker: Freeman, Underground Railroad Conductor, Businessman, Inventor

For some writers the most difficult part of a paper to write is the opening. Just as a speaker may indulge in throat-clearing and foot-shuffling, a student may circle a topic for a hundred words before reaching it. For example, someone planning to write about Disneyland might discuss the history of theme parks, Disney cartoons, the popularity of Mickey Mouse, and one or two other subjects before arriving at the topic. Such a procedure is a form of freewriting that might be a useful way of warming up your creative engine, but if you write such an irrelevant preamble, delete it, start over, and introduce your topic and thesis in one or two clear, crisp paragraphs. An opening should identify the topic, arouse a reader's interest and curiosity, and look ahead to a statement of the thesis. Every topic offers different possibilities. A paper on the silent film actor Buster Keaton might open in a number of ways:

- A factual statement.

  Joseph Frank (Buster) Keaton was born 4 October 1895, in Piqua, Kansas, where his parents were

  appearing in a vaudeville theater.

- A legend.

  According to Keaton family folklore, when Keaton was six months old he fell down a flight of stairs but did not cry. Harry Houdini, the magician, picked him up and said, "That's some buster." He remained Buster for the rest of his life.

- An incident.

  Buster Keaton's first stage appearance occurred when he was nine months old. He clambered out of the trunk where his mother had placed him to sleep and crawled on stage, where his father was doing a blackface monologue.

- A paradox.

  Although Buster Keaton never smiled on the screen, he brought smiles and laughter to millions of filmgoers.

- A comparison.

  Of the three star comedians of silent films, Charlie Chaplin and Harold Lloyd in their last years were wealthy and received many honors; Buster Keaton, however, was plagued by money worries and was nearly forgotten by many movie fans.

- A critical comment.

  Leslie Halliwell described Buster Keaton as "one of America's great silent clowns, the unsmiling little man who always came out on top despite the odds" (222).

- A description.

  Paul Gallico saw Buster Keaton as "a sad-faced little fellow wearing a flat pork-pie hat, string tie, too-big clothes, and flap shoes" (247).

The sample papers employ a variety of opening strategies. Paul Sanchez begins with a dramatized instance of animal hoarding meant to capture the reader's attention, then provides a series of very brief references to incidents that occurred within a single year to emphasize the scope of the problem. Colleen Lee's paper opens with a four-sentence summary of the story she is writing about, followed by an equally brief survey of interpretations of the story. In the subsequent paragraph, she shows how her interpretation differs from those.

The other two papers were not written for an English class, and each writer's opening reflects that. James Kebler's assignment calls for him to identify African Americans of the past who should be remembered, and he opens immediately with his thesis, followed by a concise listing of the areas in which John P. Parker excelled. Melissa Lofts begins with a straightforward statement of the well-known benefits of breastfeeding for infants, then directs her reader to her own focus—the less frequently promoted benefits for the mother herself.

Do not struggle unduly to devise a clever opening paragraph. If you have trouble finding an effective opening, start writing the main topic with which you are most comfortable. Your momentum will carry you along, and eventually an opening will suggest itself.

Closure

The opening of a paper should capture the reader's interest, set the tone of the paper, and introduce the topic. The close should leave the reader with a sense of completeness; a paper should not end in midair. The conclusion should not introduce a brand-new idea, and it should not restate the thesis verbatim. There is no formula for closing a paper, but it should be a natural recapitulation of your thesis and main points. Sometimes a pertinent quotation can be an effective close. The sample papers illustrate some forms of closure. The close of Paul's paper (pages 179–181) sums up new legislation dealing with animal hoarding and briefly returns to the anecdote with which the paper opened. Colleen ends (page 191) by drawing a conclusion about the significance of the ambivalent messages in "The Story of an Hour." James concludes (page 197) by restating the thesis in different words—the story of Parker's many achievements is an inspiration to present-day young people. Melissa closes (page 223) by suggesting that the health benefits of breastfeeding need to be more widely known.

Managing Borrowed Material

Ex. J A poor research paper is often a cut-and-paste collection of lengthy quotations looming up at close intervals in student prose. In a superior paper, more material is summarized than quoted and borrowed material blends smoothly with the text instead of standing alone with no connection to what precedes or follows.

Managing Summaries

Summary is a term with a wide range of meanings. The extent of condensation will vary depending on your purpose. If you want to sum up an author's position, you probably will state it in considerably fewer words than the author used. If you want to clarify, however, you are more likely to write a paraphrase close to the length of the author's original statement. In any type of summary, you have two challenges:

1. *Making certain that you do not unintentionally reproduce the author's language.* Compare your notes with the source and change any borrowed phrasing or enclose it in quotation marks.
2. *Signaling the beginning and end of a summary.* When there are no quotation marks, a reader may not recognize where a borrowed passage begins. You should clearly indicate where a summary starts, often by using an introductory expression like the following:

According to Morris Bishop . . .

A biography by Robert Allerton Parker describes . . .

Spencer Klaw believes . . .

The page reference would follow the borrowed material.

Managing Quotations

The smooth merging of quoted material with the text is usually achieved during revision, but a beginning can be made in the first draft. One reason for awkwardness with quotations may be uncertainty about mechanics. Some basic conventions are discussed and illustrated in the following pages.

Ways of Introducing Quotations

A verb like *said* or *wrote* introducing a quotation is ordinarily followed by a comma. Students sometimes erroneously extend this usage and place a comma before every quotation. When a brief quotation is an integral part of your sentence (usually a subject, an object, or a modifying phrase), a comma may not be needed. Also, when the word *that* precedes a quotation, a comma is seldom necessary. A colon should be used only when a complete sentence introduces the quotation. Any quotation can be introduced in more than one way. Following are five ways of introducing a brief quotation:

Mae West once remarked, "Too much of a good thing is wonderful."

Mae West described "too much of a good thing" as "wonderful."

"Too much of a good thing," purred Mae West, "is wonderful."

Mae West once remarked that "too much of a good thing is wonderful."

Mae West's persona is captured in one of her famous quips: "Too much of a good thing is wonderful."

If you introduce a quotation with a verb, do not overwork *say/said* and *write/wrote*, but look for synonyms. Most verbs in the following list would ordinarily be followed by *that*.

acknowledge	assert	declare	maintain	relate
affirm	believe	emphasize	mention	report
agree	caution	explain	note	state
allege	claim	imply	observe	suggest
argue	comment	insist	propose	think

Such terms are not interchangeable. The president *insisted* is very different from the president *implied.* Do not search for unusual or impressive verbs like *expostulated* or *asseverated.*

There is no ironclad rule for choosing the tense of such verbs, though MLA prefers the present tense. Each of the following is grammatically correct:

Thoreau reminds us that "the mass of men lead lives of quiet desperation."

Thoreau wrote, "The mass of men lead lives of quiet desperation."

Keep verb tenses consistent throughout a paper, and if you are in doubt, avoid using an introductory verb:

According to Thoreau, "The mass of men lead lives of quiet desperation."

Formatting Block Quotations

A quotation of four or more lines is usually written in block, or display, form. The entire quotation is indented one inch on the left but is not indented on the right. No quotation marks are included unless they appear within the original (as in the example). Do not indent the first line unless you quote more than one paragraph (which is seldom advisable). If there are two or more paragraphs, indent the first line of each *three* spaces. At the close of the quotation, type the citation *after* the period. The block form calls attention to the quotation, but too many block quotations will clog the flow of your prose and should be avoided. Various methods of introducing block quotations are illustrated in the sample papers.

The following example is from Susan Sniader Lanser, *The Narrative Act: Point of View in Prose Fiction* (Princeton: Princeton UP, 1981). It is longer than most block quotations because it is used for illustrations in the next section. The left margin is indented one inch in a manuscript.

> "The Story of an Hour" challenges the notion that by living for her husband a wife will also be living for herself. It suggests that even "benevolent" rule of women by men may be oppressive; it questions the assumptions that it is "monstrous" to acknowledge someone's death as one's own liberation, and that love, especially for a woman, is the most important goal. Ideologically these messages are at odds with the culture text of Chopin's time and perhaps our own. This opposition to the culture text, moreover, is hardly trivial; it threatens basic beliefs and practices about male-female relations, about women's dependency on men for survival and identity, and about the "proper" responses to love and death.
>
> If this is the message of "The Story of an Hour," it is not difficult to understand why Chopin might approach it rather gingerly, especially because a message like this from a woman writer would probably be viewed with even greater hostility than the same message coming from a man. The narrator of "The Story of an Hour" never says overtly most of what I have described, yet this ideology comes through the text, and although I have met readers who *disagree* with the textual ideology, I have never encountered a reader who failed to grasp it. (Lanser 251–52)

Blending Quotations with Your Text

A quotation must be an accurate reproduction of the original, but if the meaning and the emphasis are not altered, some exceptions are permissible.

- An initial capital letter can be changed to lowercase if only a portion of a sentence is quoted. Altered capitalization is sometimes indicated by brackets: [W]oman's. This practice is not universal, however. Learn your instructor's preference.
- When you delete words within the text you are quoting, the deletion is signaled by an ellipsis—three spaced periods. If the quotation already contains ellipses, you must enclose your own ellipses in brackets to distinguish them from the ellipses already there, as in the second example.

> "The narrator of 'The Story of an Hour' never says overtly most of what I have described, yet . . . I have never encountered a reader who failed to grasp it" (Lanser 251–52).

"His singing-voice was a full baritone . . . smooth and sweet, like his [. . .] speaking-voice"

(Mayne 52).

- A short whole phrase or clause can be quoted with no ellipsis before or after, unless the words would appear to be a full sentence without the ellipsis, as in the second example.

Susan Sniader Lanser points out that Chopin's story "threatens basic beliefs and practices about

male-female relations" (251).

Lanser uses understatement to stress her point: "Ideologically these messages are at odds with the

culture text of Chopin's time . . ." (251).

Punctuating Quotations

All forms of punctuation can be involved in quoting borrowed material. The most common uses are illustrated here.

Double Quotation Marks

The chief use of double quotation marks is to enclose language taken from a speech or a printed source. They are also used to enclose the title of an article, a story, or any other portion of a published unit, and to enclose a word used in a special sense.

"Civilization is the art of living in towns of such size that everyone does not know everyone else"

(Jaynes 150).

Hoagy Carmichael's most famous song is "Stardust."

Daphne was addicted to soap operas and began each day with her morning "serial."

Single Quotation Marks

Quoted material within a quotation is enclosed in single quotation marks. If you quote a passage that contains double quotation marks, change them to singles and use doubles to enclose the passage. Some publishers, especially in England, enclose quotations in single marks—the opposite of U.S. practice. For the sake of consistency, it is permissible to change British singles to doubles.

"'Texas political ethics' is not an oxymoron. Our guys have 'em. They just tend to have an

overdeveloped sense of the extenuating circumstances" (Ivins 203).

Period

Leaving one space after a period at the end of a sentence or after a period in a bibliographic entry is now common practice, but two spaces are still acceptable. Learn your instructor's preference and follow it consistently. Space once after a period that follows an initial in a proper name. Place a period inside quotation marks except when the quotation is followed by a citation in parentheses.

"There are eminent scholars who are convinced that America was first seen by Egyptians" (Cooke 23).

Their behavior demonstrated the truth of a well-known old saying: "Fools think alike."

Comma

Place a comma inside a quotation mark except when it follows an in-text citation.

"The Story of an Hour," which was written in 1894, can be seen as a challenge to the notion then current that love is "the most important goal" for a woman (Lanser 251).

Humor "transforms suffering and diminishes pain" (Stevens 67), but it is difficult to find these qualities in the work of most standup comedians.

Semicolon

Place a semicolon after a closing quotation mark and follow it with one space.

Our third-grade teacher called wearing a dunce cap "negative motivation"; we thought of it as punishment.

Colon

Place a colon after a closing quotation mark and follow it with one space.

All presidents before Lincoln were clean-shaven, but in the last third of the nineteenth century American men indulged in a wide variety of "hirsute adornment": Dundreary whiskers, full sideburns, imperial beards, mutton chops, Van Dykes, and many others.

Dash

Type a dash as two hyphens, leaving no space before, between, or after. Your word processing program may automatically replace the two hyphens with a dash. You may disable this feature if you like, but there is no reason to do so unless your instructor requests it. Never use a dash after a comma (as was frequently done in nineteenth-century printing). Use a pair of dashes to enclose parenthetical material and a single dash to indicate an abrupt shift in the structure of a sentence. Both uses may add emphasis to a statement, but neither should be overworked.

"The wishbone—destroyed in most commercial cutting—and the 'little drumstick,' which is the meatiest section of the wing, are the delicacies" (Blount 44).

When a group of teachers criticized baseball star Dizzy Dean for using *ain't* in his broadcasts, he replied, "There are a lot of school teachers who ain't using ain't—but they ain't eating."

Brackets

As shown on pages 72 and 111–112, square brackets are used to enclose a brief identification or some other form of clarification within a quotation. Angle brackets are used when citing a URL on an MLA Works Cited page (see page 114).

"El Greco [Doménikos Theotokópoulos] never forgot that he was of Greek descent" (Wethey 1).

"Probably the most favored tag of the early humanists of Europe comes from Terence: *homo sum; humani nil a me alienum puto* [I am a man; nothing human is foreign to me]" (Platt 184).

Salda, Michael N., ed. *The Little Red Riding Hood Project*. Vers. 1.1. U of Southern Mississippi, Oct.

2005. Web. 19 Mar. 2009. <http://www.usm.edu/english/fairytales/lrrh/lrrhhome.htm>.

Slash

Use a slash (also called a diagonal, a solidus, a virgule, and in England a stroke) to separate two closely related words and to imply that either may be chosen. It is also used to separate two or three lines of poetry written consecutively (see page 114). Space before and after a slash in this use but not when one is used in prose. Try to avoid using the *and/or* construction.

The suspect was diagnosed as obsessive/compulsive.

In "The Second Coming," Yeats predicted the breakup of modern civilization: "The best lack all

conviction, while the worst/Are full of passionate intensity" (Abrams 2: 1973).

Checklist for Writing Your First Draft

☑ I have a schedule for working on my first draft in several sessions.

☑ My notes are in a form that will allow me to locate information easily.

☑ In my draft, I have quoted only when summary or paraphrase would not be as effective as quoting.

☑ I have provided a source for each piece of information summarized, paraphrased, or quoted from an outside source.

☑ I have supplied the credentials or qualifications of a source whenever that will add to the credibility of my argument.

Exercise J

Managing Borrowed Material

Use these three passages in the exercises that follow.

Passage A Mary J. Blige's eighth studio album, "Growing Pains," defies the conventional wisdom that aging works against female entertainers. Blige has a robust, dark voice, and she moves around melodies in a pleasingly unruly way. She can irrigate a song with pain but is judicious about adding flourishes to her performances—a decision that makes her sound more like a sixties soul singer than like a modern R. & B. star. (Her 1998 live album, "The Tour," documents how comfortable Blige is with a few flat notes, and how little they matter to the fans who track her life as if it were more important than their own.) Her commercial rival and aesthetic antipode is Mariah Carey, another R. & B. singer who is selling remarkably well deep into her career. Carey, who is the more successful, offers the inhuman power of her voice, a knack for producing hit records, and undying optimism. If Carey is "Good Morning America"— all cheer and reliability—Blige is what comes later: the daytime talk show noisy with recrimination and redemption.

> Source: Frere-Jones, Sasha. "Living Pains: Mary J. Blige's Chronic Brilliance" *New Yorker*, 11 Feb. 2008. Web. 15 Mar. 2009. <http://www.newyorker.com/arts/>

Passage B A lame duck (I suppose I ought to call it *flight-challenged*) is one that is unable to keep up with the flock and is thus easy prey for predators. The phrase *lame duck* was first applied on the London Stock Exchange in the eighteenth century to brokers who could not pay their debts. Beginning in nineteenth-century America, lame duck was used to describe a congressional representative who had failed to hornswoggle the voters into re-electing him in November, but who was not due, under the Constitution, to actually be booted out until the following March. Thus freed of even the pretense of accountability to the voters, such lame ducks usually voted themselves a scandalous jackpot of perks, until the Lame Duck Amendment of 1934 put a stop to the practice.

> Source: Morris, Evan. *The Word Detective.* New York: Plume, 2001. Print.

Passage C
Q: So, do your political self and your creative self communicate at all?

A: As an artist your first loyalty is to your art. Unless this is the case, you're going to be a second-rate artist. I don't mean there's never any overlap. You learn things in one area and bring them into another area. But giving a speech against racism is not the same as writing a novel. The object is very clear in the fight against racism; you have reasons why you're opposed to it. But when you're writing a novel, you don't want the reader to come out of it voting yes or no to some question. Life is more complicated than that. Reality simply consists of different points of view.

> Source: Atwood, Margaret. Interview by Marilyn Snell. *MotherJones* July–Aug. 1997. Web. 27 Mar. 2009.

1. Write a single sentence summing up Frere-Jones's assessment of Blige's singing. Do not quote anything directly. Be sure to introduce the source.

2. Write a short paragraph summarizing the origins of the term *lame duck* (passage B). It should be no more than half the length of the passage. Do not quote directly. Be sure to introduce the source.

3. Write a one-sentence summary of the view of the relationship of art and political beliefs expressed in passage C. Do not quote anything directly. Be sure to introduce the source.

4. Write a slightly longer version of the summary of passage C in which you quote part of the sentence "But giving a speech against racism is not the same as writing a novel." Be sure to introduce the source.

5. Paraphrase Frere-Jones's contrast between Mary J. Blige and Mariah Carey (passage A), focusing on this sentence: "If Carey is 'Good Morning America'—all cheer and reliability—Blige is what comes later: the daytime talk show noisy with recrimination and redemption." Do not quote more than five words. Be sure to introduce the source.

6. Write a short paragraph describing Morris's tone (passage B). Quote no more than three or four phrases in your description. Be sure to introduce the source.

Preparing Your Final Copy

When once our labour has begun, the comfort that enables us to endure it is the prospect of its end.

The Rambler, no. 207

When you have written and revised your rough draft, you may be tempted to turn out a final copy as quickly as possible. But you should not neglect the last stage of the research process, in which you put the finishing touches on the style and form of your paper. This, after all, is the culmination of your hard work in the library and at your desk—the final product that will determine your grade. Do not let impatience or fatigue cause you to rush through this final stage. Your final copy should be as clear and correct as you can make it. Remember that what a reader sees first is what a writer does last.

Effective Revision

Revision, which literally means "to look back at" or "to see again," is a highly important but often neglected step in the writing process. It does not involve merely proofreading—just inserting a comma here and there and correcting the spelling of a few words. Effective revision is nearly as creative as the initial act of writing. It requires that you evaluate and, whenever necessary, improve the structure, content, and style of your paper.

Students in the social sciences are often required to submit an abstract—a brief summary of the essential ideas—as part of a paper. You probably will not be asked to prepare an abstract for your composition class, but preparing one on your own at this stage might be helpful. Condensing your paper without omitting any major ideas will enable you to judge the unity of your paper and identify any digressions. If you find it impossible to fit an idea into the abstract, it may not belong in the paper. An abstract written during the final phases of your project can be as useful as a prospectus is at the outset.

Revision is a specialized skill that requires a double perspective. To revise effectively requires the power Robert Burns described: "To see ourselves as others see us." Try to look at your paper as though it were written by someone else. Try to assume the role of an uninformed reader whose interest must be aroused and whose attention must be held. Try to examine your draft from a reader's point of view and remember that the test of a statement is not whether you understand it but whether a new reader will be able to.

You probably can judge your draft more objectively if you wait a few days before revising it. An elusive word or an effective combination of sentence elements may pop into your mind unexpectedly. Or you may think of a better way to organize a section of the paper. One of the ironies of composition is that these flashes of inspiration fade away as rapidly as they appear. Set aside a page in your research log for recording a fresh idea or a vivid phrase before it slips away.

Developing Your Outline

As you revise your draft, keep your basic plan in mind and have a copy of your working outline visible for guidance. Check each paragraph topic to be certain that it relates directly or indirectly to your thesis. Check each paragraph to make certain that it is unified around a single idea and that it is developed in logical sequence. If you delete a topic or rearrange the topics, record the change on your working outline.

Although you need a clear, logical plan, you also need to articulate that plan coherently in your paper. You achieve coherence (the logical and consistent relationship of parts) by adhering to a sensible plan and by providing adequate transitions between paragraphs, between subtopics, and between sentences. You will probably need more transitional markers than you expect. As the writer of the paper, you are like a driver on a familiar highway who does not need to watch for signs and landmarks, but your reader is like a driver on an unfamiliar highway who needs route signs and other directional markers. You are so familiar with the material that you anticipate what is coming next, and it is easy to underestimate the amount of guidance your readers will need. It is better to risk seeming obvious than to be obscure.

The most effective transitions are derived from the material itself. Sometimes making an outline enables you to see how material can be arranged so that one topic links up smoothly with the next. Various transitional devices—such as contrast, repetition, and echo words—are identified in Paul's paper. The most common way to connect ideas, however, is to use transitional elements—words and phrases that indicate relationships between ideas. Following are lists of some kinds of relationships and transitional elements that can express them.

Cause/Reason

accordingly	because	hence	since
as a consequence	consequently	on account of	therefore
as a result	due to	owing to	whereas

Condition

although	if	nevertheless	on condition that
at any rate	in case	nonetheless	provided that

Continuation/Addition

and	furthermore	next	moreover
additionally	as well as	in addition	not only . . . but also
again	besides	last	also
along with	further	likewise	too

Effect/Result

accordingly	consequently	then	thus
as a result	hence	therefore	

Emphasis

above all	especially	indeed	positively
absolutely	extremely	in fact	undoubtedly
certainly	importantly	of course	without question

Example

for example	namely	that is
for instance	such as	to illustrate

Opposition/Contrast

but	however	on the contrary	as opposed to
contrary to	in contrast	on the other hand	unlike
conversely	nothing like	otherwise	yet

Qualification

almost	nearly	probably
however	perhaps	somewhat

Sequence

and	initially	next	then
finally	last	second	third

Similarity/Comparison

as	in like manner	like	similarly
compared to	in the same way	likewise	too
correspondingly	just as		

Summary

in conclusion	last	therefore	in short
finally	to sum up	thus	

Time

after	hereafter	next	then
afterward	heretofore	now	thereafter
always	in the meantime	seldom	when
during	later	since	whereupon
formerly	meanwhile	sometimes	while
henceforth	never	soon	

Such functional elements are totally abstract, so it is easy to misuse them. The elements in each group are similar, but no two are identical. Two often-confused transitional words are *therefore* (for this reason) and *thus* (in this way). By attentive reading and careful writing, you can develop sensitivity to nuances in meaning and the ability to link your ideas effectively.

Writing in an Appropriate Style

Your research paper will require a somewhat more formal style than you are accustomed to using. Your instructor undoubtedly will suggest the level of formality appropriate to your topic. Contractions and the pronouns *I* and *you* are sometimes considered inappropriate in a formal style. However, if your paper will draw on your own experience, ask your instructor if using *I* occasionally is permissible, since referring to yourself as *the writer* or *this researcher* may sound clumsy. With practice you can develop a style that is dignified without being awkward or stilted. As at a formal social occasion, you try to be on your best behavior but at ease.

Using the Active Voice

Writing in a formal style sometimes encourages overuse of the passive voice. Passive verbs may suggest an objective tone, but they also tend to be wordy, indirect, and awkward. They conceal the actual subject or agent performing the action and enable the writer to evade responsibility (not surprisingly, the passive voice abounds in bureaucratic prose). Changing passive verbs to the active voice when possible and appropriate will make your prose more direct and more concise.

Passive: Elaborate dance routines were devised by Busby Berkeley in the 1930s.
Active: Busby Berkeley devised elaborate dance routines in the 1930s.
Passive: Two practices a day were scheduled by Coach Pribble.
Active: Coach Pribble scheduled two practices a day.

The passive voice, of course, is not incorrect. It is appropriate when the performer of an action is not expressed or when the object or receiver of the action is more important:

Franklin Delano Roosevelt was elected for an unprecedented fourth term in 1944.

The Internet was first developed by the Defense Department.

During the flood, our entire block was inundated.

Varying Sentence Patterns

There is no optimal length for sentences, but the greater the range from shortest to longest, the better. Sentence beginnings are especially important because of the natural inclination to start every sentence with the subject. Especially when a series of sentences all start with the *same* subject, the effect can be as sleep-inducing as a concert by metronomes. Moving a phrase or a subordinate clause to the beginning often improves the clarity as well as the rhythm of a sentence. Avoid, however, starting too many sentences with transitional elements. Submerge them within the sentence if possible, usually between the subject and the verb or the verb and its object. Like buttons, hooks and eyes, or zippers in clothing, transitional elements should join parts securely but inconspicuously.

Your style will improve if you can develop the knack of *hearing* a sentence as you are writing it. At least once during the revision process, read your paper aloud. When you read something as familiar as your paper will be by this time, your eyes have a tendency to glide over words uncritically. Because you know what is coming next, you cannot judge it as a reader would. Reading aloud slows your eye movement and enables you to identify clumsy constructions, unintentional repetition, awkward or missing transitions, and other weaknesses that you might overlook in silent reading. If you find a sentence difficult to read, perhaps it should be recast. If your sentences sound singsongy, repetitious, or choppy to you, they probably will seem more so to a reader. Look for the connections among the ideas. If one sentence deals with a cause and the next with the effect, a single sentence could express that relationship. If two short sentences identify two steps in a process, they might be combined into one sentence with a compound verb. Some students avoid writing complex sentences, possibly because they may present a punctuation problem; but complex sentences differentiate ideas, and they are sometimes thought to indicate intellectual maturity.

The following paragraph contains monotonously similar sentences. Compare it with the revised version.

<u>Original</u>

(1) Kate Chopin wrote "The Story of an Hour" in 1894. (2) It was published the same year. (3) It is deceptively short and simple. (4) Chopin takes barely over a thousand words to tell the story.

(5) Louise Mallard is a woman "afflicted with a heart trouble" (52). (6) Her sister and one of her husband's friends are very careful when they tell her that her husband has been killed in a train wreck. (7) Mrs. Mallard grieves intensely. (8) Gradually she begins to contemplate her future life without him. (9) Now she will be free to live entirely for herself, and she will not have to bend her will to his. (10) It is a prospect she welcomes with joy. (11) Suddenly her husband returns.

(12) He had not been on the train as reported. (13) Mrs. Mallard falls dead. (14) "When the doctors came," Chopin concludes, "they said she had died of heart disease—of joy that kills" (54).

<u>Revised</u>

(a) "The Story of an Hour," written and published in 1894, is deceptively short and simple.

(b) Kate Chopin takes barely over a thousand words to tell the story of Louise Mallard, a woman "afflicted with a heart trouble" (52). (c) Gently informed that her husband has been killed in a train wreck, Mrs. Mallard grieves intensely. (d) Gradually, however, she begins to contemplate her future life without him, a life in which she will be free to live entirely for herself without having to bend her will to his. (e) She welcomes the prospect with joy. (f) When her husband suddenly returns—he had not been on the train as reported—she falls dead. (g) "When the doctors came," Chopin concludes, "they said she had died of heart disease—of joy that kills" (54).

Sentence (a) gathers the relatively unimportant details of the first three sentences into a single statement. Sentence (b) combines the next two sentences by making sentence (5) into a prepositional phrase. Some more unimportant details are omitted when sentences (6) and (7) are combined in (c). When sentences (8) and (9) are combined, the writer provides a simple transition ("however") to stress the contrast, and the length of the sentence is an attempt to mirror the expansive mood of the character. Sentence (e) is shorter and more emphatic than (10), which was also less emphatic because (11) was about the same length. Sentence (f) combines three sentences to reflect the connection among the events, and the dashes help suggest the speed of the events.

Avoiding Jargon

At any given time, some high-sounding terms ("buzz words") are fashionable in the academic world, and their meaning becomes blurred because they are used so often. If you use words like *paradigm, continuum, generic, governance, optimize, parameters, prioritize, rationale, scenario,* or *viable*, be sure that they express the meaning you intend. Never use a word simply because you think it will impress a reader. Sometimes writing research papers will tempt students to elevate their vocabularies unduly. These writers often turn to a thesaurus in search of a more impressive term and select one that is not appropriate for the situation. Among the synonyms offered for the word *famous*, for instance, are *celebrated, recognized, notorious, infamous, legendary,* and *renowned.* Although all six words do represent roughly the same idea, they are far from interchangeable. In short, a thesaurus can be helpful, but use it cautiously.

Writing Concisely

A typical research paper is at least 2,500 words long. It may be the longest paper you have written so far. Unless you guard against it, you may unconsciously pad sentences, expressing ideas in as many words as possible in order to reach the prescribed length. Wordiness is a sure way to lose a reader's attention. Asked to read a hundred words to find an idea that could have been expressed in forty, a reader is likely to lose both interest and patience. An especially annoying kind of wordiness is the superfluous modifier, the meaning of which is implied by the noun or verb it modifies. For example:

> a ~~true~~ fact
> ~~basic~~ fundamentals
> a ~~free~~ gift
> unanimous agreement ~~by everyone~~
> prognosis ~~of the future~~
> green ~~in color~~
> square ~~in shape~~
> ~~close~~ proximity
> reverted ~~back~~
> followed ~~behind~~

Verb–object combinations can also be wordy.

Verb–object combination	Verb alone
made a decision	decided
reached agreement	agreed
expressed a denial	denied
made a request	requested
ventured an attempt	tried
granted permission	permitted

In revising your paper, be alert for bloated expressions like these:

Wordy	Simple
at no time	never
at the conclusion of	after
at this point in time	now
due to the fact that	because

(Continued)

Wordy	Simple
during the time that	while
for the reason that	because
in a short time	soon
in all likelihood	probably
in spite of the fact that	although
in the event that	if
in the place that	where
on or about	approximately
on the local level	locally
prior to the time that	before

Using Nondiscriminatory Language

In writing your paper, you should be sensitive to words that suggest prejudice based on ethnic, sexual, social, racial, or religious differences. Although such expressions are more likely to occur in speech than in writing, they represent the fallacy of ascribing a particular characteristic to an entire class of persons.

An issue that may arise in your research paper is the form that should be used for a title or a name. In general, do not use a title like *Mr., Mrs., Ms., Dr.,* or *Professor* with a proper name; but there are exceptions for which usage has made the title seem natural: e.g., Sir Walter Scott, Dr. Johnson, Lord Chesterfield, and Madame Curie. Give a person's full name the first time it is mentioned, and afterward use the surname alone. A combination like *Scott and Jane Austen* or *Whitman and Emily Dickinson* may suggest a sexist bias, as would referring to Dickinson as *Miss Dickinson* or as *Emily.*

Most persons today try to avoid using sexist language, which stereotypes women and men in terms of outdated roles. *Sexist* was coined by analogy with *racist* and has the same unpleasant connotations. *A lady lawyer* and *a lady doctor* imply that it is unusual for a woman to be a lawyer or a doctor, even though more than half of the law students and almost half of today's medical students are women. A major source of concern is the use of *man* as a generic term applying to persons of either gender. The most common revision is to substitute a word that is not gender-specific. For example:

Gender-specific	Generic
anchorman	anchor, anchorperson
congressman	representative, senator
fireman	firefighter
mailman	letter carrier
mankind	humanity
manmade	artificial
man on the street	average person
policeman	police officer
salesman	sales clerk, salesperson
weatherman	forecaster, meteorologist

That English is a "manmade" language is reflected in subtle and not-so-subtle ways by its grammar. Until recently, for example, the passive voice was used for women in descriptions of weddings: a woman *was given in marriage*; a man *married*, but a woman *was married*. The most obvious example of grammatical discrimination is the use of *he, his,* and *him* to refer to nouns that could be either masculine or feminine. The following sentences suggest sexual stereotyping:

1. A good bartender knows his customers by name.
2. A librarian often has to work overtime whether she wants to or not.
3. An athlete must observe a training schedule and practice regularly if he wants to succeed.
4. A nurse should complete a bachelor's degree if she hopes to advance in her profession.
5. A grocery shopper should keep her coupons in a special envelope.
6. The average voter is not concerned with party labels; he just wants honest, efficient government.
7. Everyone should complete his research by Friday.
8. Overworked physicians may neglect their wives and children.
9. An interstate truck driver must check regularly to be sure that his licenses are up-to-date.
10. Everyone in the office is entitled to his vacation time.
11. A taxpayer should keep an accurate record of his business expenses.
12. A kindergarten teacher should learn her pupils' names as soon as possible.

Sentences 1, 3, 6, 7, 8, 9, 10, and 11 imply that all bartenders, athletes, voters, students, physicians, truck drivers, office workers, and taxpayers are male. Sentences 2, 4, 5, and 12 imply that all librarians, nurses, grocery shoppers, and kindergarten teachers are female. Such sexist implications can be eliminated in several ways:

- Use *he or she, he/she.* The use of *he or she* or *he/she* is correct but can be awkward and monotonous.
- Use *s/he.* An ingenious suggestion of using *s/he* will work only for the subjective case and creates a pronunciation problem if one reads a sentence aloud.
- Use *you.* Sometimes the second-person *you*, a unisex pronoun, can be substituted for *he.*

  7. You should complete your research by Friday.

- Use the plural. Recasting a sentence to eliminate the sexist third-person pronoun is usually the best procedure. English is a rich and varied language, and there is always more than one way of expressing something. The most common revision is to make the noun plural and replace *he* with *they* (which is gender-neutral, like *you*).

  2. Librarians often have to work overtime whether they want to or not.
  3. Athletes must maintain a training schedule and practice regularly if they want to succeed.
  5. Grocery shoppers should always keep their coupons in a special envelope.
  8. Overworked physicians may neglect their families.
  9. Interstate truck drivers must check regularly to be sure that their licenses are up-to-date.

- Eliminate the pronoun.

    1. A good bartender knows all customers by name.

    4. A nurse who hopes to succeed in the profession should complete a bachelor's degree.

    6. The average voter is not concerned with party labels but just wants honest, efficient government.

    10. Everyone in the office is entitled to a vacation.

    11. A taxpayer should keep a record of business expenses.

    12. A kindergarten teacher should learn pupils' names as soon as possible.

Behavior, of course, is more important than words; but language is a basic component of human experience, and as language habits change, behavior tends to follow. Consciously avoiding the language of prejudice will help you avoid behavior motivated by prejudice.

Proofreading

Ex. K Proofreading is to revision as paring potatoes is to gourmet cooking, as mopping a floor is to interior decorating, as weeding a flowerbed is to flower arrangement—an unglamorous but essential task. Revision and proofreading are not separate processes but can be performed simultaneously. Your concerns in revision are content, style, and structure; in proofreading you look for typographical errors, misspellings, punctuation mistakes, misuse of capital letters, and similar slips.

THE WORK OF COLLEEN LEE

Chopin uses the setting to suggest that a new life may be in store for
~~The setting seems to symbolize what is happening to~~

Mrs. Mallard.   The   grief" that follows the news of her
~~Mrs. Mallard. She cries in a~~ "storm of ᵥgreif," ~~and then goes to~~

husband's death is paralleled by the weather conditions.   Looking outside, she can see
~~her room. There has evidently been a storm, but there are~~

                                                             e
"patches of blue sky showing her ᵥand there through the clouds

                                   one
that had met and piled ᵥabove the other in the west facing her

          Although Mrs. Mallard still sobs occasionally, she also
window." ~~She looked out the window and~~ feels a "delicious breath

          as she stares into one of the blue patches.   Just as rain is soon
of rain" in the air and hears birds singing ᵥ ~~Occasionally "a sob~~

  followed by sunshine and growth, Chopin seems to imply, Mrs. Mallard will again
~~came up into her throat and shook her," but she is quiet~~

  be happy, perhaps even happier than before.
~~otherwise, staring at one of the blue areas of the sky.~~

Proofreading and revision are illustrated in the preceding segment from Colleen's paper. It shows corrections of errors in punctuation and spelling (proofreading) and addition of details and substitution of more accurate words for vague or general ones (revision).

Formatting Your Paper

Although a research paper is evaluated primarily on its content, its overall appearance is also important. Many papers are now submitted electronically, and they, too, should follow appropriate formatting conventions. Look over the Checklist on the inside back cover of this text. Your instructor will undoubtedly specify some aspects of the format, so the following suggestions should be modified to meet those specifications. When you have typed the final copy, read and correct your manuscript carefully and make any necessary corrections.

MLA Handbook does not recommend a title page or an outline page, but many instructors require both. The title of your paper should be concise but accurate. It should not be enclosed in quotation marks, underlined, written in full capitals, or followed by a period. Center the title and below it type your name, your class section, your instructor's name, and the date. Because you will receive no special credit for decoration, don't waste your time on ribbons, pictures, or fancy lettering. A title page should be neat but not gaudy.

If an outline is required, it should follow the title page. In addition to reviewing it for logic, parallelism, and general neatness, check the symbols, indentation, and other outlining conventions. Use one of the outlines in Chapter 6 as a model.

Type your last name and the page number as a running head in the upper right-hand corner of each page: for example, Lee 7. It is a safeguard against pages being mislaid or lost. According to MLA, it should be a half-inch from the top of the page and should end flush with the right margin. MLA also recommends one-inch margins. You should use your word processing program to position your header and to begin your text one inch from the top of the page. Some instructors prefer more generous margins—perhaps an inch and a half at the top, bottom, and both sides. Indent each paragraph five spaces (half an inch).

If there is no title page, endorse the paper on the left. One inch from the top of the page, type your name, your instructor's name, your class section, and the date:

James Kebler

Professor Jericho

African American Studies 100

12 May 2009

Use the word processing program to center the title (rather than trying to center it visually on the screen).

If a sentence ends in the last line of a page, be sure to continue with the next sentence unless you have reached the end of a paragraph. Try to avoid an "orphan" (the first line of a new paragraph at the bottom of a page) or a "widow" (the final line of a paragraph at the top of a page). Most word processing programs make it easy to do so.

Unless your instructor specifies otherwise, double-space throughout—block quotations, endnotes, and entries in Works Cited.

Before typing the list of sources in Works Cited, be certain that your sources are in alphabetical order and that every work you cited is represented. Hanging indentation is customary in Works Cited because it facilitates locating an item in an alphabetical list. The first line is flush with the left margin, and any additional lines are indented five spaces. Learn how to create a hanging paragraph with the word processing program you are using instead of forcing a line break or inserting tabs. This will allow you to make corrections, change printers, or change the font without having to adjust the entry.

Be certain that the pages of your paper are in proper order and are numbered sequentially. Do not use the abbreviation p. or any form of punctuation with a page number.

Fasten the pages with a paper clip rather than staple them. Often an instructor will want to detach the Works Cited page in order to refer to it while reading the paper.

If you are required to submit rough drafts along with your finished paper, keep printouts of early versions of your paper.

Keep a copy of your paper when you submit it. Because you may be asked to authenticate a citation or rewrite a portion of your paper, retain your notes, your rough drafts, and your computer disk until the paper has been graded and returned.

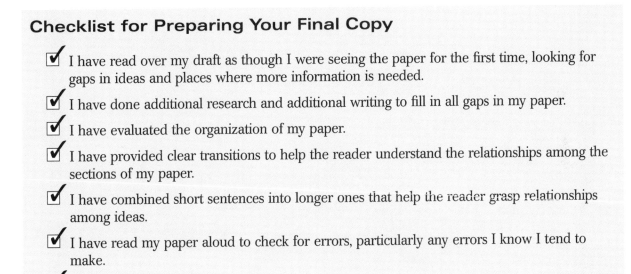

Checklist for Preparing Your Final Copy

☑ I have read over my draft as though I were seeing the paper for the first time, looking for gaps in ideas and places where more information is needed.

☑ I have done additional research and additional writing to fill in all gaps in my paper.

☑ I have evaluated the organization of my paper.

☑ I have provided clear transitions to help the reader understand the relationships among the sections of my paper.

☑ I have combined short sentences into longer ones that help the reader grasp relationships among ideas.

☑ I have read my paper aloud to check for errors, particularly any errors I know I tend to make.

☑ I have verified that the paper follows the format specified by my instructor.

Exercise K

Proofreading and Revision

1. Turn the following short, choppy sentences into a paragraph of no more than seven sentences.

    (1) Some Americans opposed slavery in the eighteenth century. (2) The abolition movement was not effectively organized until the generation before the Civil War. (3) The abolitionists regarded slavery as a moral evil. (4) They demanded immediate emancipation of all slaves. (5) They were often attacked by mobs. (6) They continued their crusade. (7) They supported other reforms: temperance, pacifism, and women's rights. (8) Many Northerners disliked slavery. (9) Some of them disapproved of the abolitionists' extreme tactics. (10) Some Southerners disapproved of slavery. (11) They were offended by the violent actions and language of the abolitionists. (12) Abolitionists experienced many setbacks. (13) Abolitionists were one of the most effective protest groups in American history.

2. Exchange your revision of the sentences in the preceding exercise with a classmate. How do your revisions differ? Explain to each other why you combined the sentences as you did. For example, you may have combined two sentences to show a contrast or to clarify a cause-and-effect relationship.

3. Revise the following paragraph to reduce the wordiness. If you alter the quotation, be sure to follow the guidelines in Chapter 7 for managing borrowed material.

    When animal hoarding occurs, large numbers of animals are generally confined in a relatively small space. When such crowding occurs in these close quarters, property damage is almost always going to happen. It is unavoidable, in fact. The Hoarding of Animals Research Consortium (HARC) studied seventy-one cases of animal hoarding. After reviewing those cases, they concluded that in a "typical" case "household interiors were coated, often several inches high, with human and animal urine and feces, sometimes to an extent that floors buckled" (128). Newspaper accounts of animal hoarding incidents almost always describe the condition of the property in graphic terms that emphasize such details as the accumulated human and animal waste. These graphic accounts are frequently accompanied by photographs of the destruction caused by the confined animals. Under such conditions as these, cleanup or repair may not be a viable alternative or even a possibility, and several newspaper accounts mention that houses were condemned or sometimes even had to be demolished once they have been vacated (Murray; Eckstein; Cullen).

4. The following paragraph contains numerous mechanical errors, wordy expressions, and inappropriate words that are typical of early drafts. Proofread the paragraph and make the necessary corrections.

Robert Frosts favorite poem, "Stopping by Woods on a Snowy Evening, is short and simple but it has been interpreted in a number of different ways. Frost simply describes how he stopped to watch snow falling in a woods, enjoyed the scene untill he remembered that he had "promises to keep, and drove on. Many critics find in the poem a conflict between what a person has to do and what he enjoys. The poet feels a sense of gilt because he forgets his responsibilities for a time. Other critics have made an interpretation of the poem that is more sinister. The woods are said to represent oblivion and the temptation to linger and enjoy the scene is a death-wish. Frost disliked this interpretation, and did not except it.

Documenting a Paper MLA Style

> *Mark what ills the scholar's life assail.*
>
> "The Vanity of Human Wishes"

In writing your research paper, you use facts and opinions found in books, periodicals, electronic media, and nonprint sources to support your ideas. You can use the actual language, or you can summarize the material in your own words. In either case, you must document the borrowed information. Documentation—acknowledgment of indebtedness to a source—takes a variety of forms or styles. Classes in English and other humanities generally use the style developed by the Modern Language Association (MLA). The MLA approach to documentation is simple and efficient, consisting of two parts:

1. A list of the sources used in a paper that serves as a general acknowledgment of indebtedness to each. Headed *Works Cited*, this list follows the final page of the text.
2. Separate citation of each borrowed fact or opinion. The source and the page number, enclosed in parentheses, follow the borrowed material.

Together, the list of works cited and individual citations allow a reader to retrieve further information from the sources and to verify the accuracy of your argument. Carelessness will make it impossible to do either of those things, and it might even lead to charges of academic dishonesty. For these reasons, then, painstaking attention to documentation is essential.

Listing Sources

Ex. L Do not be intimidated by the large number of examples in this section. The checklists in Figures 9.1 and 9.2 will help you locate the information you need quickly. Figure 9.1 is an index to examples of bibliographic forms. When you have mastered the basic forms for books and periodicals (sections 1, 26, and 27), you will see that the other forms are variations or elaborations of these basic forms. The checklist of special situations (Figure 9.2) is keyed to the examples as well. These lists are not absolute, and in almost every paper a situation will arise that is not covered by a standard form. Do not hesitate to ask for assistance when you encounter a perplexing, out-of-the-ordinary situation. Together with your instructor you can devise a form that is consistent with MLA style (see section 6 for an illustration).

Books

1. Book, standard form
2. Anonymous book
3. Anthology (entire)
4. Book in a series
5. Book published before 1900
6. Collaborator
7. Corporate author
8. Dissertation
9. Edition
10. Editor
11. Government publication
12. Introduction/afterword
13. Legal source
14. Letter, published
15. Multiple authors/editors
16. Multivolume work
17. Musical score
18. Pamphlet
19. Pseudonym
20. Reference work
21. Republished book
22. Selection in an anthology
23. Title within a title
24. Translation
25. Works by the same author/editor

Periodicals

26. Journal, standard form
27. Magazine, standard form
28. Advertisement
29. Anonymous article
30. Cartoon or comic strip
31. Interview, published
32. Letter to the editor
33. Multiple authors/editors
34. Newspaper
35. Review
36. Title within a title
37. Translation

Web Publications

38. Nonperiodical publications appearing only on the Web
39. Nonperiodical publications appearing previously in print
40. Nonperiodical publications appearing previously in a medium other than print
41. Periodical publications retrieved from an online database
42. Periodical publications appearing only on the Web

Nonprint or Unpublished Sources

43. E-mail
44. CD-ROM
45. Digital file
46. Film
47. Interview, personal, telephone
48. Lecture
49. Letter, personal
50. Manuscript material
51. Microform
52. Performance
53. Recording
54. Television/radio program
55. Works of art

FIGURE 9.1 Standard sources

Abbreviations 11
Approximate date (c.) 50
Bimonthly magazine 27
Capitalization of titles 1
Condensed page numbers 22
Congressional Record 11
Cross-reference 22
Dictionary 20
Discontinuous paging 27
Editorial 34
E-mail 43, 47
Encyclopedia 20
Et al. 15
Filmstrip 46
Foreword 12
Hanging indentation 1
Identifying term 12
Italicized titles 1
Journal without volume number 26, 31
Monthly magazine 27
Preface 12
Public document 11
Publishers' names 1
Publisher's imprint 4
Quotation marks for titles 26
Sections of a newspaper 34
Slide 55
Subtitle 1
Two publishers 6
University press 15
Unpaged source 12
Unpublished work 8, 50
Untitled article 35
URLs 38
Videocassette 46
Volume numbers of books 16
Weekly magazine 27
Work in progress 16

FIGURE 9.2 Special situations

Checklist of Bibliographic Forms

The numbered examples illustrate most of the kinds of sources you are likely to use. When you prepare a source note for a work that is somehow out of the ordinary, use the checklist to find an example that it resembles.

Figure 9.2 lists some special situations that may prove troublesome. Each is keyed to the section where it is illustrated and briefly explained. If you use an anthology or any collection of pieces by different authors, pay particular attention to the description of cross-referencing in section 22, which can save you considerable time and trouble.

Examples: Books

1. Book, Standard Form

The basic entry for a book consists of three main elements—the author, title, and publication information. Sometimes, however, additional information will be needed. The following list outlines the possible components and the sequence in which they are arranged. (See Figure 9.3 to see where to find this information.)

1. Name of the author, editor, compiler, or translator of the book (or section of the book) being cited
2. Title of individual section of book
3. Title of book
4. Editor, translator, or compiler of book if an anthology
5. Edition (if not first)
6. Number(s) of the volume(s) used

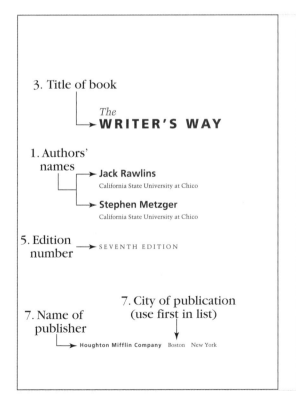

FIGURE 9.3 Title and copyright pages

7. City of publication, name of publisher, year of publication
8. Inclusive page numbers of individual section used
9. Medium (*Print*)
10. Name of series and volume number (if any)

These examples illustrate the information in a basic entry (items 1, 3, 7, and 9 in the preceding list).

Grolnick, Wendy S. *The Psychology of Parental Control: How Well-Meant Parenting Backfires*. Mahwah:

Erlbaum, 2003. Print.

Holmes-Eber, Paula. *Daughters of Tunis: Women, Family, and Networks in a Muslim City*. Boulder: Westview,

2003. Print.

Guidelines for MLA Works Cited (Books)

- Each line after the first is indented half an inch (hanging indentation), making it easier to locate a name in an alphabetical list.
- The author's name is inverted. It should be written as it appears on the title page (C. S. Lewis, not Clive Staples Lewis). Titles and degrees, however, are omitted (for example, Ph.D., M.D., Sir, Colonel).
- Copy the title from the title page, not from the cover or the spine of a book. Reproduce it accurately. Articles and prepositions are not capitalized except at the beginning of a title or a subtitle. The title of a book or any work published as a unit is italicized. Forgetting to italicize is such a common fault that you should check each book title (and any other element of the entry requiring italics) before you print your text.
- A subtitle is also italicized. It is introduced by a colon unless the main title closes with a question mark, an exclamation point, or a dash.
- If more than one city is listed on the title page, cite only the first. MLA style does not identify the state after an American city. Follow a foreign city with an abbreviation of the country if needed: Naples, It.
- Shorten the publisher's name (see Appendix A).
- Cite the year of publication from the title page. If none appears there, look on the copyright page (inverse of the title page) and use the most recent copyright date. If there is no copyright date, write *n.d.*
- Identify the medium (*Print*).
- Provide any additional information required (such as the name of a series).

2. Anonymous Book

When a work is published without an author's name, begin the entry with the title. Alphabetize it according to the first main word, ignoring *a, an,* or *the.* Do not use the word *Anonymous* if the author's name is known but not given on the title page; if you learn the author's name, include it in brackets (see the second example).

Fodor's 2008 San Francisco. New York: Fodor's, 2008. Print.

[Klein, Joe]. *Primary Colors: A Novel of Politics*. New York: Random, 1996. Print.

3. Anthology (Entire)

Begin the citation of an anthology or any similar collection of pieces by various authors with the name of the editor. For the citation of a selection from such a work, see section 22.

Brown, Stewart, and John Wickham, eds. *The Oxford Book of Caribbean Stories*. New York: Oxford UP, 1999.

>   Print.

Cheney, Patrick, and Anne Lake Prescott, eds. *Approaches to Teaching Shorter Elizabethan Poetry*. New York:

>   MLA, 2000. Print.

Phillips, Caryl, ed. *The Right Set: The Faber Book of Tennis Stories*. New York: Faber, 1997. Print.

Witalec, Janet, ed. *Twentieth-Century Literary Criticism*. Vol. 133. Detroit: Gale, 2003. Print.

4. Book in a Series

The name of a series is placed at the end of the entry, following the medium. It is not italicized or placed in quotation marks. The number assigned to the book within the series, if any, is included. The following example also illustrates a publisher's imprint, a subsidiary operation specializing in a particular type of book. Cite the imprint first and follow it with a hyphen and the name of the main publisher (for example, Anchor-Doubleday, Mentor-NAL, Crown-Random, or Belknap-Harvard UP). In recent years, so many publishing companies have expanded and absorbed other publishers that your instructor may prefer that you simply cite the publisher named first on the title page.

Rice, Marcelle Smith. *Dawn Powell*. New York: Twayne-Macmillan, 2003. Print. Twayne's United States

>   Authors Ser. 715.

5. Book Published before 1900

It is not necessary to cite the publisher of a book published before 1900. However, some instructors may prefer that you include this information.

Wilson, Henry. *History of the Rise and Fall of the Slave Power in America*. 6th ed. 3 vols. Boston, 1872. Print.

6. Collaborator

Autobiographical books by nonliterary celebrities are often produced with professional assistance, which is acknowledged, if at all, by *with, as told to*, or a similar phrase. The *MLA Handbook* provides no explicit directions for this situation. One possibility is simply to treat the names of both equally, as multiple authors (see section 15). Since the wording on the title page of the book suggests a subordinate role for the collaborator, however, you may want to indicate that. To do so requires improvising a form consistent with MLA style. In this case you might cite the collaborator by using whatever phrase appears on the title page. Include the collaborator in Works Cited but not in parenthetical citations.

Conrad, Richard T., with Jill LaForge Jones. *"What Shall We Do about Mom?" A New Look at Growing Old*.

>   New York: TAB-McGraw, 1993; Bradenton: Human Services Inst., 1993. Print.

This example illustrates four somewhat unusual situations:

a. A publisher's imprint (see also section 4, above)
b. Quotation marks in a book title (see also section 23)
c. Two U.S. publishers of the same work, separated by a semicolon
d. A subtitle not requiring a colon because the main title ends with a question mark

7. Corporate Author

When an institution, a committee, or some other group is designated as the author, it is cited in the author position even when the same group is the publisher.

National Osteoporosis Foundation. *How Strong Are Your Bones?* Rev. ed. Washington: NOF, 1996. Print.

Student Conservation Assn. *The Guide to Graduate Environmental Programs*. Washington: Island, 1997. Print.

8. Dissertation

You can find listings of dissertations classified by subject in *Comprehensive Dissertation Index*, published by University Microfilms International. You are not likely to use a dissertation, except perhaps one written at your own school; but if you do, list it like the second example: After the title add *Diss.* (not italicized or enclosed in quotation marks), the university, and the year. If you use an abstract from *Dissertation Abstracts International (DAI)*, identify the university and the year the degree was granted, the volume of *DAI*, and the page number. Note that the title of any unpublished work, regardless of its length, is enclosed in quotation marks.

Ford, Bridget. "American Heartland: The Sentimentalization of Religion and Race Relations in Cincinnati

and Louisville, 1820-1860." Diss. U of California, Davis, *DAI* 63 (2003): 2984. Print.

Taylor, Nikki Marie. "'Frontiers of Freedom': The African American Experience in Cincinnati, 1802-1862."

Diss. Duke U, 2001. Print.

9. Edition

After the title of a book other than a first edition, designate the edition as identified on the title page. See section 7 for an illustration of a revised edition.

Gilderhus, Mark T. *History and Historians: A Historiographical Introduction*. 5th ed. Upper Saddle River:

Prentice, 2003. Print.

10. Editor

The editor of a republished work by another author is identified after the title. When used in this position, *Ed.* means "edited by" and is not made plural if there are two or more editors. The editor of a collection of essays, stories, and so on is identified before the title; *ed.* here means "editor," and *eds.* is used if there are two or more editors. In the first example, the original publication date is identified after the title. The second example is a book with two subtitles.

Algren, Nelson. *The Man with the Golden Arm*. 1949. Ed. Daniel Simon and William J. Savage, Jr. New York:

Seven Stories, 1999. Print.

Kesselman, Amy, Lily D. McNair, and Nancy Schniedewind, eds. *Women: Images and Realities:*

  A Multicultural Anthology. 2nd ed. Mountain View: Mayfield, 1999. Print.

Shields, Christopher, ed. *The Blackwell Guide to Ancient Philosophy.* Malden: Blackwell, 2003. Print.

11. Government Publication

Federal, state, county, and city governments issue an enormous number of documents each year—bills, statutes, reports, regulations, statistics, records of hearings, executive orders, speeches, and so on. Because they vary greatly in form, documentation often presents problems. Ordinarily no author is named, so the government and the agency issuing the document are cited first. A title is italicized. A congressional publication includes the branch (HR or S), the session of Congress, and the type of document. As always, keep the same basic order and omit whatever is not available. Abbreviations are used freely:

Comm. Committee	**Doc.** Document
Cong. Congress	**GPO** Government Printing Office
Cong. Rec. *Congressional Record*	**Sess.** Session
Dept. Department	

MLA practice with abbreviations consisting of all capital letters is not to include space between the letters and not to follow the abbreviation with a period. An abbreviation containing lower-case letters is followed by a period.

Congressional Record illustrates some of the complexity to expect when you use public documents. The official record of the proceedings and debates of the U.S. Congress, it is published daily when Congress is in session. *Congressional Record* consists of four sections: the Daily Digest, the House section, the Senate section, and the Extension of Remarks. The Daily Digest at the end of each issue summarizes that day's activities and can be used as a table of contents for that issue. The sections for the House and Senate contain proceedings for each chamber of Congress. The Extension of Remarks consists of tributes, comments, and other information supplementing statements made on the House or Senate floor. Print publication began in 1873, and material from volumes 140 (1994) to the present is available online (http://www.gpoaccess.gov/crecord/index.html). The database is usually updated daily; the date of the publication refers to the date the proceedings were recorded, not necessarily the date of delivery. Because of the bulk of the annual volumes, many libraries have *Congressional Record* only on microfilm or CD-ROM. To cite *Congressional Record* you need to give only the title (abbreviated), the date, and the page number:

Cong. Rec. 20 Mar. 1997: H190. Print.

In this example H stands for House; you would use S or E for Senate or Extension of Remarks, respectively.

Reports of congressional hearings often contain useful information, but searching it out requires patience. Reports of lengthy hearings are published serially in pamphlets, which are collected in bound volumes after the hearings are completed. Publications of other agencies are cited as in the first five examples that follow. Municipal and state publications often do not designate a publisher. If you cite two or more works issued by the same government, substitute three hyphens for the name in each entry after the first. If you also cite more than one work by the same agency, use an additional three hyphens in each subsequent entry. The following examples also illustrate how to alphabetize government documents.

Ohio. Dept. of Health. *Nursing Home and Rest Home Licensure Law.* Columbus: State of Ohio, 1993. Print.

United States. Cong. House. Subcommittee on the Constitution of the Committee on the Judiciary. *Assisted*

Suicide in the United States. 104th Cong., 2nd sess. Serial no. 78. Washington: GPO, 1996. Print.

---. ---. Senate. Committee on the Judiciary. *The Innocence Protection Act of 2002*. 107th Cong., 1st sess.

Serial No. J-107-315. Washington: GPO, 2002. Print.

---. Dept. of Agriculture. *Agricultural Statistics 2002*. Washington: GPO, 2002. Print.

---. Dept. of Education. *Youth and Tobacco: Preventing Tobacco Use among Young People: A Report of the*

Surgeon General. Washington: GPO, 1995. Print.

12. Introduction/Afterword

Cite the introduction, afterword, foreword, or preface when you actually use it in your paper. Include the identifying term that appears in the book. Such terms are not italicized or enclosed in quotation marks. Give the name of the author or editor of the work after the title, preceding the name with *By* or *Ed.* Use lowercase Roman numerals only if they are used in the source. In the third example, *N. pag.* means there is no pagination. The first example is a republished book (see item 21).

Cowley, Malcolm. Introduction. *Leaves of Grass, The First (1855) Edition*. By Walt Whitman. 1987. New York:

Barnes, 1997. vii-xxxvii. Print.

Gates, Henry Louis, Jr. "A Negro Way of Saying." Afterword. *Their Eyes Were Watching God*. By Zora Neale

Hurston. New York: Harper, 1990. 195-205. Print.

Gould, Stephen Jay. Foreword. *The Far Side Gallery 3*. By Gary Larson. Kansas City: Andrews, 1988. N. pag. Print.

13. Legal Source

Legal references are of two general types: laws and court cases. They are even more varied and formidably complicated than government publications. Attorneys and legal writers use abbreviations that seem like a secret code to most laypersons. Translate them when necessary for clarity. If you use a number of legal references, consult the latest edition of *The Blue Book: A Uniform System of Citation* (Cambridge: Harvard Law Rev. Assn.).

References to the United States Code (USC) begin with the title number.

20 USC. 6a. 1995. Print.

This citation identifies the title number (20), the section in which this information appears (6a), the year, and the medium. References to the USC are alphabetized as though United States Code were spelled out; if you have more than one USC reference, arrange them numerically by the title number.

To cite an act in the list of works cited, give the name of the act, its Public Law (Pub. L.) number, the date it was enacted, and its Statutes at Large (Stat.) cataloging number. Titles of laws and legislative acts are never italicized or enclosed in quotation marks.

Swift Rail Development Act of 1994. Pub. L. 103-440. 2 Nov. 1994. Stat. 108.4615. Print.

For a legal case, cite the parties to the suit, the case number, the name of the court, and the year the case was decided. Titles are shortened; the full title of the case in the example is

Eurus Kelly Waters, Petitioner-Appellant v. Walter Zant, Warden Georgia Diagnostic and Classification Center, Respondent-Appellee. Names of cases are italicized in the text of a paper but not in bibliographic entries or in notes.

Waters v. Zant. No. 88-8935. US Ct. of Appeals, 11th Circuit, Atlanta. 1992. Print.

14. Letter, Published

If you use more than one letter from a collection, cite the source as in the first example and identify individual letters in the text of your paper. If using only one letter, follow the second example, including the date and the number (if any) of the letter. Close with the page reference.

Donne, John. *Selected Letters*. Ed. P. M. Oliver. New York: Routledge, 2002. Print.

James, Henry. "To Henry Adams." 21 Mar. 1914. Letter 280 of *Henry James: A Life in Letters*. Ed. Philip

Horne. New York: Viking, 1999. 533-34. Print.

15. Multiple Authors/Editors

If a work has two or three authors or editors, cite them in the order in which they are listed on the title page. Invert only the first name. Separate the names with commas. If there are more than three authors or editors, cite the name that appears first on the title page and follow it with the abbreviation *et al.* (and others). The first of the following examples has four authors. In citing books like the first example, University Press is abbreviated UP, written without periods and without a space. The letters are placed where they appear in the official name of the press: Indiana UP, State U of New York P, UP of Mississippi.

Brownson, Ross C., et al. *Evidence-Based Public Health*. New York: Oxford UP, 2003. Print.

Schwartz, David, Steve Ryan, and Fred Wostbrock. *The Encyclopedia of TV Game Shows*. New York: Facts,

1999. Print.

Shekhar, Shashi, and Sanjay Chawla. *Spatial Databases: A Tour*. Upper Saddle River: Prentice, 2003. Print.

16. Multivolume Work

Numerous variations are possible when you use a work of more than one volume. From the following examples, choose one like the work you are citing and use it as a model. This is one of the few occasions in MLA style for using the abbreviation *vol.* If you use only one volume of a multivolume work, identify the number of the volume just before the publication data, as in the first example.

The Republic of Letters: The Correspondence between Thomas Jefferson and James Madison, 1776-1826. Ed.

James Morton Smith. Vol. 3. New York: Norton, 1995. Print.

If you use all the volumes of a multivolume work, cite the total number of volumes just before the publication data and cite specific volumes in the text of your paper. Note the inclusive dates of publication in the second example.

Cook, Blanche Wiesen. *Eleanor Roosevelt*. 2 vols. New York: Viking, 1999. Print.

Rampersad, Arnold. *The Life of Langston Hughes*. 2 vols. New York: Oxford UP, 1986-88. Print.

A volume with an individual title can be cited without reference to other volumes in the work:

Proust, Marcel. *Within a Budding Grove*. Trans. C. K. Scott Moncrieff and Terence Kilmartin. Rev. D. J.

    Enright. New York: Random, 1992. Print.

An alternative procedure is to cite the complete work after the citation of the volume you used:

Proust, Marcel. *Within a Budding Grove*. New York: Random, 1992. Vol. 2 of *In Search of Lost Time*. Trans.

    C. K. Scott Moncrieff and Terence Kilmartin. Rev. D. J. Enright. 3 vols. 1992. Print.

For a work still in progress, write the date after the number of volumes; follow the date with *one* hyphen and a space.

Oberg, Barbara B., ed. *The Papers of Benjamin Franklin*. 37 vols. to date. New Haven: Yale UP, 1959-. Print.

17. Musical Score

A published musical score is cited like a book:

Elgar, Edward. *Falstaff*, Op. 68. London: Novello, 1913. Print.

18. Pamphlet

To cite a pamphlet, follow the basic order for citing of a book and omit whatever is unavailable. As the examples show, publication data for pamphlets are often incomplete. The abbreviation *n.p.* means "no place of publication" when it appears to the left of the colon and "no publisher" when it appears on the right side; *n.d.* means "no date of publication." When an abbreviation follows a period, it is capitalized.

Effective Lawn Care. Detroit: n.p., n.d. Print.

Games for Children. N.p.: n.p., n.d. Print.

Rosenbaum, Michael E. *The Amazing Superfood of the Orient*. N.p.: Sun Wellness, 1998. Print.

19. Pseudonym

If you identify an author's real name in Works Cited, enclose it in brackets, but this is unnecessary if you give it in the text of your paper. Do not identify a well-known pseudonym like Mark Twain or George Eliot. If you need to learn an author's real name, you may find it in the library catalog or in a dictionary of pseudonyms.

Mayne, Xavier [Edward Irenaeus Prime Stevenson]. *Imre: A Memorandum*. 1906. New York: Arno, 1975. Print.

20. Reference Work

You need not cite publication data for standard reference works, but you should identify the edition (if given) and the year of publication. Less familiar works like the second example are cited in full. If you use a dictionary for more than one definition, give only the title and cite each definition in the text of your paper. If an encyclopedia article is signed, begin the entry with the author's name. List an unsigned article by its title. Major articles are signed in the *Americana*. Articles in the *Macropaedia* volumes of *Britannica* are signed with initials, which are identified in the *Propaedia* volume. Volume and page numbers are unnecessary in a work that is alphabetically arranged.

De Santillana, Giorgio. "Galileo." *The New Encyclopaedia Britannica: Macropaedia*. 15th ed. 2002. Print.

"Istanbul." *Islamic Desk Reference*. New York: Brill, 1994. Print.

Park, David. "Determinism." *McGraw-Hill Encyclopedia of Science and Technology*. 8th ed. 1997. Print.

"Roadrunner." *Encyclopedia Americana*. 1999 ed. Print.

"Rorem, Ned." *Who's Who in America*. 2003 ed. Print.

"Scapegoat." Def. 4b. *Random House Unabridged Dictionary*. 2nd ed. 1993. Print.

21. Republished Work

For a book reissued by a different publisher (often a paperback version of a hardback original), give the date of the original publication immediately after the title.

Cooper, James Fenimore. *The Pathfinder*. 1840. Ed. William P. Kelly. New York: Oxford UP, 1992. Print.

22. Selection in an Anthology

To cite one selection from an anthology or a similar collection, as in the first example, give the author and title of the selection, then the title of the collection, its editor or editors, the publication data, and inclusive page numbers of the selection. To cite a previously published article, follow the form of the third example. After a complete citation of the original publication data for the article, add *Rpt. in*, the title of the collection, the editor, the publication facts, and the page numbers.

If you use two or more selections from an anthology, cite the anthology in its proper alphabetical location and make a cross-reference to that entry, citing just the editor(s) and inclusive page numbers (see section 3, above, for the full Works Cited entry for the collection edited by Brown and Wickham). Note that page numbers above 100 are condensed by reducing the second number to the last two digits.

Kastan, David Scott. "Impressions of Poetry: The Publication of Elizabethan Lyric Verse." *Approaches to*

   Teaching Shorter Elizabethan Poetry. Ed. Patrick Cheney and Anne Lake Prescott. New York: MLA,

   2000. 156-60. Print.

Markham, E. A. "Mammie's Form at the Post Office." Brown and Wickham. 270-73. Print.

Parrinder, Patrick. "*News from Nowhere, The Time Machine*, and the Break-Up of Classical Realism." *Science*

   Fiction Studies 3 (1976): 265-74. Rpt. in *Twentieth-Century Literary Criticism*. Ed. Janet Witalec.

   Vol. 133. Detroit: Gale, 2003. 247-54. Print.

Silvera, Makeda. "Caribbean Chameleon." Brown and Wickham. 399-402. Print.

23. Title within a Title

When the title of a book contains a title or phrase in quotation marks, retain the quotation marks. When the title of a book contains a book title or other italicized word or phrase, you may either enclose the embedded italicized words in quotation marks or remove the italics from those words. The following example contains the title of a short story ("The Yellow Wall-Paper") and the title of a novel (*Herland).* The example is given twice to demonstrate both options for handling the italicized title. Ask your instructor's preference and follow that method consistently.

Knight, Denise D., and Cynthia J. Davis, eds. *Approaches to Teaching Gilman's "The Yellow Wall-Paper" and*

Herland. New York: MLA, 2003. Print.

Knight, Denise D., and Cynthia J. Davis, eds. *Approaches to Teaching Gilman's "The Yellow Wall-Paper" and*

"*Herland*." New York: MLA, 2003. Print.

24. Translation

The name of a translator follows the title of the work except when the translation itself is your primary concern (third example).

Flahault, François. *Malice*. Trans. Liz Heron. London: Verso, 2003. Print.

Homer. *The Odyssey*. Trans. Robert Fagles. New York: Viking-Penguin, 1997. Print.

Lattimore, Richard, trans. *The Odyssey of Homer*. New York: Farrar, 1998. Print.

25. Works by the Same Author/Editor

When you list two or more works by the same author or editor, give the name only in the first entry. In subsequent entries, type three hyphens and a period and space once before the title of the work. List the works alphabetically. If the author is also the first author in a multiple-author item following the list, repeat the author's name; do not use the three hyphens. However, if you have two or more books by the same multiple authors, the three hyphens should be used for all entries after the first, as in the fourth and fifth examples.

Woodward, Bob. *Bush at War*. New York: Simon, 2002. Print.

---. *The Choice*. New York: Simon: 1996. Print.

---. *Veil: The Secret Wars of the C.I.A., 1981-1987*. New York: Simon, 1998. Print.

Woodward, Bob, and Carl Bernstein. *All the President's Men*. 2nd ed. New York: Simon, 1994. Print.

---. *The Final Days*. New York: Simon, 1976. Print.

Woodward, Bob, and Marga Hogenboom. *Autism: A Holistic Approach*. Edinburgh: Floris, 2000. Print.

Examples: Periodicals

Periodicals include a variety of scholarly journals, popular magazines, and newspapers. Depending on the sort of periodical you are citing, you will need to include some or all of the following elements in your citation.

1. Author's name
2. Title of the article (in quotation marks)
3. Name of the periodical (italicized)
4. Series number or name (if needed)

5. Volume number (for scholarly journal)
6. Issue number (if needed)
7. Publication date
8. Inclusive page numbers
9. Medium
10. Any additional information needed

As you look at the examples in this section, pay particular attention to the distinctions among the various kinds of periodicals. Those distinctions determine which elements are included and how they are treated. Most of the variations and, therefore, most of the problems occur in the publication data. An initial *The* as in *American Scholar* or *Atlantic Monthly* can be omitted. (This is not done with book titles.)

26. Journal, Standard Form

For most topics you should use more scholarly journals (generally quarterlies) than popular magazines. Most journals, like the first example, are paged continuously throughout a volume. Cite the volume number (an Arabic numeral without the abbreviation *vol.*), enclose the year of publication in parentheses, follow it with a colon, and give the inclusive page numbers of the article (not just the pages used in your paper). See Figure 9.4 to see how to find the appropriate information.

Nicolaisen, Peter. "Thomas Jefferson, Sally Hemmings, and the Question of Race: An Ongoing Debate."

Journal of American Studies 37 (2003): 99-118. Print.

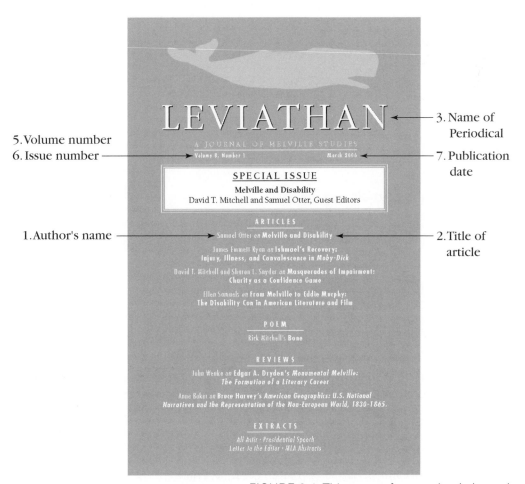

FIGURE 9.4 Title page of an academic journal

For a journal in which page numbering begins over in each issue, follow the same form but add a period and the issue number after the volume number with no space between them. The issue will be identified on the cover or on the contents page of a journal. A quarterly that has no volume number is identified by the number of the issue (second example). The second example is also a double number.

Dussere, Erik. "Subversion in the Swamp: *Pogo* and the Folk in the McCarthy Era." *Journal of American Culture*

26.2 (2003): 134-41. Print.

Molesworth, Charles. "The Art Scene." *Salmagundi* 137/138 (2003): 41-47. Print.

27. Magazine, Standard Form

Do not cite a volume or issue number for a weekly, monthly, or bimonthly magazine. Give the date of the issue immediately after the name of the magazine. Follow it with a colon and the page numbers. Months except for May, June, and July are abbreviated in Works Cited and in parenthetical citations but not in the text of a paper. Do not use the abbreviations *p.* or *pp.*; it is understood that numbers after a colon refer to pages. If an article is not paged consecutively, type a plus sign after the number of the first page (third example).

Masland, Tom. "Wars without End." *Newsweek* 14 July 2003: 28-31. Print.

Orleans, Susan. "The Lady and the Tigers." *New Yorker* 18-25 Feb. 2002: 95–102. Print.

SerVaas, Cory. "A Call to Arms!" *Saturday Evening Post* May-June 2003: 52+. Print.

28. Advertisement

You might need references like these in a paper on advertising.

Chevron. Advertisement. *New Yorker* 16 Mar. 2009: 29. Print.

Subaru. Advertisement. ABC. 5 Sept. 2009. Television.

29. Anonymous Article

Most periodical articles are signed, but if you cite one published without an author's name, begin the entry with the title. In the list of works cited, it should be alphabetized by the first word (excluding *a*, *an*, and *the*).

"Unjust, Unwise, Un-American." *Economist* 12 July 2003: 9. Print.

30. Cartoon or Comic Strip

Cite a cartoon or comic strip with the artist's name, the title of the comic strip (if any) in quotation marks, and the identifying term *Cartoon* or *Comic strip* (neither italicized nor in quotation marks). Do not treat lengthy dialogue beneath a cartoon as a title. The rest of the entry follows the standard form for the newspaper or magazine in which it appears.

Adams, Scott. "Dilbert." Comic strip. *Columbus Dispatch* 7 July 2009: D4. Print.

Roberts, Victoria. Cartoon. *New Yorker* 16 Mar. 2009: 79. Print.

31. Interview, Published

Begin a citation with the name of the person interviewed. If the title does not indicate that it is an interview, include the identifying term after the title. See section 41 for an interview in an online source, section 47 for the citation of an interview that you conduct yourself, and section 54 for an interview on radio or television.

Gordimer, Nadine. "'A Feeling of Realistic Optimism': An Interview with Nadine Gordimer." By Karen Lazar.

Salmagundi 113 (1997): 150-65. Print.

Miller, Arthur. "The Art of Theater II." Interview with Christopher Bigsby. *Paris Review* 152 (1999):

209–24. Print.

32. Letter to the Editor

A letter to the editor in a periodical is frequently assigned a heading that serves as a title (first example). The identifying term *Letter* is still necessary.

Bay, Don. "Kangaroo Court-Martial." Letter. *Nation* 21-28 July 2003: 2. Print.

Morrow, Jack. Letter. *Harper's* Feb. 2000: 6-7. Print.

33. Multiple Authors/Editors

As with a book (section 15), two or three authors are cited in the order in which they appear. If there are more than three authors (the article in the first example has eight), cite the first author and follow the name with a comma and *et al.*

Arluke, Arnold, et al. "Press Reports of Animal Hoarding." *Society and Animals* 10 (2002): 113-35. Print.

Axia, Vanna D., and Thomas S. Weisner. "Infant Stress Reactivity and Home Cultural Ecology of Italian

Infants and Families." *Infant Behavior and Development* 25 (2002): 255-68. Print.

Campbell, Laura A., Timothy A. Brown, and Jessica P. Grisham. "The Relevance of Age Onset to the

Psychopathology of Generalized Anxiety Disorder." *Behavior Therapy* 34 (2003): 31-48. Print.

34. Newspaper

Material that can be cited from a newspaper varies greatly. The examples illustrate an unsigned news item, signed news stories, a syndicated column, and an editorial. If the city is not part of the name of the paper, include it in brackets as in the third example. Of course, you do not designate a city for a national publication like *Wall Street Journal* or *USA Today*. If an edition is specified on the masthead (e.g., late ed., city ed.), identify it after the date because other editions may be paged differently. If the newspaper is divided into sections, designate the section along with the page number; follow whatever form is used in the newspaper. Identify an editorial as such after its title (last example).

"A Decade of Denial." *USA Today* 15 July 2003: 12A. Print.

Miller, Sara B. "A Skill to Help Women Shine." *Christian Science Monitor* 16 July 2003: 15. Print.

Ryback, Deborah Caulfield. "Animal Hoarding Is Increasing." *Star Tribune* [Minneapolis] 25 Aug. 1999:

1A. Print.

Schlesinger, Arthur, Jr. "The Imperial Presidency Redux." Editorial. *Washington Post* 28 June 2003, final

ed.: A25. Print.

35. Review

The basic form for citing a book review can be adapted to other types of reviews. Full citation of a review includes the reviewer's name and then the title of the review in quotation marks. Follow the title with *Rev. of* and the name of the work being reviewed, a comma, the word *by*, and the author's name. Finally, give the periodical and the publication data. Follow this basic order, omitting whatever is inapplicable or unavailable. If the review is unsigned and untitled like the final example, begin with *Rev. of*, but alphabetize the entry by the first main word in the title of the work being reviewed (*Y*). The examples illustrate two books, a television series, a film, and the performance of a play.

Applebaum, Anne. "The Worst of the Terror." Rev. of *Stalin's Last Crime: The Plot against Jewish*

Doctors, by Jonathan Brent and Vladimir P. Naumov. *New York Review of Books* 17 July 2003:

14-17. Print.

Franklin, Nancy. "Unbuttoned." Rev. of *Queer as Folk*. *New Yorker* 15 Jan. 2001: 94-96. Print.

Johnson, Malcolm. "The Good, the Bad, and the Elderly: Aging Action Stars Run Out of Gas at the Box

Office." Rev. of *Terminator 3: Rise of the Machines*. *Hartford Courant* 2 July 2003: D1. Print.

Wolf, Matt. Rev. of *The Master Builder*, by Henrik Ibsen. *Variety* 30 June-13 July 2003: 35. Print.

Rev. of *Y: The Descent of Man*, by Steve Jones. *Economist* 2 Nov. 2002: 82–83. Print.

36. Title within a Title

When the title of an article contains double quotation marks, change them to singles and enclose the title of the article in double quotes. Italicize a book, play, or film title that appears in the title of an article. The example illustrates both possibilities.

Nachbar, Jack. "'Nobody Ever Loved Me That Much': A *Casablanca* Bibliography." *Journal of Popular Film*

and Television 27.4 (2000): 42-46. Print.

37. Translation

As in the citation of a translated book (example 24), the name of the translator follows the title of the work.

Weigel, Sigrid. "Secularization and Sacralization, Normalization and Rupture: Kristeva and Arendt on

Forgiveness." Trans. Mark Kyburz. *PMLA* 117 (2002): 320-23. Print.

Examples: Web Publications

Many valuable resources are available on the World Wide Web, but the wide variety of forms they take makes consistent documentation something of a challenge. The following documentation forms follow the organizational scheme presented in the latest *MLA Handbook* (2009), which groups Web sources into five categories: nonperiodical publications that appear only on the Web, nonperiodical publications that have also appeared in print, nonperiodical publications that have appeared in some medium other than print, periodical publications retrieved from an online database, and periodical publications appearing only on the Web. Each of these categories is described briefly below.

38. Nonperiodical Publications Appearing Only on the Web

Nonperiodical Web publications are not released on a regular schedule (even though they may be updated frequently). The first category identified by MLA is publications that appear only on the Web. Included here are such things as Web pages hosted by organizations, scholarly projects that make data and documents available to researchers, individual home pages, and—perhaps surprisingly—Web sites sponsored by magazines, newspapers, and other news organizations. Typically, the Works Cited entry for a Web-only nonperiodical source will contain the following elements, arranged in this order:

1. Name of author, editor, compiler, or translator of the work
2. Title of the work (in italics if it stands alone, in quotation marks if it is part of a larger work); untitled works should be identified with a general descriptive term, such as *Home page* (without italics or quotation marks)
3. Title of the overall Web site (in italics) if different from item 2
4. Version or edition of the site
5. Publisher or sponsor of the site, followed by a comma; use *N.p.* if not identified
6. Date of posting (day, month, year) as given; use *n.d.* if no date given
7. Medium (*Web*)
8. Date you accessed site (day, month, year)

Except for item 5, each of the above elements is followed by a period. MLA no longer recommends including the URL of the Web site, noting that URLs routinely disappear or change and that they are often long and unwieldy and thus highly susceptible to error. Moreover, it is often easier to find a Web site by using online search tools than by typing in the URL. If, however, you believe that a reader could not find your source without the URL—or if your instructor requires that you provide the URL—it should be included at the end of the Works Cited entry, after the access date. Enclose it in angle brackets. Divide it, if necessary, only after a slash.

In the following example, the eight elements listed above are identified by number (note that 2 and 3 are combined). Although the placement of the URL is shown for the sake of illustration, it typically is not included.

1   2 / 3   4

Salda, Michael N., ed. *The Little Red Riding Hood Project*. Vers. 1.1.

5   6   7   8

U of Southern Mississippi, Oct. 2005. Web. 19 Mar. 2009.

(URL, if required)

<http://www.usm.edu/english/fairytales/lrrh/lrrhhome.htm>.

The following examples of nonperiodical Web-only publications include a professional organization, scholarly projects, and radio-, television-, and magazine-related sites.

Folsom, Ed, and Kenneth M. Price, eds. *The Walt Whitman Archive*. U of Nebraska–Lincoln, Jan. 2009. Web.

30 Apr. 2009.

Harris, Richard. "Antarctic Ice May Melt, But Not for Millennia." *National Public Radio*. Natl. Public Radio,

19 Mar. 2009. Web. 27 Mar. 2009.

Haseltine, Wiliam. "George Costakis and the Survival of Russian Art." *The Atlantic.com*. Atlantic Monthly

Group, 19 Mar. 2009. Web. 25 Mar. 2009.

Limansky, Nicholas E., ed. Home page. *The Legacy of the Diva*. N.p., n.d. Web. 30 July 2008.

NCTE Standing Committee Against Censorship. "Guidelines for Dealing with Censorship of Nonprint and

Multimedia Materials." *NCTE: National Council of Teachers of English*. NCTE, Oct. 2004. Web. 15 May

2009.

"New Prison Photo of Charles Manson Released." *CNN.com*. Cable News Network, 19 Mar. 2009. Web.

19 Mar. 2009.

Tobin, Thomas J., ed. *The Pre-Raphaelite Critic: Periodical Criticism of the Pre-Raphaelite Movement

1846-1900*. N.p., 3 Mar. 2008. Web. 17 May 2009.

Tyre, Peg. "Struggling School-Age Boys: A New Study Says Parents Are Right to Worry about Their Sons."

Newsweek. Newsweek, 8 Sept. 2008. Web. 24 May 2009.

39. Nonperiodical Publications Appearing Previously in Print

A number of nonperiodical works on the Web are also available in print form. Common examples include books and journal articles scanned for inclusion in databases or scholarly projects, as well as a wealth of government documents. If you have a source that falls into this category, begin your Works Cited entry with the information you would include for the print equivalent of the item, stopping before the medium (*Print*). Follow that information with these items:

1. Title of the Web site or database you used (in italics)
2. Medium (*Web*)
3. Date you accessed site (day, month, year)

If your instructor requires that you include the URL, place it at the end of the citation in angle brackets.

    The *Little Red Riding Hood* illustration below, for instance, begins with the form used for a book printed before 1900. That is followed by the name of the scholarly project from which it was obtained, the medium, and the date of access. If the Works Cited form calls for inclusive page numbers but the online version you are using does not include pagination, use the abbreviation *n. pag.* in place of page numbers (see the Dickens example, below).

Dickens, Charles. "Old Lamps for New Ones." *Household Words* 15 June 1850: n. pag. *The Pre-Raphaelite*

    Critic: Periodical Criticism of the Pre-Raphaelite Movement 1846-1900. Web. 17 May 2008.

Little Red Riding Hood. Cincinnati, 1884. *Little Red Riding Hood Project*. Web. 21 May 2008.

United States. Cong. Senate. Committee on the Judiciary. *Advancing Justice through DNA Technology Act of*

    2003. 108th Cong., 1st sess. S.1700. THOMAS, 2003. Web. 30 Apr. 2009.

---. Dept. of Agriculture. *Agricultural Statistics 2008*. 2008. *Natl. Agricultural Statistics Service*. Web. 27

    May 2009.

Walker, H. Wilfred. *Wanderings among South Sea Savages and in Borneo and the Philippines*. New York:

    Scribner's, 1909. *Project Gutenberg*. Web. 28 Mar. 2009.

If you wish, you may provide additional information about the database or Web site:

Little Red Riding Hood. Cincinnati, 1884. *Little Red Riding Hood Project*. Ed. Michael N. Salda. U of

    Southern Mississippi. Web. 21 May 2008.

40. Nonperiodical Publications Appearing Previously in a Medium Other Than Print

While you should expect to work mostly with text that has been put online, you may find that you need to refer to images or sound published on the Web. Again, the basis of the Works Cited entry will be the form used for the image, music, or film in its original form. However, the medium of original publication is dropped, and the entry ends with the title of the database or website (in italics), the medium (*Web*), and the date of access. If required, the URL (in angle brackets) would follow the access date. Shown below are entries for a photograph, a film, and a painting found online.

Fellig, Usher. *Drunken Men in the Bowery*. 1943. International Center of Photography Midtown. *Weegee's*

    World: Life, Death and the Human Drama. Web. 9 June 2009.

Queen of the Amazons. Dir. Edward F. Finney. Screen Art, 1946. *Internet Archive*. Web. 20 Mar. 2009.

Van Gogh, Vincent. *The Postman Joseph Roulin*. 1889. Museum of Modern Art, New York. Web. 16 May 2008.

41. Periodical Publications Retrieved from an Online Database

The value of online databases in finding articles in scholarly journals and magazines was discussed at length in Chapters 2 and 3. Use of the database to retrieve the source is the key distinguishing feature of this category. Works Cited entries for these items are based on the form used for the medium in which the work originally appeared. Although most of the sources retrieved in this way will be associated with print, you may retrieve other kinds of material from an online database (the Aracagök illustration, for example, is an article found in an exclusively online journal). To create an entry for a source taken from an online database, begin with the appropriate form, and omit the medium (usually *Print*). Conclude the entry with the name of the database (in italics), the medium (*Web*), and the access date. (Should your instructor require you to include the URL, add it to the end of the citation in angle brackets.) The following examples include articles from online and print journals, magazines, and newspapers.

Aracagök, Zafer. "Whatever Image." *Postmodern Culture* 13.2 (2003): n. pag. *Project Muse*. Web. 20 May

2008.

Cullen, Sandy. "Convicted Cat Hoarder At It Again, Health Department Says." *Wisconsin State Journal* 6

Sept. 2007: B1. Web. *LexisNexis*. 14 Nov. 2007.

Hoarding of Animals Research Consortium. "Health Implications of Animal Hoarding." *Health and Social*

Work 27.2 (2002): 125-36. *Academic Search Complete*. Web. 17 May 2008.

McDermott, Kevin. "Illinois Bill Would Treat Pet Hoarders as Ill." *St. Louis Post-Dispatch* 5 Feb. 2001: B1.

LexisNexis. Web. 17 May 2008.

Stoddard, Maynard Good. "The Dog That Owned Me." *Saturday Evening Post* Mar.-Apr. 2000: 52-53.

Academic Search Complete. Web. 24 July 2009.

Welter, Barbara. "The Cult of True Womanhood: 1820–1860." *American Quarterly* 18 (1966): 151–74.

JSTOR. Web. 30 Apr. 2009.

42. Periodical Publications Appearing Only on the Web

Some periodicals are published only on the Web. If you retrieve one of those publications from a database, you should use the form given in section 41 above. However, if you go directly to the online journal, you should use the form illustrated in this section. (The first example in sections 41 and 42 shows how you would cite the same article if you had used a database or gone directly to the journal's Web site, respectively.) The basic form follows that of the print periodical. A publication of this type often does not have page numbers; if that is the case, use *n. pag.* in place of page numbers. The entry concludes with the medium of publication (*Web*) and date of access. (As always, if you are required to supply the URL, add it at the end of the entry in angle brackets.)

Aracagök, Zafer. "Whatever Image." *Postmodern Culture* 13.2 (2003): n. pag. Web. 20 May 2008.

Harrison, Stanley D. "Cyborgs and Digital SoundWriting: Rearticulating Automated Speech Recognition

Typing Programs." *Kairos* 5.1 (2000): n. pag. Web. 17 May 2008.

Hinduja, Sameer, and Jason R. Ingram. "Self-Control and Ethical Beliefs on the Social Learning of

Intellectual Property Theft." *Western Criminology Review* 9.2 (2008): 52-72. Web. 17 July 2009.

Powell, Jessica Ernst and Erin M. Rebhan. "Manuscripts of the Mexican Inquisition: The Witchcraft

Case against Catalina de Miranda (1650-67)." *eHumanista* 4 (2004): 217-39. Web. 14 July

2009.

Examples: Nonprint or Unpublished Sources

43. E-Mail

To cite e-mail sent to an individual, give the name of the writer, the title of the message (the subject line) in quotation marks, a description that includes the name of the recipient, and the date the message was sent. In the first example, the word *author* refers to the person writing the paper in which the e-mail is being cited.

Rogers, Marcia. Message to the author. 15 Jan. 2008. E-mail.

Taylor, Heidi. "Re: Macrobiotics." Message to Johnson C. Smith. 26 Dec. 2009. E-mail.

44. CD-ROM

The CD-ROM databases in the first group of examples that follow are updated periodically because they cover journals, magazines, newspapers, annual bibliographies, and other sources published periodically. A full citation consists of the following items:

1. Author (if given). If an editor, compiler, or translator is identified, give that person's name, followed by the appropriate abbreviation (*ed.*, *comp.*, *trans.*)
2. Publication information for the printed source or print equivalent (including title and date of print publication)
3. Title of database (italicized)
4. Vendor (distributor)
5. Electronic publication date
6. Publication medium (*CD-ROM*)

If you cannot locate some of this information, provide what is available.

DeHart, Ganie B. "Gender and Mitigation in Four-Year-Olds' Pretend Play Talk with Siblings." *Research on*

Language and Social Interaction 29 (1996): 81-96. Abstract. *Sociofile*. SilverPlatter. Dec. 1996.

CD-ROM.

Gibson, James M. "An Old Testament Analogue for 'The Lottery.'" *Journal of Modern Literature* Mar. 1984:

1+. *MLA International Bibliography*. SilverPlatter. July 1997. CD-ROM.

Sung, Kiho. "Iconoclasm in the Fiction of Joseph Conrad." U of Missouri-Columbia, 1995. *DAI* 57 (1995):

1953A. *Dissertation Abstracts Ondisc*. UMI-Proquest. Mar. 1997. CD-ROM.

The CD-ROM databases in the second group of examples are not in continual revision like the first group but are issued once like books. An entire work is cited like a book, and a portion of a work is cited like a selection in an anthology. A full citation contains the following items:

1. Author (if given). If an editor, compiler, or translator is identified, give that person's name, followed by the appropriate abbreviation (*ed.*, *comp.*, *trans.*).
2. Title of publication (italicized)
3. Name of editor, compiler, or translator (if applicable)
4. Edition or version (if applicable)
5. Place of publication
6. Name of publisher
7. Date of publication
8. Publication medium (*CD-ROM*)

If some of this information is not provided, supply what is available. The first example illustrates how to cite a portion of a nonperiodical CD-ROM database that has a print equivalent.

Coleridge, Samuel Taylor. "An Ode to the Rain." *The Complete Works of Samuel Taylor Coleridge*. Ed. Ernest

Hartley Coleridge. Vol. 1. Oxford: Clarendon, 1912. 382-84. *English Poetry Full-Text Database*. Rel. 2.

Cambridge, Eng.: Chadwyck, 1993. CD-ROM.

"Microwave." *Random House Unabridged Dictionary*. 2nd ed. New York: Random, 1993. CD-ROM.

45. Digital File

You may wish to refer to a digital file that you did not locate on the Web. For example, a friend might send you a sound file or image attached to an e-mail message, or an organization you have contacted might send you a brochure in the form of a PDF file. If you need to cite a file of this sort, look for the most appropriate form in this section of the book as the starting point. When you create the Works Cited entry, identify the type of file as the medium you consulted (e.g., *PDF, MP3, JPEG*, Microsoft Word), followed by the word *file*. The following examples illustrate how to cite an unpublished Word document and a PDF provided by an organization. Note that the name of a software program is italicized.

Smith, Stephen, Jr. "Moving Toward the Light: A Study of Near-Death Experiences." 1 Apr. 2009. *Microsoft*

Word file.

Unitarian Universalist Association of Congregations. *The Real Rules: Congregations and the IRS: Guidelines*

on Advocacy, Lobbying, and Elections. Washington. 28 Mar. 2008. PDF file.

46. Film

The basic elements of a film citation are the title, the director, the distributor, and the year. The writer, performers, and producer are often included, as shown in the examples. If you are concentrating on the work of one person, begin the entry with that person's name.

On the Waterfront. Dir. Elia Kazan. Perf. Marlon Brando, Eva Marie Saint, Karl Malden, Lee J. Cobb, and Rod

Steiger. Columbia, 1954. Film.

Parker, Alan, and Laura Jones, adapt. *Angela's Ashes*. By Frank McCourt. Dir. Alan Parker. Prod. David Brown

    and Scott Rudin. Perf. Emily Watson, Robert Carlyle, and Gerard McSorley. Paramount, 1999. Film.

Cite a filmstrip, videocassette, or digital video disc (DVD) like a film, but include the appropriate identifying term for the medium. If a film is reissued in another medium, include the original release date, if possible.

The Age of Reason. Films for the Humanities and Sciences, n.d. Filmstrip.

Mansfield Park. By Jane Austen. Screenplay by Ken Taylor. Dir. David Giles. Prod. Betty Willingate. Perf.

    Anna Massey, Bernard Hepton, and Angela Pleasence. 1983. CBS/Fox Video, 1987. Videocassette.

Midnight Express. Screenplay by Oliver Stone. Dir. Alan Parker. Perf. Brad Davis and Irene Miracle. 1978.

    Columbia/Tristar, 1998. DVD.

47. Interview, Personal, Telephone

For an interview that you conduct, give the name of the person interviewed, the type of interview, and the date. For the citation of an interview on radio or television, see example 54.

Bascom, Elizabeth. Telephone interview. 8 Oct. 2008.

Thorp, Martin. Personal interview. 13 Oct. 2008.

48. Lecture

The speaker's name, the title (if any) in quotation marks, the occasion and the sponsoring organization (if relevant), the place, and the date are the basic elements in a full citation. If there is no title as in the first example, use the identifying term *Lecture*.

Halsey, R. Jason. History 110. Lake Forest College. 25 Oct. 2008. Lecture.

DeVine, Christine. "Altered States: Charles Dickens's Two Trips to America." MLA Convention. Marriott,

    Washington, D.C. 30 Dec. 2005. Lecture.

49. Letter, Personal

Cite a letter that you received in this way (TS indicates typescript):

Thomas, James. Letter to the author. 6 Jan. 2008. TS.

50. Manuscript Material

In a short research paper, you are not likely to use unpublished letters, diaries, or other manuscript material unless it is reproduced on the Web or available in a special collection in your school library. Follow standard bibliographic form as closely as possible. Use the appropriate identifying term and include any special designations used by the repository (e.g., Folder C, File 41). The abbreviation *c.* in the fourth example means *circa* (about) and is used for approximate dates. The third example illustrates how to cite manuscript material reproduced on the Web. *MS* indicates a manuscript (a handwritten document); *TS* identifies a typescript.

Fitzgerald, F. Scott. Letter to Maxwell Perkins. 14 Oct. 1940. MS. Firestone Lib., Princeton.

Twain, Mark. Letter to Henry H. Rogers. 8 June 1904. MS. Collection of Peter A. Salm, New York.

Whitman, Walt. "All Thine!" 1871. *The Walt Whitman Archive*. Web. 18 May 2008.

Wolfe, Thomas. Letter to George P. Baker. c. June 1922. MS. Thomas Wolfe Collection. U of North Carolina,

Chapel Hill.

51. Microform

After the title and publication data, identify the medium and give its number (if any).

LeClair, Mary C., and James C. Hanson. "A Comparison of Homeless and Nonhomeless Adolescents." ED 399

331. Arlington: ERIC Reports, 1995. Microfiche.

Plumb, J. H. "Our Last King." *American Heritage*. June 1960: 5+. Microfilm. Reel 2.

U.S. Census of Population, 1970. New Haven: Research Publns., n.d. Microfilm. Reel 80.

52. Performance

The listing of a performance includes the title of the work in italics, the names of key people involved in performance and production, the name of the theater or concert hall, the city, the date, and the identifying term *Performance*. The theater and city are separated by a comma; all other elements are separated by periods. As with a film (section 46), if you are concentrating on a particular element of the performance (such as the choreographer, in the second example), begin the citation with that element.

The Master Builder. By Henrik Ibsen. Perf. Patrick Stewart and Sue Johnston. Albery Theater, London. 18

June 2003. Performance.

Sebastian, Stuart, chor. *Dracula*. Dayton Ballet. Victoria Theatre, Dayton. 26 Oct. 2008. Performance.

53. Recording

A spoken recording (first example) begins with the author and title of the work being read, followed by information about the reader, medium, and publication. Do not italicize the title of a musical composition identified by form, number, or key (second example). If you refer to one song, you can cite it either by the composer (fifth example) or performer (final example). To cite printed material accompanying a recording, give the author's name, the title of the material (if any), and a description of the material (third and fourth examples). Use an identifying term like *CD, LP, Audiotape,* or *Audiocassette* to identify the medium.

Andrews, Donna. *Crouching Buzzard, Leaping Loon*. Read by Bernadette Dunne. Books on Tape, 2003.

Audiocassette.

Beethoven, Ludwig. Symphony no. 6 in F, op. 68. Nicolaus Esterházy Sinfonia. Cond. Béla Drahos. Naxos,

2002. CD.

Corneille, Thomas. Libretto. *Médée*. Music by Marc-Antoine Charpentier. Les Arts Florissants. Cond. William

Christie. Erato, 1995. CD.

Robinson, Harlow. "A Russian Fondness for Nostalgia." Booklet. *Russia Cast Adrift*. By Georgii Sviridov.

Philips, 1996. CD.

Rorem, Ned. "That Shadow, My Likeness." Perf. Thomas Hampson and Craig Rutenberg. *To the Soul*. EMI,

1997. CD.

Scruggs, Earl, Doc Watson, and Ricky Skaggs. "Ridin' That Midnight Train." *Three Pickers*. Rounder, 2003. CD.

54. Television/Radio Program

The basic items of information are the title of the individual episode (if appropriate) in quotation marks; the name of the program (italicized); the names of the persons mainly responsible for production and performance; the network; call letters and city of the station (if relevant); the date; and the medium. A comma separates the station and the city; periods separate all other items. An entry may begin with the name of an individual, if that is the emphasis in the paper (fourth example). Programs vary so much that some sensible improvisation may be necessary.

Beckett, Wendy. Interview. "Bill Moyers in Conversation with Sister Wendy." PBS. WXEL, West Palm Beach.

6 Oct. 1997. Television.

Candaele, Kelly. "Mom the Baseball Player." *Morning Edition*. Natl. Public Radio. WYSO, Yellow Springs. 17

July 2003. Radio.

Daniel Deronda. By George Eliot. Adapt. Andrew Davies. Dir. Tom Hooper. Perf. Hugh Dancy, Romola Garai,

Hugh Bonneville. 2 episodes. Masterpiece Theatre. Introd. Russell Baker. PBS. WGBH, Boston. 30-31

Mar. 2003. Television.

Davies, Andrew, adapt. *Daniel Deronda*. By George Eliot. Dir. Tom Hooper. Perf. Hugh Dancy, Romola Garai,

Hugh Bonneville. 2 episodes. Masterpiece Theatre. Introd. Russell Baker. PBS. WGBH, Boston. 30-31

Mar. 2003. Television.

"Seabiscuit." *The American Experience*. Narr. Scott Glenn. Writ. Michelle Ferrari. Dir. Stephen Ives. PBS.

WGBH, Boston. 28 July 2003. Television.

55. Works of Art

When you are citing the work of art itself (the fourth example), begin with the artist's name and follow it with the title of the work (in italics), the date it was completed, the medium of the work, the museum housing the work, and the city where the museum is located. The museum and the city are separated by a comma; other items, by periods. If you use a reproduction, give the artist, title, date, and repository; follow these with your source, the publication data, and the number of the reproduction (if any). If you use a slide, identify the producer and the number of the slide. The third example illustrates how to cite a painting reproduced on the Web.

Homer, Winslow. *Snap the Whip*. 1872. Butler Inst., Youngstown. New York: Sandak, n.d. PB 590. Slide.

O'Keeffe, Georgia. *Cow's Skull–Red, White and Blue*. 1931. Metropolitan Museum of Art, New York. *Georgia*

O'Keeffe. By Charles C. Eldredge. New York: Abrams, 1999. 118. Print.

Van Gogh, Vincent. *The Postman Joseph Roulin*. 1889. Museum of Modern Art, New York. Web. 16 May

2008.

Wyeth, Andrew. *Christina's World*. 1948. Tempera. Museum of Modern Art, New York.

In-Text Citation

The first time you document a paper in MLA style, you will find the most innovative feature to be *in-text citation*. It is also the most efficient time-saver. To identify a source, type the first main word in the Works Cited entry (usually the author's last name) and the page reference immediately *after* the borrowed material. A reader then can easily identify the source by turning to the list of Works Cited. If you cite an entire work in your text, no parenthetical citation is necessary, but you will, of course, list the source in Works Cited. Place a citation at the end of the ideas being cited, usually at the close of a sentence. It follows the borrowed material and precedes your closing punctuation.

You must acknowledge material taken from any source except your own mind and imagination, whether it is a direct quotation, a paraphrase or summary of an author's opinion, a map, a picture, a table of statistics, or any other material from an outside source. However, unless they are included as part of something you are quoting, facts that are common knowledge available in various reference books—for example, the capital of Wyoming, the names of Columbus's ships, or the murderer of John Lennon—need not be cited even if you did not know them before you did your research. If you are in doubt as to whether a citation is needed, it would be prudent to include one.

Examples: Print Sources

The first three illustrations show the three ways you can handle parenthetical citations for print sources in general. Despite variations in types of source, the pattern will remain the same. The rest of the illustrations are keyed to the list of examples in Figure 9.1 so that you can compare a citation with its bibliographic counterpart.

Author and Page Number in Parentheses

Note that there is no comma between the author's name and the page number.

Before the 1590s most lyric poetry in England did not appear in print (Kastan 156).

In sixteenth-century England, print was "not the natural environment of lyric poetry"

(Kastan 156).

Author Cited in Text, Page Reference in Parentheses

According to David Scott Kastan, print was "not the natural environment of lyric poetry" in

sixteenth-century England (156).

Entire Work Cited in the Text

David Scott Kastan examines the emergence of print as a common medium for lyric poetry in

sixteenth-century England.

Anonymous Work (2, 29)

When no author is given, a work is alphabetized according to its title in the list of Works Cited. Use a short form of the title—starting with the first key word of the title—as you would the author's name. Punctuate the shortened title appropriately—the first example is for the title of a book, the second for a newspaper article.

The travel guide characterizes the people of the Haight-Ashbury district as predominantly "either

under 25 or over 50" (*Fodor's* 83).

The military commissions were criticized as "a shadow court system outside the reach of either

Congress or America's judiciary" ("Unjust" 9).

Corporate Author (7)

Twenty-five million Americans, 80% of them women, are threatened by osteoporosis (National

Osteoporosis Foundation 2).

Government Publication (11)

A portion of a reference often can be cited in the text (second example).

Norton urged that Pennsylvania Avenue be opened to traffic if it could be done without

endangering the President's safety (*Cong. Rec.* 20 May 1997: H2936).

The House Subcommittee on the Constitution was informed that the Christian Medical and Dental

Society opposes physician-assisted suicide in any form (*Assisted Suicide* 405).

Introduction/Afterword (12)

Malcolm Cowley argues that the first version of the poem that eventually became "Song of Myself"

is "one of the great inspired (and sometimes insane) prophetic works" that appear from time to

time in the West (xi).

One of the most striking features of the book is the way Hurston "constantly shifts back and forth between the literate narrator's voice and a highly idiomatic black voice" (Gates 203).

Legal Source (13)

Blind persons are authorized to operate vending facilities on any Federal property (20 USC 6a).

Although Waters admitted to two murders and sexual assault, his death sentence was reversed because he had received ineffective counsel (Waters v. Zant).

Letter, Published (14, 32)

In 1914 when Henry Adams complained about the "unmitigated blackness" of life, Henry James agreed that they were "lone survivors" whose past seemed "at the bottom of an abyss"; even so, he asserted, life continued to interest him (533–34).

According to Jack Morrow, the United States favors free trade except for Cuba, which would be a source of inexpensive sugar (7).

Multiple Authors/Editors (15, 33)

When you cite a work by two or three authors or editors, give the last name of each in the order in which they appear on the title page. If there are more than three, cite the first name, followed by *et al.* with no intervening comma.

In 1931 Hot Springs, New Mexico, changed its name to Truth or Consequences, and annual Truth or Consequences festivals are still being held (Schwartz, Ryan, and Wostbrock 237).

Press reports of animal hoarding often "reflect the confusion of various officials or experts" and thus may confuse readers as well (Arluke et al. 133).

Multivolume Work (16)

The volume number and the page reference are separated by a colon and one space. The abbreviations *vol.* and *p.* are not used. The second and third examples show two different ways of handling the same work. One is written with a short title, the other with a volume number. Use the one corresponding to the way the work has been entered on the Works Cited page. Note, too, that a comma is used between the name of an author and title, though not with a volume number.

On 10 February 1938, Mrs. Roosevelt spoke at a meeting sponsored by the National Negro Congress and created a controversy when she said, "We still do tolerate slavery in several ways" (Cook 2: 35).

"The contempt which my father had for my kind of intelligence was so far tempered by affection that, in practice, his attitude towards everything I did was one of blind indulgence" (Proust, *Budding Grove* 35).

"The contempt which my father had for my kind of intelligence was so far tempered by affection that, in practice, his attitude towards everything I did was one of blind indulgence" (Proust 2: 35).

Reference Work (20)

Page references are not necessary in a work that is arranged alphabetically unless the entry being cited is more than a page long, as in the first example. If you cite a specific definition, give its designation after the abbreviation *def.*, as in the final example. The examples illustrate an encyclopedia article, a biographical reference work, and a dictionary definition.

Jesuits claimed that Galileo's defense of the Copernican system would harm religion "more than Luther and Calvin put together" (De Santillana 639).

He has been on the faculty at the Curtis Institute since 1980 ("Rorem").

Tessie Hutchinson is often considered a scapegoat, "a person or group made to bear the blame for others or to suffer in their place" ("Scapegoat," def. 4b).

Selection in an Anthology (22)

According to Kastan, print was "not the natural environment of lyric poetry" in sixteenth-century England (156).

Works by the Same Author/Editor (25)

If you use two or more works by the same author or editor, you must include the title in your citation. Author and title are separated by a comma. Any information included within your text should not be repeated in the parentheses, as the second example illustrates.

The impressively calm demeanor of General Colin L. Powell may have been encouraged by a motto under the glass on his desk: "Never let them see you sweat" (Woodward, *Veil* 374).

In *The Choice* Woodward writes that he was "perplexed" by Pat Buchanan's "strange mixture of personality traits" (147).

Interview, Published (31)

Cite the last name of the person interviewed. For citing a nonprint interview, see the following section.

> Although *Death of a Salesman* is a sad play, the playwright admitted, "I did a lot of laughing when
>
> I was writing the play because some of Willy Loman's ideas are so absurd and self-contradictory
>
> that you have to laugh about them" (Miller 214).

Examples: Web and Other Nonprint Sources

Nonprint sources are cited exactly the same way as print materials. That is, you need to provide the information—the first element of the entry in your Works Cited—that will take your reader to that entry. Supply additional information to help someone locate the ideas you have quoted or summarized, if you can. Some online journals, for example, reproduce the print version; others (such as *Postmodern Culture*) number the paragraphs. In such cases, you can provide the page number (or paragraph number) just as you would with a print source. In many more cases, however, you will be unable to provide any further information for your readers. If you are quoting an Internet document, your readers will still use your Works Cited to locate the source and then can easily search the site to locate anything you have quoted. In other situations, you can provide contextual clues that would help a reader locate the material, such as identifying the final scene of a film or noting that an anecdote was used to open a lecture. Some of the following examples include a description of the source, which not only helps establish the authority of that source but also leads the reader not to question the absence of a page number. The illustrations include articles retrieved from a variety of Web sources (38–42), a lecture (48), a radio program (54), and a painting (55).

> Reviewing *Christ in the House of His Parents*, Dickens described the central figure in
>
> John Everett Millais's painting as "a hideous, wry-necked, blubbering, red-headed boy,
>
> in a bed-gown."
>
> The Hoarding of Animals Research Consortium reports that in one case ammonia levels reached 152
>
> ppm (130).
>
> Aracagök points out "the difficulty that arises when giving an example of the concept of example"
>
> (par. 42).
>
> Professor Halsey began his lecture by characterizing the 1876 campaign as the "most vicious
>
> display of partisan politics" yet seen in the state.
>
> Describing a 1945 photograph of his mother playing professional baseball, Candaele compared the
>
> blowing folds of her uniform skirt to "the fins of an old Cadillac."
>
> In *The Postman Joseph Roulin* (1888), van Gogh represents the subject in his uniform, looking
>
> directly at the viewer, his right eyebrow slightly raised.

```
1. Indirect citation
2. Authors with the same last name
3. Anonymous works with the same title
4. Two or more sources in a citation
5. Work often reprinted
6. Shortened title
7. Poetry
8. Work with numbered divisions
9. Graphic material
10. Foreign titles
```

FIGURE 9.5 In-text citations: special situations

Methods of quoting or documenting out-of-the-ordinary material, listed in Figure 9.5, are illustrated in the following.

1. Indirect Citation

To document the source of a quotation that you find in a source you are using, identify the writer or speaker in the text and give your source in the citation; introduce the citation with *qtd. in.* Your first thought in such a situation, however, should be to look for the original source because it may contain other usable material.

An investigator for the Animal Humane Society of Hennepin County, who pointed out that the agency

was "already strapped for money," estimated that this case would cost $30,000 (qtd. in Rybak 1A).

2. Authors with the Same Last Name

If you cite two or more authors with the same last name, include their initials in the parenthetical citations:

(M. Moore 21)

(T. Moore 166)

If two or more authors have the same first initial and the same last name, spell out their first names:

(Marianne Moore 112)

(Merrill Moore 28)

3. Anonymous Works with the Same Title

If you have two or more anonymous works with the same title, find some publication information that will distinguish them and add it to the title in the parenthetical citation. In the following example, the name of the overall Web site has been added to distinguish between two Internet documents with the same title.

Although the scarlet ibis is not considered an endangered species globally ("Scarlet Ibis," *Bronx Zoo*),

its numbers are declining in Trinidad, where it is a protected species ("Scarlet Ibis," *Birds in Surinam*).

4. Two or More Sources in a Citation

If you need to acknowledge two or more sources in the same citation, separate the references with semicolons.

> Since Van Wyck Brooks published *The Ordeal of Mark Twain* in 1920, many other authors have attempted to analyze Twain's marriage and his wife's influence on his work (see DeVoto 207-09; Geismar 259-61; Harris 135–73; Kaplan 278–79; Sanborn 447–48).

5. Work Often Reprinted

Page references are not always helpful when a work has been published in a number of editions. Include the chapter after the page reference, separated by a semicolon.

> In *Great Expectations,* Dickens's dislike of class distinctions is suggested when Estella scornfully dismisses Pip as lower class because he calls knaves jacks, has coarse hands, and wears thick boots (65; ch. 8).

6. Shortened Title

When you refer to a title several times in your paper, you can reduce it to a key word, to a phrase, or to initials. You can do this most simply by designating the short form the first time you mention the title.

> In *The Portrait of a Lady* (*Portrait*), Henry James described a young American woman whose naive idealism destroys her chance for happiness.

> Robert Penn Warren based his novel *All The King's Men* (*ATKM*) on the career of Huey P. Long.

7. Poetry

Two or three lines of poetry can be written consecutively with a slash separating the lines. One space precedes and one follows the slash.

> Readers disagree as to what kind of choice Robert Frost referred to when he wrote, "Two roads diverged in a wood, and I— / I took the one less traveled by, / And that has made all the difference" ("The Road Not Taken").

A longer passage is written in block form (see pages 110–111). It is indented one inch and is not enclosed in quotation marks. As much as possible, follow the indentation of the original. If there is no room for the citation after the last line, type it on the next line so that it ends flush with the right margin.

> Poe begins "For Annie" by hailing Annie's death as a release from the suffering that came with her illness, then suggests that life itself is an illness to be overcome:

> Thank Heaven! the crisis—
>
> > The danger is past,
>
> And the lingering illness
>
> > Is over at last—
>
> And the fever called "Living"
>
> > Is conquered at last. (42)

8. Work with Numbered Divisions

A play, a poem, the Bible, or any other work divided into numbered sections is cited like the following examples. In the citation of a play, upper- and lowercase Roman numerals are sometimes preferred instead for act and scene: III.iii.155–60. Books of the Bible, as in the third example, are usually abbreviated and are not italicized.

> In his effort to poison Othello's mind and make him suspicious of Desdemona, Iago cleverly
>
> stresses the importance of a spotless reputation:
>
> > Good name in man and woman, good my lord,
> >
> > Is the immediate jewel of their souls.
> >
> > Who steals my purse steals trash; 'tis something, nothing;
> >
> > 'Twas mine, 'tis his, and has been slave to thousands;
> >
> > But he that filches from me my good name
> >
> > Robs me of that which not enriches him
> >
> > But makes me poor indeed. (*Othello* 3.3.155–60)

> The Byronic hero is a world-weary man who has experienced everything and found it boring: "He,
>
> who grown aged in this world of woe, / In deeds, not years, piercing to the depths of life, / So
>
> that no wonder waits him . . ." (*Childe Harold's Pilgrimage* 3.5.37–39).

> God blessed Adam and Eve and gave this promise: "Be fruitful and multiply, and replenish the
>
> earth, and subdue it, and have dominion over the fish of the sea, and over the fowl of the air, and
>
> over every living thing that moveth upon the earth" (Gen. 1.26).

9. Graphic Material

Your paper should not be overloaded with illustrative material like maps and graphs, but if you use any, make certain that they are relevant to your thesis and are not just window dressing. If your paper contains several illustrations, you can put them in an appendix and refer to them in the text of your paper as Figure 3, Table 2, and so on. If you include an illustration in your paper, place it as close as possible to the discussion to which it relates.

A table is a listing of statistics and is assigned a number. The word *Table*, a number, and a brief title are usually placed *above* the material. The source is identified briefly in a credit line below the table and is fully documented in Works Cited.

A graph, picture, map, diagram, or any other pictorial material is labeled *Figure* and assigned a number. The word *Figure*, the number, and a brief title are usually placed *below* the illustration. A credit line identifies the source, which also is listed in Works Cited.

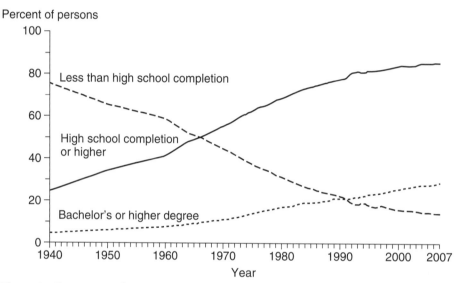

Figure 1.   Percentage of persons 25 years old and over, by highest level of educational attainment: Selected years, 1940 through 2007

Source: *Digest of Education Statistics: 2007*
    http://nces.ed.gov/programs/digest/d07/figures/fig_03.asp

10. Foreign Titles

If you use a work translated from a foreign language, the title will almost certainly be in English; but if you use the original, write the title and the author's name as they appear in the source. In French, Italian, and Spanish, the first word of a title and of a subtitle as well as proper nouns are capitalized. In German, capitalize the first word of a title and of a subtitle as well as all nouns. Diacritical marks are available on most computers; if you cannot insert them or your printer will not handle them, draw them in as neatly as possible.

Martin, Jean-Yves. "Mondialité et identités." *La Pensée* 319 (1999): 75-84. Print.

Garcia, Gustavo V. "(Anti)platonismó en *La destrucción o el amor.*" *Hispania* 82 (1999): 733-39. Print.

Krolow, Karl. "Sechs späte Gedichte." *Monatshafte* 41 (l999): 301-04. Print.

Table 1. Projected number of participants in educational institutions, by level and control of institution: Fall 2007

	[In millions]						
Participants	All levels (elementary, secondary, and postsecondary degree-granting)	Elementary and secondary schools			Postsecondary degree-granting institutions		
		Total	Public	Private	Total	Public	Private
1	2	3	4	5	6	7	8
Total	**83.5**	**62.9**	**55.9**	**6.8**	**20.7**	**15.3**	**5.4**
Enrollment	73.7	55.8	49.6	6.2	18.0	13.5	4.5
Teachers and faculty	4.6	3.7	3.2	0.5	0.9	0.6	0.3
Other professional, administrative, and support staff	5.2	3.4	3.1	0.3	1.8	1.2	0.6

NOTE: Includes enrollments in local public school systems and in most private schools (religiously affiliated and nonsectarian). Excludes federal schools. Excludes private preprimary enrollment in schools that do not offer kindergarten or above. Degree-granting institutions grant associate's or higher degrees and participate in Title IV federal financial aid programs. Data for teachers and other staff in public and private elementary and secondary schools and colleges and universities are reported in terms of full-time equivalents. Detail may not sum to totals because of rounding.

Source: *Digest of Education Statistics: 2007*

   http://nces.ed.gov/programs/digest/d07/tables/dt07_001.asp?referrer=report

Explanation and Reference Notes

In your reading, you will encounter many notes consisting entirely of citations—identifying the sources of borrowed material. However, notes often supply additional information (explanation notes) or suggest additional sources (reference notes). Students often ignore such notes, but they can be very helpful. They may contain facts or opinions that relate to your thesis or they may furnish useful leads to other sources. You may wish to include such notes in your own paper as well.

Explanation notes contain information that pertains to some aspect of a topic but is not directly supportive of the thesis. They should be used sparingly in most student papers because something that does not pertain to the thesis probably does not belong in the paper. But if you want to include an amusing or interesting sidelight on your topic, consider putting it in a note (see page 3 of Paul's paper and page 3 of James's paper.). Explanation notes can also be a convenient way of identifying individuals or events and of defining terms.

Reference notes direct the reader to another section of your paper or, more often, to a book or an article. A source that supports one of your statements is usually introduced by *See also*; one that contradicts or contrasts with your statement is usually introduced by *Compare* or *But see*.

The two types of notes are sometimes combined; the same note may cite a source, include a comment, and suggest one or more supplementary sources. Sources cited in notes are, of course, included in Works Cited.

To write a note of either kind, type a numeral (a superscript) in the text a half-space above the line. In the text a note number follows any punctuation except a dash. In the note itself, the number is not raised but kept in line with the text. The number is followed by a period, and the note is indented like a regular paragraph. Notes can be presented either at the bottom of the page as footnotes or as endnotes on a separate page headed *Notes* and placed after the text but before *Works Cited.* Your word processing program will allow you to insert the note in either location. A brief reference (e.g., "see Schwab ch. 6") can be made in the text, but if the reference is long enough to impede the sentence flow, it should be written as a reference note. Many student papers contain neither explanation nor reference notes.

Sample Papers

The following sample papers, as well as the one in Chapter 10, have been revised somewhat to illustrate as many aspects of research writing as possible. The papers offered are not models of perfection, of course, but they represent excellent student writing and may suggest ways in which you can improve your paper.

Comments on the facing pages of the first paper point out the basic organization, transitional devices, management of quotations and summaries, forms of documentation, and other aspects of structure and style. The efficiency of MLA style is demonstrated by the fact that there are more than forty in-text citations, which would have required at least three pages of endnotes. Conserving paper, however, is not as beneficial as facilitating the use of brief quotations that can be smoothly blended with the text of the paper.

1   Your last name and the page number should appear in the upper right-hand corner of each page, including the first one. Do not use the abbreviation *p.*, and do not use any punctuation with the number. Set it up as a header that will appear automatically rather than type it in on each page. It should be placed half an inch from the top of the page and flush right.

2   MLA style does not call for a separate title page. This endorsement begins on the first line of the first page of the paper. It consists of your name, your professor's name, the class you are taking, and the date you are submitting the paper. If your professor asks for a separate title page, he or she will probably give you specific directions about what to include. If not, you would include the title of your paper, followed by the information in the endorsement. Type the title about a third of the way down the page, centered, with the rest of the information on the next lines. It should be double-spaced and look something like this:

Understanding and Dealing with Animal Hoarding

Paul Sanchez

Professor O'Connor

English 110

15 May 2009

3   Center your title on the next line after the endorsement. Do not underline it, put it in quotation marks, follow it with a period, or type it in all capitals. The body of the paper begins on the next line. If you have a separate title page, the title of your paper would appear again as the first line of this page.

4   Paul begins with an anecdote intended to lead the reader into the topic by evoking a familiar type of news story.

5   The last two sentences of this paragraph introduce the topic of the paper and give the thesis in general terms.

6   This paragraph begins the discussion of the extent of the problem of animal hoarding. It uses a series of examples from newspapers from around the country—mostly stories retrieved from online sources—to demonstrate how widespread the problem is.

7   There are no page numbers for any of these citations because they all come from online sources that do not have page or paragraph numbers.

8   This sentence uses information taken from two different sources. The parenthetical citations are placed so that it is clear which piece of information came from which source.

9   Paul is using two sources by Noel, so a shortened form of the title of the article is included to distinguish between them.

1 Sanchez 1

2 Paul Sanchez

Professor O'Connor

English 110

15 May 2009

3   Understanding and Dealing with Animal Hoarding

4   Microphone in one hand, the reporter stands in front of a procession of men and women passing with

animal carriers in each hand. Mrs. Smith's neighbors had complained of the smell, the reporter explains,

then points to the house with her free hand. Inside, other men and women, wearing what appear to be gas

masks, are placing listless, bony Chihuahuas into more carriers. In a voiceover the reporter relates that

nearly sixty dogs and a dozen cats were removed from Mrs. Smith's two-bedroom house, concluding that

they will be available for adoption at a local animal shelter. Viewers do not see Mrs. Smith, nor does

anyone say why—or how—she came to be living with so many animals that she could not care for.

5   Although this account of Mrs. Smith is fictional, almost everyone has seen, read, or heard similar news

stories. Details may vary, but the overall pattern of these reports is similar. Intervention by police or some

other agency reveals the presence of a large number of animals crowded into a person's home and living

under deplorable conditions. This phenomenon, known as animal hoarding, is more widespread than these

isolated local stories might suggest. It is a serious problem and needs to be understood so that it can be

dealt with effectively.

6   Incidents of animal hoarding are reported all over the country. A sampling of news stories from a single

year (2007) will illustrate. For instance, in August, sixty-two live cats and six dogs were removed from a

12,000-square-foot mansion in Saddle River, New Jersey; twenty-six dead animals were later removed from

7 the garage, and another twenty cats were believed to be still "running through the walls" (Murray). In

8 September, 663 cats were rescued from a compound near Pahrump, Nevada (Peters), and eighty-eight small

dogs were discovered in a home near Sun, Louisiana, in October (Chapple). Also in October, after

authorities had seized 160 cats, 105 dogs, and thirty-five birds in Lee County, Illinois, they found an

9 additional 200 dead pets (Noel, "Dark Tale").

10 Bill Stephenson's title is given to indicate his authority.

11 Paul needs to indicate that Stephenson is being quoted in Lonetree's newspaper article. Simply including Lonetree's name would confuse readers, who might think that Paul had cited the wrong source or omitted Stephenson from the Works Cited page. The last citation in this paragraph comes from an anonymous article, so a shortened version of the title, enclosed in quotation marks, is used in place of an author's name. The article is alphabetized under "Las Cruces" on the Works Cited page.

12 The word *estimates* echoes the beginning of the previous paragraph and helps unify the paper. The word *equally* also links the new topic (the estimated number of cases nationally) with the previous topic (the number at state and local levels).

13 In an earlier draft, Paul had explained how Lockwood had gathered the information he used to reach this conclusion:

THE WORK OF PAUL SANCHEZ

A decade ago, in 1994, Randy Lockwood stated that the Humane Society of the United States (HSUS) received two or three calls a week from local agencies needing assistance with animal hoarding cases and that each of the ten regional offices of the HSUS had been involved in two or three cases in the previous year. On that basis, he calculated that "at least several thousand" people in this country were involved in hoarding animals (18).

As Paul read back through his draft, he realized that he was reproducing far too much of Lockwood's original wording:

The Humane Society of the United States (HSUS) receives two to three calls a week from local

agencies requesting information or assistance in dealing with collectors, and each of our

10 regional offices has become actively involved in two to three interventions involving collectors

in the last year.

As Paul revised the wording, he also realized that most of it was irrelevant to his point and cut most of it.

14 Paul is using more than one source by Patronek, so he uses a shortened version of the title to distinguish between them.

15 Again, Paul uses a shortened form to distinguish between two articles by Noel.

16 The costs have been arranged in ascending order, with the second example used to suggest that costs are likelier to be higher than first estimated. The highest dollar amount comes from the source, so Paul tries to capitalize on it.

17 A corporate author (HARC)

There is no national database tracking animal hoarding, so it is difficult to estimate how common

such incidents are. Individual news reports suggest that they are not isolated, often referring to previous

10 investigations carried out by the same local agencies. Bill Stephenson, the animal control supervisor in St.

Paul, Minnesota, says he sees a case of animal hoarding "about once every three to five years" (qtd. in

11 Lonetree). In Gwinnett County, Georgia, authorities estimate that the average number of hoarding cases is

about two a month; in nearby Fulton County, officials had investigated four cases in the first six months of

2007 (Eckstein). In Las Cruces, New Mexico, animal control had investigated four animal hoarding cases

between mid-May and late July 2007 ("Las Cruces Pets").

12   Estimates of the total number of annual cases nationally are equally varied. On the basis of the number of

13 calls received by the Humane Society of the United States (HSUS) and its ten regional offices, Randy

Lockwood calculated that "at least several thousand" people in this country were involved in hoarding

animals (18). More recently, drawing on data gathered nationally, Gary J. Patronek estimated that anywhere

from 700 to 2,000 cases of animal hoarding occur annually in the United States, concluding that the likely

14 number is between 1,200 and 1,600 cases per year ("Hoarding" 83). No matter which of these estimates is

15 closest to the actual number of cases, it is clear that incidents of animal hoarding occur frequently enough

to warrant serious attention.

Equally difficult to calculate are the costs of dealing with animal hoarding, though it is evident that

they are high. It is impossible, of course, to assign a dollar value to animal suffering and death, but caring

for the rescued animals involves significant sums of money. For example, medical costs alone for the 663

cats that were seized in Nevada were $36,500 for the first six weeks, with total costs predicted to exceed

$100,000 (Peters). The cost of caring for 300 animals rescued in Illinois was initially estimated to range

16 between $30,000 and $100,000 (Noel, "Dark Tale"), but a later account revised the estimate to $127,500

(Noel, "Hundreds"). As long ago as 1994 a pair of cases in Loudoun County, Virginia, exceeded $135,000

(Handy, "Handling, Part 2"), a figure that would undoubtedly be substantially higher today.

Other types of costs are involved as well. When large numbers of animals are confined in a small

space, property damage is unavoidable. After studying seventy-one case reports, the Hoarding of Animals

17 Research Consortium (HARC) concluded that in a "typical" case "household interiors were coated, often

18 A content note

19 A reference to several sources that provide the same information

20 In this paragraph Paul has tried to select telling statistical evidence as well as details that will play on a reader's emotions. The content note provides some additional details.

21 Transition into next major section of the paper repeats the key points of the first section.

22 Series of similar examples to establish reliability of the claim

23 Transition bridges previous topic (women as hoarders) to discussion of behaviors common to both genders.

several inches high, with human and animal urine and feces, sometimes to an extent that floors buckled"

(128). Newspaper accounts of individual incidents almost always describe the condition of the property in

graphic terms and frequently accompany the story with photographs of the destruction caused by the

18 confined animals.[1] Under such conditions cleanup or repair may not be a viable alternative, and several

newspaper accounts mention that houses are condemned and sometimes must be demolished once they

19 have been vacated (Murray; Eckstein; Cullen).

20   The accumulated clutter and animal waste with which animal hoarders live also pose significant health

risks. In the cases reviewed in the HARC study, conditions were such that the possibility of "maintaining

basic personal hygiene" was rated as "very much impaired" in 74.2% of the homes, including unusable

toilet facilities in 53.1% of the homes (128). Several individual cases further highlight the dangers. In one

instance, an eighty-year-old woman's hair was so filthy and matted that her head had to be shaved; in

another, a couple's two children had to repeat kindergarten and first grade because of repeated absences

due to respiratory infections (129).[2]

21   Together, the various costs associated with animal hoarding and the widespread nature of the

phenomenon point to the seriousness of the problem. A logical first step in dealing with it is trying to

22 understand hoarders themselves. Studies point to a number of common elements. Perhaps most striking is

that the majority of hoarders are women who live alone. One early investigation found that more than two-

thirds of the people involved were women, 70% of them unmarried (Lockwood 18). Almost twenty years

later, using a larger sample, Patronek found that 76% of those cases were female, and 72% were described

as single, divorced, or widowed ("Hoarding" 84). In a 2002 follow-up study, HARC found that 83.1% of the

hoarders in its sample were women and that 71.8% were unmarried (126).

     A number of hoarders—male and female alike—share other traits as well. Many observers point to

23 evidence of delusions. All the participants in a HARC-sponsored project to interview animal hoarders stated

their belief in a special ability to communicate with animals; in addition, all maintained that their animals

were well cared for and healthy, despite obvious evidence to the contrary (Frost). This inability to

recognize actual conditions appears repeatedly in accounts of animal hoarding. In 58% of the cases

24 Specific evidence from one source (Patronek) used to support a generalization from another source (Frost)

25 A striking individual example that will be given a more general application with statistics from another source (see item 26)

26 The generalization from one source (Frost) used to suggest that a striking individual example (Greenberger) may not be an isolated case (see item 25); also note use of square brackets to alter the quotation.

27 Evidence from one source used in support of another

28 Source of article included to give added credibility

29 Application of general theory to specific situation

30 Transition that emphasizes the structure of the argument being summarized

31 Evidence from another source (Patronek) used to support Frost's analysis

24 reviewed by Patronek, the "hoarder would not acknowledge to the investigating officer that a problem existed" ("Hoarding" 84).

25 As well as denial, hoarders may show signs of paranoia. A Boston woman claimed that the inspectors had planted the sixty dead cats found in her apartment (many of them in trash bags in the freezer) and accused judges of conducting an unfair trial and of carrying out a vendetta intended to "ruin [her]

26 credibility" (Greenberger). According to Randy Frost, "delusional levels of paranoia regarding the actions and intentions of animal control officers" occur "frequently" in these cases.

27 Lockwood also observed that the onset of the condition often coincided with "the early or sudden loss of a loved one, usually a parent or sibling" (19). Information gathered in the HARC-sponsored interviews indicates that hoarders' childhoods were often marked by "chaotic, inconsistent and unstable parenting" and that animals frequently provided stability and emotional security (Frost).

28 Taken together, these traits have led researchers to suggest several tentative explanations for the hoarding of animals. In an article written for *Psychiatric Times*, Frost provides a brief summary of the various theories. Because hoarders so frequently cannot recognize the actual conditions around them and even show signs of paranoia, some believe that hoarding is a form of delusional disorder. The tendency to hoard other objects in addition to animals has led other researchers to associate animal hoarding with obsessive-compulsive disorder (OCD), of which hoarding is a common symptom. Studies suggest that hoarding in general may be an attempt to control the environment or avoid the difficulty of making decisions or the distress of parting with a loved possession. On this basis Frost theorizes that animal

29 hoarders' failure to secure treatment for sick animals is a form of avoiding such difficulties; likewise, not removing dead animals may be a refusal to acknowledge the animal's death and a way to avoid feelings of guilt or responsibility.

30 Another explanation considered by Frost is the attachment model, which suggests that an individual who has experienced early parental detachment (usually in the form of absence, neglect, or abuse) and cannot establish close relationships in adulthood turns to animals to replace the missing bond. Similarly,

31 other researchers report that hoarders say that they regard the animals as friends or surrogate children (Patronek, "Hoarding" 84).

32 Summary of section that starts transition into next major section of paper

33 Beginning of next major section of the paper

34 Citation for work with two authors

35 *Work* echoes earlier paragraph, helps connect theoretical and practical levels of issue.

36 Summary statement at end of paragraph leads to next phase of paper.

37 Repetition of *complexity* helps unify paragraph and suggests reason for summarizing Handy's two-part online article.

38 Beginning of summary of Handy's article

39 Content note providing more detail about repeat offenders

32   Frost concludes his survey of these theories by suggesting that no single explanation is sufficient: "Like many psychological conditions, the causes of animal hoarding are probably multiple and, therefore, assessments of emotions, behavior and thoughts must be multifaceted to point the way to successful treatment."

33   Although that conclusion seems very sensible, it is very difficult to put into practice. A number of factors have to be considered, each one a challenge in its own right. For instance, even though Frost describes animal hoarding as a psychological condition, the current *Diagnostic and Statistical Manual of Mental Disorders* (1994) of the American Psychiatric Association does not recognize it as a syndrome

34 (Campbell and Robinson 17). Although researchers like Frost and Patronek and organizations like HARC have done groundbreaking work in this area, no truly comprehensive, scientific study has yet been carried out. Thus, much work still remains to be done in this area.

35   That work is important for highly practical reasons. If animal hoarding is not recognized as a psychiatric problem, it is more difficult for agencies to intervene when a case arises. According to HARC, a "recurring theme" in the case reports they studied was difficulty in getting human health agencies involved in animal hoarding cases; even when health risks from self-neglect were evident, agencies would withdraw from cases if the current criteria for mental incompetence were not met (129). With a clearer

36 understanding of the condition and its causes, it would be possible to establish clearer medical and legal guidelines for intervention.

37   That clearer understanding would also make it easier to develop more effective strategies for intervention. Because of the complexity of the typical animal hoarding situation, HARC suggests that it would be necessary to involve a number of agencies, such as public health, fire, police, housing, mental health, aging, adult protective services, and animal control agencies, in addition to veterinarians and perhaps legal services (131). The real complexity of these situations and the need for cooperation among a variety of agencies are both evident in a two-part article addressed to directors of shelters. In the first part,

38 Geoffrey L. Handy outlines the difficulty in determining whether to bring criminal prosecution against a hoarder or to attempt some other type of intervention. As Handy and others point out, it is often difficult

39 to get a conviction, and hoarders have an extremely high rate of relapse.[3] Because prosecution is difficult

40 Outline note

THE WORK OF PAUL SANCHEZ

Handy, part 1 (online)   dealing w/hoarders

(1) cooperate in hopes they will get help for animals and maybe give some up

(2) get court order limiting how many they can keep; often can get agency involved to supervise

(3) bring in social services—housing, public safety, mental health, aging

41 Reference to "second part" of article helps distinguish between sources without page numbers.

42 Citation for article with eight authors

43 Transition echoes "difficulties" and "legal."

44 Citation for online government document; two sources cited

45 Citation of work without an author

46 Conclusion mentions key points to give a sense of summary without repeating much material and refers back to opening anecdote.

and does not really address the cause of the problem, Handy also outlines three strategies

commonly used for intervention: (1) cooperating with the hoarder to immediately improve conditions for the animals and subsequently getting the hoarder to give up some of them; (2) obtaining a court order that limits the number of animals the person can keep, often under the supervision of some agency; and (3) involving social service agencies that deal with mental health, housing, public safety, or aging.

The second part of Handy's article summarizes the legal grounds on which animals can most often be removed (such as violations of animal cruelty laws). Because laws vary greatly from one location to another, agencies must work closely with local officials and attorneys. Once the necessary legal actions have been taken, Handy recommends forming one or more five-person teams, each including a veterinarian and photographer. His directions to the photographer documenting the rescue and to the entire team about their actions and even their dress are full of cautions about the legal implications of their behavior and how it might be perceived in a courtroom. Even when convictions are obtained, however, there may be no requirement that the person seek help. In fact, according to a review of press coverage of animal hoarding cases, judges "rarely suggested or required" counseling (Arluke et al. 124).

A recent development may help reduce difficulties in taking legal action against animal hoarders and in obtaining help for them. In August 2001 the governor of Illinois signed legislation that specifically addresses animal hoarding. The law defines an animal hoarder as someone with a large number of companion animals who cannot care properly for them and who is unable to recognize the severity of the situation. It also recommends psychiatric evaluation for an adult convicted under that law and requires an evaluation for a minor (Illinois; McDermott). Although this is the first state law dealing with animal hoarding, similar legislation has been proposed in New Mexico, Vermont, and Montana, and lawmakers in Wyoming and Idaho are discussing similar revisions for existing laws ("Lawmakers").

Such legislation is an encouraging sign for those concerned about the problem of animal hoarding. In recognizing the condition, laws like these may indirectly encourage official recognition in a medical sense. More important, such legal provisions make it easier for local agencies to intervene on behalf of suffering animals. Most important of all, it makes it likelier that the hoarder will get the help that he or she needs much sooner than in the past. Then, perhaps, stories like Mrs. Smith's will become less familiar.

47 Endnotes supply incidental information not directly supportive of the thesis or cite additional sources. Although the note number in the body of the paper is presented as a superscript, in the note itself the number is on the same line as the text and followed by a period. The note is indented like a paragraph.

48 Note refers the reader to another source for a more detailed discussion of a secondary point; citation refers to a specific section of an article with eight authors.

49 Note supplies additional evidence that is related to evidence presented in the paper but from a slightly different perspective.

50 Note supplies an anecdote that would extend an already long summary.

51 Note directs the reader to other sources and combines citations in a single set of parentheses.

47   Notes

48   1. For a detailed analysis of typical press coverage, see Arluke et al. 119–21.

49   2. The risk may involve others besides the occupants of the home. One of the HARC cases involving

dogs led to a flea infestation at a nearby school for emotionally disturbed children and the closing of the

school (129).

        3. Handy cites a case in which authorities rescued over fifty animals, only to discover that the person

50 had obtained more than twenty more animals within two days. A number of other writers call attention to

recidivism as a potential problem or mention that a specific individual has previously been involved in a

51 similar case (see, for example, Arluke et al. 118; Cullen; Eckstein; Lockwood 21; Noel, "Dark Tale";

Patronek, "Problem" 6).

Works Cited

52 Arluke, Arnold, et al. "Press Reports of Animal Hoarding." *Society and Animals* 10.2 (2002): 113-35. Print.

53 Campbell, Carol S., and James W. Robinson. "Animal Hoarding." *Encyclopedia of Criminology and Deviant Behavior*. Ed. Clifton D. Bryant. Vol. 1. Philadelphia: Brunner-Routledge, 2001. 17-19. Print.

54 Chapple, Charlie. "Mistreated Dogs Need New Homes: 88 Found Suffering during Drug Raid." *Times-Picayune* [New Orleans] 3 Oct. 2007: 1. *LexisNexis*. Web. 14 Apr. 2009.

55 Cullen, Sandy. "Convicted Cat Hoarder At It Again, Health Department Says." *Wisconsin State Journal* 6 Sept. 2007: B1. *LexisNexis*. Web. 12 Apr. 2009.

56 Eckstein, Sandra. "Officials Sniff Out Animal Hoarders." *Atlanta Journal-Constitution* 29 July 2007, main ed.: 6M. *LexisNexis*. Web. 13 Apr. 2009.

57 Frost, Randy. "People Who Hoard Animals." *Psychiatric Times* 17.4 (2000): n. pag. Web. 14 Apr. 2009.

58 Greenberger, Scott S. "'Animal Hoarding' Said To Be Symptom of a Mental Illness." *Boston Globe* 12 May 2003: B1. *LexisNexis*. Web. 13 Apr. 2009.

59 Handy, Geoffrey L. "Handling Animal Collectors, Part 1: Interventions That Work." *Shelter Sense* May-June 1994: n. pag. Web. 14 Apr. 2009.

60 ---. "Handling Animal Collectors, Part 2: Managing a Large-Scale Rescue Operation." *Shelter Sense* July 1994: n. pag. Web. 14 Apr. 2009.

61 Hoarding of Animals Research Consortium. "Health Implications of Animal Hoarding." *Health and Social Work* 27 (2002): 125-36. Print.

62 Illinois. 92nd General Assembly. Public Act 92-0454. 21 Aug. 2001. Web. 1 May 2009.

63 "Las Cruces Pets Shipped to No-Kill Shelter in Texas." *Las Cruces Sun-News* 21 July 2007. *LexisNexis*. Web. 14 Apr. 2009.

64 "Lawmakers Tackle Animal Hoarding." *JAVMA News* 1 May 2003. Web. 14 Apr. 2009.

65 Lockwood, Randy. "The Psychology of Animal Collectors." *Trends* 9.6 (1994): 18-21. Print.

66 Newspaper article retrieved from a database

67 Newspaper article retrieved from a database

68 Newspaper article retrieved from a database

69 Newspaper article retrieved from a database

70 Article from journal with continuous pagination

71 Second item by same author; magazine article; double issue; interrupted pagination indicated with + after page number of first page of article

72 Newspaper article retrieved from a database

66 Lonetree, Anthony. "St. Paul House Condemned after Discovery of Animal Hoarding." *Star Tribune*

[Minneapolis] 9 Aug. 2007. *LexisNexis*. Web. 14 Apr. 2009.

67 Murray, Brian T. "Scores of Dead, Dying Cats Found in New Jersey Mansion." *Newhouse News Service*, 16 Aug.

2007. *LexisNexis*. Web. 14 Apr. 2009.

68 Noel, Josh. "Dark Tale Found Behind Doors." *Chicago Tribune* 21 Oct. 2007. LexisNexis. Web. 13 Apr. 2009.

69 ---. "Hundreds of Woman's Seized Pets Given to Humane Society: Woman Gives Hundreds of Them to Shelter."

Chicago Tribune 24 Oct. 2007. LexisNexis. Web. 13 Apr. 2009.

70 Patronek, Gary J. "Hoarding of Animals: An Under-Recognized Public Health Problem in a Difficult-to-Study

Population." *Public Health Reports* 114 (1999): 81-87. Print.

71 ---. "The Problem of Animal Hoarding." *Municipal Lawyer* May-June 2001: 6+. Print.

72 Peters, Sharon. "Rescuers Rush to Aid of 663 'Hoarded' Cats: Neglect Reported at Nevada Compound: Two Pets

Reunited with Grateful Owners." *USA Today* 4 Sept. 2007, final ed.: 8D. LexisNexis. Web. 13 Apr. 2009.

Colleen Lee

Professor Diaz

English 1301

5 May 2010

"A Monstrous Joy": Ambivalent Messages in "The Story of an Hour"

In "The Story of an Hour," written and published in 1894, Kate Chopin takes barely over a thousand words to narrate the story of Louise Mallard, a woman "afflicted with a heart trouble" (76). Informed as gently as possible that her husband has been killed in a train wreck, Mrs. Mallard grieves intensely. Soon, however, she begins to envision a future in which she will be free to live entirely for herself, and she welcomes the prospect with joy. When her husband suddenly returns a short time later—he had not been on the train as reported—she falls dead. "When the doctors came," Chopin concludes, "they said she had died of heart disease—of joy that kills" (79). This brief story is widely recognized as a powerful critique of the place of women in the society of Chopin's day. Emily Toth, for example, characterizes the story as "a criticism of the ideal of self-sacrifice" in women (*Kate Chopin* 25) and as an attack on marriage, "an institution that traps women" (*Unveiling* 10). Similarly, Barbara C. Ewell writes that Chopin's narrative "indicts the conventional view of female devotion" (90). Susan Sniader Lanser goes still further, describing the message of this story as a threat to "basic beliefs and practices about male-female relations, about women's dependency on men for survival and identity, and about the 'proper' responses to love and death." Lanser says that Chopin takes a "rather gingerly" approach to the topic because such a message would be even more unacceptable coming from a woman than a man, but she adds that readers never fail to grasp Chopin's message, even when they disagree with it (251-52).

In her analysis of Chopin's story, Lanser concentrates on how Chopin's handling of point of view and the conventions of fiction conveys that message without stating it directly. I believe that Chopin's "gingerly" approach is actually rather daring because it risks misinterpretation. That is, Chopin includes some elements that might allow a reader to conclude that Mrs. Mallard's death is a form of "poetic justice," punishment for her desire to be free of her husband. Readers are, in effect, receiving contradictory messages and must decide which to accept. In addition, the tension between these messages seems to reflect Chopin's own somewhat ambivalent views on the subject.

One reason that Chopin's message is so effective is that she does not state it immediately but unfolds it gradually, letting more conventional views about the role of women dominate the first part of the text. The story is half over before the idea of freedom from marriage is even introduced. Up to that point, Mrs. Mallard is presented as an admirable woman who matches or even surpasses the ideals of the time. Those ideals have been neatly summed up by Barbara Welter as four "cardinal virtues—piety, purity, submissiveness and domesticity" (152). Welter, who draws on a large number of the conduct manuals written for women in the first half of the nineteenth century, concludes that submission was "perhaps the most feminine virtue" (158). According to these guidebooks, a woman's subordinate role was decreed by God and should be embraced. As George Burnap put it in *The Sphere and Duties of Woman*, a true woman "feels herself weak and timid. She needs a protector" (qtd. in Welter 159).

Mrs. Mallard is described in terms that put her clearly into this category. The care taken by her husband's friend Richards and by her sister Josephine suggests that she is in need of a protector. In this case, her vulnerability is not due to any weakness in character but to a physical condition over which she has no control. At the same time, readers see the strength of her feelings for her husband. Chopin implies that those feelings set her apart from most women. Instead of a typical "paralyzed inability" to understand the news of her husband's death, she weeps "with sudden, wild abandonment" when she receives the news (76). This display of passion is followed by isolation, as she withdraws to her room alone. Chopin's comment that the lines in Mrs. Mallard's face "bespoke repression" (77) seems to echo Burnap's description of a woman's life as "a series of suppressed emotions" (qtd. in Welter 162). She continues to sob involuntarily, like a child crying in its sleep (77), a comparison that suggests the cardinal virtue of purity. Her purity is also suggested when the forbidden thought of freedom—still not named—begins to rise to her consciousness, and she struggles heroically against it, "striving to beat it back with her will" (77). Even then, she knows that she will weep again when she sees her husband's "kind tender hands" and the face that had looked at her only with love (78). In these respects Mrs. Mallard's feelings and actions mark her as an exemplary wife according to the views of the time.

Only at this point does Chopin begin to make a more direct criticism of the relationships between men and women, and that criticism is presented in ways that reduce its immediate force. For example, she is not critical only of men. Both men and women believe with a "blind persistence" that "they have a right to impose a private will upon a fellow-creature" (78). The motivation behind such actions might be kind as well as cruel (though no less a crime in either case). Chopin also softens criticism by presenting it in ways that suggest uncertainty. Her description of Mrs. Mallard's feelings about her husband is a good example: "And yet she had loved him—sometimes. Often she had not. What did it matter!" (78). In this case, the question is finally set aside as unimportant.

The most striking way in which Chopin uses uncertainty is in her presentation of the notion of freedom itself. It is first associated with the view from Mrs. Mallard's upstairs bedroom window. Looking down she sees treetops "all aquiver with the new spring life," and she feels the "delicious breath" of rain in the air (77). As she looks into the blue sky visible through the clouds, she hears a distant song and the "twittering" of "countless sparrows" in the eaves (77). The thought of freedom emerges from this scene, "reaching toward her through the sounds, the scents, the color that filled the air" (77). Lanser comments that this peaceful scene connects Mrs. Mallard with "what is natural, life-affirming, innocent, and good" and that the "extremely conventional" language used to describe it prepares readers to accept her thoughts in the same positive way (257–58).

At the same time, though, Chopin's language undercuts the sense of innocence and goodness in ways that Lanser does not examine. The thought of freedom is an unidentified "something" that is "creeping out of the sky" toward Mrs. Mallard, seeking to "possess" her. When she begins to recognize this "thing" and strives "to beat it back with her will," the attempt proves futile, for her will is "as powerless as her two white slender hands would have been" (77-78). The language here is equally conventional, though in this case it is associated with sexual assault. The description of Mrs. Mallard's eventual defeat is also sexually suggestive: "When she abandoned herself a little whispered word escaped her slightly parted lips" (78). It is only then that the notion of freedom is stated explicitly. Is Mrs. Mallard's reaction an affirmation of the freedom natural to all humans? Or is it an expression of her depravity as she surrenders her purity?

Chopin herself raises but seems to dismiss such questions: "She did not stop to ask if it were or were not a monstrous joy that held her. A clear and exalted perception enabled her to dismiss the suggestion as trivial" (78). Later, however, Chopin's choice of language casts some doubt on the clarity of that perception. Love is subordinate to "this *possession* of self-assertion" (78, emphasis added), an ambiguous statement that could refer either to something that Mrs. Mallard owns or to something that owns her. To say that someone's "fancy was running riot" usually suggests that a person is not thinking clearly, and the incomplete sentence following that statement may demonstrate some incoherent thinking as she envisions her future of freedom from her husband (79). Conventionally, a reference in fiction to "a feverish triumph" (79) in someone's eyes precedes some sort of collapse, and readers familiar with that convention would expect that this triumph is an illusion. These statements all point to another convention of popular fiction with which readers would have been familiar as well. As Welter puts it, for a woman to lose her sexual purity "in the women's magazines at least, brought madness or death" (154). That generalization could readily be applied to Mrs. Mallard's story as well, for she experiences something approaching madness and then death. From this perspective, then, Chopin's story would seem to support the status quo by showing Mrs. Mallard being punished for even thinking about abandoning her husband and, with him, the four cardinal virtues of women.

Some of the mixed messages in the story may lie in its connection to the author's own life. In *Unveiling Kate Chopin*, Emily Toth records a number of striking similarities between "The Story of an Hour" and the death of Chopin's father, probably the most important event in her childhood. Chopin grew up in St. Louis, the daughter of Eliza and Thomas O'Flaherty, a wealthy businessman. O'Flaherty was one of the prominent men invited to ride the first train across the newly built Gasconade Bridge to Jefferson City, Missouri, on 1 November 1855. When the bridge collapsed, he was among those killed. Eliza O'Flaherty inherited a large estate. She never remarried, so she retained legal control over her property and her children (if she had remarried, her husband would have had control over both). Toth points out some additional similarities as well. Like Louise Mallard, Eliza O'Flaherty had a sister named Josephine. "Louise" sounds like "Eleeza," the French pronunciation of "Eliza" (10). In Toth's earlier biography of Chopin, she provides another link to this story. Letters and other papers belonging to Kate and her childhood friend Kitty Garesché describe their pleasure in climbing the tall trees in the garden of

Kate's St. Louis home. Toth concludes that Louise Mallard's "first image of freedom," the tops of the trees, is drawn from a happy memory of the author's childhood (*Kate Chopin* 43).

Eliza O'Flaherty's story is quite different from that of Louise Mallard, of course, and Toth writes that Chopin had to disguise her mother's story to make it publishable: "A story in which an unhappy wife is suddenly widowed, becomes rich, and lives happily ever after . . . would have been much too radical, far too threatening, in the 1890s" (*Unveiling* 10). Other documents suggest that the story may reflect more complicated feelings on Chopin's part. According to Seyersted, Chopin wrote "The Story of an Hour" on 19 April 1894, when the many favorable reviews of *Bayou Folk* began to appear and make her "national fame . . . an acknowledged fact" (57-58). By that time she had been a widow for a dozen years as well. It is clear from any biography of Chopin that her own marriage was not happy and that she was eager to be recognized as a writer. In light of those facts, then, a portion of a diary entry for 22 May 1894 is rather surprising:

> If it were possible for my husband and my mother to come back to earth, I feel that I would
> unhesitatingly give up every thing that has come into my life since they left it and join my
> existence again with theirs. To do that I would have to forget the past ten years of my growth—
> my real growth. But I would take back a little wisdom with me; it would be the spirit of perfect
> acquiescence. (qtd. in Seyersted 58–59)

The attitude expressed here is quite different from that expressed in "The Story of an Hour," written only a month earlier: "What could love, the unsolved mystery, count for in the face of this possession of self-assertion which she suddenly recognized as the strongest impulse of her being!" (78). The diary entry shows something of Chopin's own ambivalence. She recognizes growth and obviously values it highly; at the same time, though, she values "perfect acquiescence" (submission) as "wisdom."

It is important to recognize the ambivalence expressed in the diary and, I believe, in the short story as well. It does not lessen Chopin's criticism of the condition of women—clearly, something is wrong in the Mallard household, even if Louise Mallard seems to be recognizing it only at this moment. At the same time, though, the recognition that this joy might be "monstrous," that it might even kill, prevents the story from being simplistic. The question Mrs. Mallard dismisses is not so trivial after all. Instead, Chopin's story asks readers to consider the complexities of the relationships between men and women and consider the consequences for both parties when one attempts to impose his or her will on the other.

Works Cited

Chopin, Kate. "The Story of an Hour." *A Vocation and a Voice*. Ed. Emily Toth. New York: Penguin, 1991.

    76–79. Print.

Ewell, Barbara C. *Kate Chopin*. New York: Ungar, 1986. Print.

Lanser, Susan Sniader. *The Narrative Act: Point of View in Prose Fiction*. Princeton: Princeton UP, 1991.

    Print.

Seyersted, Per. *Kate Chopin: A Critical Biography*. Baton Rouge: Louisiana State UP, 1969. Print.

Toth, Emily. *Kate Chopin*. New York: Morrow, 1990. Print.

---. *Unveiling Kate Chopin*. Jackson: UP of Mississippi, 1999. Print.

Welter, Barbara. "The Cult of True Womanhood: 1820–1860." *American Quarterly* 18 (1966): 151–74.

    JSTOR. Web. 30 Apr. 2010.

James Kebler

Professor Jericho

African American Studies 100

12 May 2009

John P. Parker: Freeman, Underground Railroad Conductor, Businessman, Inventor

Although John P. Parker (1827-1900) is not well known, he is certainly among those African

Americans of the past whose accomplishments should be remembered. By any standard, Parker led an

extraordinary life. Born into slavery, he purchased his own freedom while still a teenager, then went on

to assist approximately a thousand fugitives escaping slavery, frequently risking his life to do so. In

addition, he was an inventor and a successful businessman as well. His achievements in any one of those

areas are impressive; together, they are truly remarkable.

Most of the details of Parker's early life would have been forgotten completely if not for the work

of a journalist who interviewed him in the 1880s. Frank M. Gregg was conducting research into stories

about the Underground Railroad, the process by which slaves were assisted in escaping from the South.

Gregg had grown up in Ripley, Ohio, which had been an important "terminal" on the Underground

Railroad, and he returned there to speak with people who remembered those days. He was soon directed

to Parker by the children of several of the well-known white Abolitionists of the town. He was already

acquainted with Parker, describing him as "a man who rarely talked, never bragged," but he was not

aware of Parker's involvement in helping slaves escaping from the South (qtd. in Parker 19). Astonished

at what he learned, Gregg spent the night talking and taking notes. He put those notes into a rough

draft but never published the manuscript, which was eventually deposited at Duke University. It was

finally published in 1996, more than a century after it was written (Sprague 15-16).

Parker was born in Norfolk, Virginia, to a white father and a slave mother. At the age of eight he

was sold and walked in chains to Richmond. In the account he gave to Gregg, Parker recalled that the

old man he was chained to was kind to him and that he later saw the old man beaten to death. Parker

tried to conceal his hatred of slavery, but "it rankled and festered," so that he became "obstinate and hateful." As a result, Parker was soon sold again, this time marching in a slave caravan from Richmond to Mobile, Alabama, a journey of well over eight hundred miles. Parker told Gregg of several incidents on this long journey in which he also acted out his anger "like a mad bull hitting out in every direction against my enemies" (Parker 26-27).

In Mobile, he became a servant in the household of a physician, where he seems to have been treated unusually well, making friends with the doctor's sons, who secretly taught him to read and write. When he was 16, he was apprenticed to a plasterer, where he was beaten so seriously that he had to be hospitalized. Parker fled the hospital and made his way to New Orleans, where he was captured and eventually returned to the doctor in Mobile.

Parker told Gregg that the doctor continued to treat him well, not only not punishing him for his escape but placing him in an iron foundry owned by a friend so that he could learn a trade. Parker quickly became very skillful but was, he admitted, "always in trouble and could not keep a job" (66). His success created envy among his fellow workers, and he squandered his earnings, which the doctor had allowed him to keep. Parker was soon involved in fights and sent to a foundry in New Orleans, where he was quickly dismissed as well. Knowing that on his present course "the cotton fields of Alabama would see [his] finish," Parker resolved to gain his freedom (65). He finally persuaded one of the doctor's patients, a Mrs. Ryder, to purchase his freedom and let him repay her over two years. "At this time I was 18," Parker recalled, "strong as an ox, and working like a steam engine, under high pressure" (67). Despite several serious setbacks, Parker was able to repay Mrs. Ryder within eighteen months, received his freedom papers, and requested a "passport" to Indiana, where he intended to work in the iron foundries (68).

Parker went to Indiana in 1845 but seems to have relocated in Ohio very soon, since he told Gregg that he was working as an iron molder in Cincinnati when his first encounter with a runaway slave took place in that same year (Parker 90). Located on the Ohio River, the southern boundary of a free state, Cincinnati was an important "station" on the Underground Railroad, and many escaping slaves passed through the city on their way to Canada. Parker, who was to become an important "conductor" in this operation, said that he entered into the enterprise unwillingly, being persuaded by a barber with whom he was sharing lodgings to help him assist two young women in escaping. To do so, they went to the nearby town of Ripley, which was also on the Ohio River and another important station on the Underground Railroad.[1]

Parker's determination and resourcefulness are evident in his detailed account of that first venture (91-96). Despite the danger and several near disasters (beginning with the barber's decision to abandon the effort), Parker said that the experience "prompted" his relocation to Ripley, a thriving city where there was an iron foundry. First, though, he moved with his wife (he had married in 1848) to Beechwood Factory, Ohio, where he opened a general store. After moving to Ripley in 1850, he worked as an iron molder and by 1854 had established his own business, the Phoenix Foundry (Sprague 8). At the same time his business was prospering, he continued secretly to help slaves escape the South.

Parker's account of his activities often downplays his own bravery, but it is clear that he was aggressive in the rescue attempts, often venturing onto slave owners' properties to lead slaves to the Ohio River and cross with them. An especially memorable example of his determination and courage (bordering on recklessness) occurred when a white man who worked in Parker's foundry accused Parker of helping fugitives and dared him to steal his father's slaves. Parker denied his involvement, but that same night he slipped into Kentucky to make contact with the people he would soon persuade to go with him to freedom. The rescue itself proved unusually complicated, causing Parker to return a number of times and finally requiring him to steal the infant child of the slaves from the bedroom of the sleeping owner, who evidently anticipated the attempt and was armed (Parker 105-07). The success of this particular rescue led authorities in Kentucky to post a reward of $1000 for him "dead or alive"(Parker 127). Clearly, Parker was, as he was later characterized, "a bold, perfectly fearless man, who was not contented to ferry the slaves who came to the river, but invaded the enemy's country and led his people out of bondage" (Ripley Sesquicentennial 26). Additionally, after the Union army began accepting African American soldiers in 1863, Parker recruited for the 27th Regiment, U.S. Colored Troops, and has been credited with the majority of enlistments for that regiment, mostly from Kentucky (Levstik 481).

It is uncertain exactly how many Parker led to freedom. In the 1890s Wilbur Henry Siebert, an Ohio historian, interviewed W. R. Campbell (son of a prominent Ripley Abolitionist), who told him that Parker was "the direct means of plucking over 1,000 slaves from bondage" (78). According to J. Blaine Hudson, Parker estimated that he rowed an average of one fugitive across the river every week and sent "another" 300 or more to the Union army (152). Using that figure, even a conservative estimate would be that Parker made over 725 weekly trips across the Ohio between 1850 (the year he moved to Ripley) and the end of the Civil War in 1865. Parker himself gave Gregg two different numbers. For a time he kept a detailed record of the people he assisted, but following the passage of the Fugitive Slave Law in 1850, which imposed severe penalties for anyone helping slaves escape, he burned the list, which then contained 315 names (100). At another point he told Gregg that he had assisted 440 people on their way to Canada, again mentioning the list he had destroyed (127). No matter what the number, Parker repeatedly risked his livelihood and his life on the behalf of others.

While Parker was intent on rescuing others from slavery, he was not neglecting his growing business. By 1859, the Phoenix Foundry was producing castings for a variety of farm and industrial equipment; the business did well during the Civil War, and in 1866 he built a machine shop near the foundry (Ripley Sesquicentennial 36). An article in an 1869 issue of the Little Rock *Arkansas Freeman* quoted Parker as saying that he produced engines varying from ten to twenty-five horsepower, Dorsey's reaper and mower, and a sugar mill ("which has thus far given universal satisfaction") and that he intended to add a line of steel plows later in the year (qtd. in Sprague 10). By 1868, Parker's business and property were estimated to be worth between $8,000 and $10,000, and by 1882, that net worth was estimated to be about double, between $15,000 and $20,000 (Sprague 10). According to Edith M. Gaines, Parker had up to twenty-five employees during the 1870s and 1880s (31). Parker's business ventures were thus a significant part of the local economy during and after the Civil War, and when Ripley celebrated its sesquicentennial in 1962, the commemorative book produced for the occasion stated that no one of the time "was more prominently identified with the prosperity of the town than John Parker" (Ripley Sesquicentennial 92).

The significance of that achievement and its continuing recognition is even greater when Parker's race is considered. Despite what historian Louis Weeks calls the "massive inequities of Ohio's legal and social regulations," Parker succeeded in becoming "a reputable businessman and prominent citizen of

Ripley" (162). There is evidence that Parker himself saw his achievements in context of race and that he believed participation in business and manufacturing was an effective pathway to full equality. In fact, Parker appears to have seen this as a more effective pathway than political lobbying, for the *Arkansas Freeman* article also quotes him as saying that "a plow made by a black man, tells for us more than a hundred first class speeches" (qtd. in Sprague 10).

This comment gives additional significance to Parker's achievement in yet another field. He was a successful inventor and held at least three patents: one issued in 1884 for a follower screw used in a tobacco press (U.S. Patent No. 304,552), another in the following year for a portable tobacco press (U.S. Patent No. 318,215), and a third in 1890 for a "soil pulverizer" (U.S. Patent No. 442,538) (Genheimer). According to W. E. B. Dubois, a total of only 77 patents had been issued to African Americans by 1886, and only 55 African Americans held more than one patent in 1901 (qtd. in Weeks 155). As an early holder of multiple patents, then, Parker is a distinguished figure.

As an inventor, businessman, Underground Railroad conductor, and determined seeker of freedom, Parker certainly deserved to be remembered. Although conditions have changed radically since the time he lived, his story can inspire future generations.

Note

1. One story associates Ripley with the origin of the term Underground Railroad. When Tice Davids escaped across the Ohio River in 1831, his owner looked for him in Ripley and, unable to locate him, is supposed to have said that Davids "must have gone off on an underground railroad" (Blight 3).

Works Cited

Blight, David W. "The Underground Railroad in History and Memory." Introduction. *Passages to Freedom: The Underground Railroad in History and Memory*. Ed. Blight. Washington: Smithsonian, 2004. 1-10. Print.

Gaines, Edith M. *Freedom Light: Underground Railroad Stories from Ripley, Ohio*. Cleveland: New Day, 1991. Print.

Genheimer, Bob. "Underground at the Underground Railroad: Testing at John P. Parker's House and Foundry Site in Ripley, Ohio." *Current Research in Ohio Archaeology* 15 Oct. 2001. Web. 7 May 2009.

Hudson, J. Blaine. *Fugitive Slaves and the Underground Railroad in the Kentucky Borderland*. Jefferson: McFarland, 2002. Print.

Levstik, Frank R. "Parker, John P." *Dictionary of American Negro Biography*. Ed. Rayford W. Logan and Michael R. Winston. New York: Norton, 1982. 480-81. Print.

Parker, John P. *His Promised Land: The Autobiography of John P. Parker, Former Slave and Conductor on the Underground Railroad*. Ed. Stuart Seely Sprague. New York: Norton, 1996. Print.

Ripley Sesquicentennial Historical Committee. *Ripley, Ohio: Its History and Families*. N.p.: n.d. Print.

Siebert, Wilbur Henry. *The Mysteries of Ohio's Underground Railroads*. Columbus: Long's, 1951. Print.

Sprague, Stuart Seely. Preface. *His Promised Land: The Autobiography of John P. Parker, Former Slave and Conductor on the Underground Railroad*, by John P. Parker. Ed. Sprague. New York: Norton, 1996. 7-16. Print.

Weeks, Louis. "John P. Parker: Black Abolitionist Entrepreneur, 1827-1900." *Ohio History* 80 (1971): 155-62. Web. 30 Apr. 2009.

Checklist for Documenting a Paper MLA Style: Works Cited and In-Text Citation

☑ I can identify the category of every work that I will cite—such as whether it is a book, a journal with continuous pagination, an online newspaper, and so on.

☑ I know how to locate each kind of source within this chapter.

☑ I can explain each element of the citation forms I have used—such as author, title, volume number, issue number, publication date, access date, and so on.

☑ I have verified that every piece of borrowed information has a parenthetical citation identifying the source.

☑ I have not repeated any information from my text unnecessarily in the parenthetical citations.

☑ I have verified that every parenthetical citation has a corresponding entry on the Works Cited page.

Exercise L

Listing Sources in Works Cited

Use the following information to assemble a Works Cited page for a paper about Oscar Wilde. In some cases, you have been given more information than is needed.

1. author: Douglas Murray
   title of book: Bosie
   subtitle of book: A Biography of Lord Alfred Douglas
   publisher: Hyperion
   place: New York
   date: 2000

2. author: Richard Ellmann
   title of book: Oscar Wilde
   publisher: Alfred A. Knopf
   place: New York
   date: 1988

3. author: Lord Alfred Douglas
   title of book: The Collected Poems of Lord Alfred Douglas
   publisher: AMS
   place: New York
   date: 1976
   other information: originally published by Martin Secker (London, 1919)

4. author: Gary Schmidgall
   title of book: The Stranger Wilde
   subtitle of book: Interpreting Oscar
   publisher: Dutton
   place: New York
   date: 1994

5. author: Richard Jenkyns
   title of article: Leprous Spawn
   online journal: The New Republic
   retrieval information: Academic Search Complete database
   date of issue: August 28, 2000
   date of posting: August 24, 2000
   date of access: April 12, 2008
   other information: review of Douglas Murray's *Bosie:
                          A Biography of Lord Alfred Douglas* (item 1 above)

6. author: Oscar Wilde
    title of book: Poems
    online publisher: Bartleby.com
    URL: http://www.bartleby.com/143/
    date of posting: July 1999
    date of access: April 12, 2008
    additional information: originally published by Robert Brothers (Boston, 1881)

7. author: Oscar Wilde
    title of poem: Impression: Le Reveillon
    title of book: Poems
    online publisher: Bartleby.com
    URL: http://www.bartleby.com/143/53.html
    date of posting: July 1999
    date of access: April 12, 2008
    additional information: originally published by Robert Brothers (Boston, 1881)

8. author: Julia Wood
    title: The Bosie Web Site
    date of posting: October 1998
    date of access: October 23, 2003
    URL: http://members.tripod.com/~MarkSweeney/

9. title of Web site: The Trials of Oscar Wilde
    name of editor: Douglas O. Linder
    date of latest update: January 14, 2000
    date of access: April 12, 2008
    URL: http://www.law.umkc.edu/faculty/projects/ftrials/wilde/wilde.htm

10. author: Nancy Jane Tyson
     title of essay: Caliban in a Glass
     subtitle of essay: Autoscopic Vision in *The Picture of Dorian Gray*
     title of anthology: The Haunted Mind
     subtitle of anthology: The Supernatural in Victorian Literature
     pages: 101–121
     editors of anthology: Elton E. Smith and Robert Haas
     place: Lanham, MD
     publisher: Scarecrow Press
     date: 1999

11. author: James Raeside
     title of article: The Spirit Is Willing But the Flesh Is Strong
     subtitle of article: Mishima Yukio's Kinjiki and Oscar Wilde
     journal: Comparative Literature Studies
     volume: 36
     issue: 1
     date: 1999
     pages: 1–23
     additional information: pagination is continuous throughout the volume in this journal

Documenting a Paper APA Style

Of composition there are different methods.

"Alexander Pope," *Lives of the Poets*

In research papers that you write for your composition and literature classes, you will probably be asked to follow MLA style. In other disciplines, other styles are preferred. There is, in fact, no field in which procedures are completely uniform. While gathering material for your paper, you will find bibliographic entries and notes in diverse styles, which you should convert to the style you are using. The system you are most likely to encounter is APA style, which is described in the *Publication Manual of the American Psychological Association,* 5th ed. (Washington: APA, 2001). With some variations, APA style is used in education, nursing, and in most of the social sciences.

As in MLA style, APA documentation has a twofold purpose: to list all of the sources used in a paper and to identify the specific location of each item of borrowed material. Although the purposes are the same, the means of accomplishing them differ considerably.

The style of documentation found in the *Publication Manual* was developed for use by professionals in the field of psychology, and for that reason it may present particular challenges for undergraduate students. Whereas students are likely to draw a good deal of specific information from secondary sources, research psychologists are much more likely to cite only the overall findings of a study, often grouping similar studies in a single parenthetical reference. Likewise, the range of acceptable secondary sources is much narrower—it would be very unusual, for instance, to find an advertisement or a cartoon cited by one of these researchers. If you cannot find the type of source you are using in the following list or in the APA manual itself, consult your instructor to work out the most appropriate way of handling that source.

Listing References

In APA style the sources used in a paper are listed alphabetically on a separate page headed with the word *References*. It follows the final page of the text. Many of the examples that follow are keyed to the bibliographic examples in Chapter 9.

Examples: Books

Standard Book (1)

Differences from MLA style are enumerated following the examples.

Grolnick, W. S. (2003). *The psychology of parental control: How well-meant parenting backfires*. Mahwah, NJ:

Lawrence Erlbaum.

Holmes-Eber, P. (2003). *Daughters of Tunis: Women, family, and networks in a Muslim city*. Boulder, CO:

Westview.

1. Authors' given names are reduced to initials. The names of all authors are inverted, and the last two names are joined by an ampersand (&) rather than by the word *and*.
2. The date of publication is placed in parentheses immediately after the author's name.
3. Only proper nouns and the first word of a title and subtitle are capitalized.
4. The place of publication and the publisher are separated by a colon. Except for major cities, APA style uses the two-letter postal abbreviation to identify the state in which the publisher is located.
5. Publishers' names are shortened by the omission of abbreviations like *Co.* or *Inc.*, but they are given more fully than in MLA style. Names of university presses are written in full.

Anthology (3)

The listing of an edited collection of pieces by various authors begins with the editor's name followed by (*Ed.*). For the citation of one selection, see the Selection in an Anthology entry later in this chapter.

Phillips, C. (Ed.). (1997). *The right set: The Faber book of tennis*. New York: Faber.

Corporate Author (7)

When the author and the publisher are identical, the word *Author* designates the publisher. The APA manual uses the term *Group author* for such a work.

National Osteoporosis Foundation. (1996). *How strong are your bones?* Washington, DC: Author.

Multiple Works by the Same Author/Editor (25)

Several works by the same author are arranged in the order of publication date, starting with the earliest.

Patronek, G. J. (1999). Hoarding of animals: An underrecognized public health problem in a difficult-to-

study population. *Public Health Reports, 114*(1), 81-87.

Patronek, G. J. (2001, May-June). The problem of animal hoarding. *Municipal Lawyer,* 6-9, 19.

Two works by the same author published in the same year are arranged alphabetically with a lowercase letter added after the year to distinguish between them.

Gould, S. J. (2001a). The evolutionary definition of selective agency, validation of the theory of hierarchical

selection, and fallacy of the selfish gene. In R. S. Singh, C. B. Krimbas, D. B. Paul, & J. Beatty (Eds.),

Thinking about evolution: Historical, philosophical, and political perspectives (pp. 208-234). New York:

Cambridge University Press.

Gould, S. J. (2001b). The interrelationship of speciation and punctuated equilibrium. In J. B. C. Jackson, S.

Lidgard, & F. K. McKinney (Eds.), *Evolutionary patterns: Growth, form, and tempo in the fossil record*

(pp. 196-220). Chicago: University of Chicago Press.

Unpublished Dissertation (8)

Taylor, N. M. (2001). *"Frontiers of freedom": The African American experience in Cincinnati, 1802-1862.*

Unpublished doctoral dissertation, Duke University.

Edition (9)

Information pertaining to the title (e.g., *Rev. ed.*) is enclosed in parentheses and placed after the title with no intervening punctuation.

Gilderhus, M. T. (2003). *History and historians: A historiographical introduction* (5th ed.). Upper Saddle

River, NJ: Prentice-Hall.

Editor (10)

Shields, C. (Ed.). (2003). *The Blackwell guide to ancient philosophy*. Malden, MA: Blackwell.

Government Publication (11)

If there is no author, give the name of the specific department, office, or agency that produced the report; give a higher department only if the office producing the report is not well known. Provide any identifying number as well.

Gabrel, C. S. (2000). *Characteristics of elderly nursing home current residents and discharges: Data from the*

1997 National Nursing Home Survey (DHHS Publication No. PHS 2000-1250).

U.S. Department of Education. (1997). *Projections of education statistics to 2007* (Report No. NCES

97-382). Washington, DC: U.S. Government Printing Office.

Multiple Authors/Editors (15, 33)

All authors (up to six) are listed in References, the last two being joined by an ampersand (&). For more than six authors, list the first six and use et al. to represent the others (the first example has eight authors). In the text, if there are three, four, or five authors, all of them are named in the first citation, and the first author's name plus *et al.* is used thereafter. For six or more authors, the first author's name plus *et al.* is used in every citation.

Arluke, A., Frost, R., Steketee, G., Patronek, G., Luke, C., Messner, E., et al. (2002). Press reports of animal

hoarding. *Society and Animals, 10*(2), 113–115.

Axia, V. D., & Weisner, T. S. (2003). Infant stress reactivity and home cultural ecology of Italian infants and

families. *Infant Behavior and Development, 25,* 255–268.

Multivolume Work (16)

Inclusive dates of publication follow the author's name. The number of volumes in parentheses follows the title with no intervening punctuation. The second example illustrates how to cite a single volume with an individual title.

Proust, M. (1992). *In search of lost time: Vol. 2. Within a budding grove* (C. K. Scott Moncrieff & T.

Kilmartin, Trans.; rev. D. J. Enright). New York: Random House. (Original work published 1919)

Rampersad, A. (1986–1988). *The life of Langston Hughes* (Vols. 1-2). New York: Oxford University Press.

Reference Work (20)

If an entire reference work is cited, the lead editors are named, and the editorial staff is indicated by *et al.* If one article is cited, the editors are omitted but the volume and page are included. Publication data are given for all reference works.

Chernow, H. A., & Vallasi, G. A. (Eds.). (1993). *The Columbia encyclopedia* (15th ed.). New York: Columbia

University Press.

Miller, A. W. (1995). Herod Agrippa I. In *Encyclopedia americana* (Vol. 14, p. 145). Danbury, CT: Grolier

Encyclopedia.

Selection in an Anthology (22)

Infante, G. C. (1999). The doors open at three. In S. Brown & J. Wickham (Eds.), *The Oxford book of*

Caribbean stories (pp. 80-90). New York: Oxford University Press.

Translation (24, 37)

The name of a translator in parentheses follows the title with no intervening punctuation. The translator's name is not inverted, and the abbreviation *Trans.* is used.

Flahault, F. (2003). *Malice* (L. Heron, Trans.). London: Verso.

Examples: Periodicals

Journal (26)

Differences from MLA style are enumerated following the examples.

Dussere, E. (2003). Subversion in the swamp: Pogo and the folk in the McCarthy era. *Journal of American*

Culture, 26(2), 134-141.

Nicolaisen, P. (2003). Thomas Jefferson, Sally Hemmings, and the question of race: An ongoing debate.

Journal of American Studies, 37, 99-118.

1. The author and date are positioned the same as for a book.
2. The title of an article is not enclosed in quotation marks; only proper nouns or proper adjectives and the first word of a title or subtitle are capitalized.
3. Both the volume number and the title of a journal are italicized.
4. If a journal is paginated separately in each issue (see Dussere example), the issue number is given in parentheses after the volume number, with no intervening space.

Magazine (27)

Differences from MLA style are enumerated following the examples.

Masland, T. (2003, July 14). Wars without end. *Newsweek, 142*, 28-31.

Orleans, S. (2002, February 18-25). The lady and the tigers. *The New Yorker,* pp. 95-96, 98-102.

1. The issue date (year first) follows the author's name.
2. Months are spelled out, and military style is not used for dates (February 24, not 24 Feb.).
3. A volume number is included. If there is no volume number, the abbreviations *p.* and *pp.* are used for pages. Inclusive pages are given, including all pages for discontinuous pagination (see Orleans example).

Newspaper (34)

An identifying term like *Editorial* is enclosed in brackets. The abbreviations *p.* and *pp.* are used for pages.

A decade of denial. (2003, July 15). *USA Today,* p. 12A.

Schlesinger, A., Jr. (2003, June 28). The imperial presidency redux [Editorial]. *The Washington Post,* p. A25.

Review (35)

The work being reviewed is identified in brackets.

Applebaum, A. (2003, July 17). The worst of the terror [Review of the book *Stalin's last crime: The plot*

against Jewish doctors]. *New York Review of Books,* pp. 14-17.

Examples: The Internet and Other Electronic Media

In 2007, the APA issued the *APA Style Guide to Electronic References* (available online from www.apa.org/books/). This new publication further simplified citation forms for documenting electronic and Internet sources. The new forms follow the same general pattern as the equivalent print forms, with retrieval information added. The following examples illustrate some of the most common types of sources. If you need to carry part of a URL or Digital Object Identifier (DOI) onto a subsequent line, you can divide it after a slash or before a period. Note that no period follows the URL or DOI.

Article from an Online Periodical (41)

For an online journal article that has been assigned a DOI, provide the DOI at the end of the reference citation (first example). If there is no DOI, give the full URL (for open-access content—second example) or the URL of the home page of the journal (for content available only to subscribers—third example). If you use the final version of the article and know that the content will not change, no retrieval date is necessary.

Laser, J., Luster, T., & Oshio, T. (2007). Risk and promotive factors related to depressive symptoms among

Japanese youth. *American Journal of Orthopsychiatry* 77, 523-533. doi: 10.1037/0002-9432.77.4.523

Mitka, M. (2008). New evidence-based guidelines focus on treatment of children with asthma. JAMA:

Journal of the American Medical Association 299(10), 1122-1123. Retrieved from http://jama

.ama-assn.org/cgi/content/full/299/10/1122

Pear, R. (2008, March 23). Gap in life expectancy widens for nation. *The New York Times*. Retrieved from

http://www.nytimes.com

Multipage Internet Document

To cite an entire Web site (which the *APA Publication Manual* refers to as an *Internet document*), use the publishing organization as the author, provide the most recent date on the site's main page, and provide the retrieval date along with the URL of the main page of the document (first example). To cite only a portion of a document with a separate URL, include the title of that section and the URL for that specific section (second example). If no author or sponsoring organization is identified, begin with the title of the document (third example); if no date is provided, use *n.d.* (no date) to indicate the omission (third example).

Benton Foundation. (2005). *Citizen's guide to the public interest: Obligations of digital television broadcasters.*

Retrieved March 25, 2008, from http://www.benton.org/pioguide/index.html

Benton Foundation. (2005). Ensuring that television serves the full spectrum of America. In *Citizen's guide*

to the public interest: Obligations of digital television broadcasters. Retrieved March 25, 2008, from

http://www.benton.org/pioguide/diversity.html

Bschool.com (n.d.). Retrieved March 25, 2008, from http://www.bschool.com/

Message Posted to a Newsgroup, Online Forum, or Electronic Mailing List

Matheson, A. (2003, April 29). Re: Source for paradigm activities [Msg. 9506]. Message posted to

gopher://lists.Princeton.EDU:70/0R113215-114504-/aeelist/logs/log9506

Following the name of the author and the date of the posting, provide the subject line of the posting and, if given, the number of the message. After the descriptive phrase *Message posted to,* supply the retrieval information. Remember, however, that individual private e-mail messages would be cited parenthetically as personal communication and not included in the References at the end of the paper.

E-Mail Communications (43)

E-mail should be cited parenthetically within the text as personal communications but not included in the reference list. The in-text citation would be given in this form:

> M. Pearce (personal communication, December 5, 2008) suggested . . .

In-Text Citation

Like MLA, APA uses parenthetical citations in the body of the paper to indicate the source of borrowed material. In APA, an author's surname and the publication date are the basic elements. Researchers in psychology and the social sciences cite entire works more often than single pages, and direct quotation is relatively rare. However, page numbers are needed whenever you refer to a specific portion of a document, whether you are quoting, paraphrasing, or summarizing. Use the abbreviation *p.* or *pp.* to indicate the page(s) on which the borrowed information appears.

The elements of a citation are separated by commas. Abbreviations like *p., pp., vol., para.,* and *chap.* are used when necessary. A typical citation consists of the author's last name and the year of publication.

> One analysis of Civil War soldiers North and South (McPherson, 2001) indicates that . . .

If the author's name is part of the text, only the year is cited parenthetically.

> McPherson (2001) finds that . . .

If an author is cited more than once in the same paragraph, the date is necessary only in the first citation.

If a direct quotation is used, the page reference is the third element in the citation.

> "Actors in silent movies had no specific identity; they lived the emotional lives their audiences
>
> chose to project onto them" (Eyman, 1997, p. 301).

Note how the placement of these pieces of information varies when the attribution and quotation are integrated with the writer's own words.

> Eyman (1997) has suggested that performers in silent films "had no specific identity" apart from
>
> those projected by their viewers (p. 301).

You may also identify larger portions of text.

> One study (Eyman, 1997, chap. 2) starts from an unusual premise . . .

The names of multiple authors are joined with an ampersand (&) rather than the word *and* in parenthetical citations—but not in the body of the paper.

Although one research team (Strauss & Howe, 1997) was able to obtain similar results, . . .

Strauss and Howe (1997) reached a similar . . .

If no author is given, a shortened form of the title with the date is used. Note that quotation marks and capitals are used with the title.

A recent editorial ("Health Care Heavies," 1997) opposed the plan . . .

In citing something from an online source, use the name of the author (if available) or a shortened title and date just as for a print source. If the source shows page numbers, the citation would look just like it would for a print source.

(Johnson & Garcia, 2004, p. 14)

If the paragraphs are numbered, use those numbers when quoting directly. Use the ¶ symbol if it is available in the word processing program you are using; otherwise, use the abbreviation *para.*

(Montgomery, 2003, ¶ 17)

(Montgomery, 2003, para. 17)

In some cases, other simple descriptions of the location can be provided.

(Li, 2001, Conclusion section, para. 1)

If no identifying number is provided or a description is impractical, however, you can omit this final element of the citation. Most browsers will allow readers to search for the quoted material.

Personal letters, telephone calls, e-mail messages, and other material that cannot be recovered by a reader are cited as personal communication in the text but are not listed in References.

J. R. Miller (personal communication, January 8, 2008) said that . . .

Sample Paper: APA Style

Some differences between MLA and APA styles of page layout can be observed in the sample paper that follows. See Figure 10.1 for a checklist of these.

Melissa Lofts decided to use her research project to answer a question of great personal importance. She was already planning to breastfeed the child she was expecting but was uncertain how long she should do so. She quickly learned the recommendations of professional healthcare agencies and was struck by the health advantages of breastfeeding not only to the child but to the mother as well. Because the latter was the most surprising thing she learned, she decided to use that information to help persuade mothers to follow those recommendations.

- There is always a title page. It includes the header and page number, a running head, the title, and the author's name and affiliation (for students, usually the class name and number). The running head is an abbreviated form of the title that would be used at the top of each page if the paper were published. Some instructors will ask you to omit it, but it has been included here to illustrate all the features of APA style.
- Page numbering begins with the title page, and the title page itself is numbered.
- The abstract appears on a separate page, which is numbered page 2. The abstract should be typed as a single paragraph in block style (without indentation). It should be no more than 120 words.
- Instead of your last name, use the first two or three words of the title with the page number as a page header. The shortened title and the page number are separated by five spaces. This header appears on every page, including the title page.
- Quotations of forty or more words (about four lines) are indented half an inch from the left margin.
- If notes are used, include them on a separate page headed *Footnotes*. (If the paper were published, these notes would be set as footnotes, hence the seemingly inappropriate heading.)

FIGURE 10.1 APA page layout

1   The header appears on every page of the paper, including the title page. It consists of the first few words of the title and the page number. There are five spaces between the short title and the page number.

2   The running head is the shortened title that will appear at the top of the page in a journal when this paper is published. It appears on the first line of the title page (and nowhere else in the paper) and is capitalized as shown here. For an undergraduate class, you may not need to include a running head. Ask your instructor to be sure.

3   The endorsement is centered approximately halfway down the title page. It consists of the title, the name of the author, and the author's institutional affiliation. The key words of the title are capitalized, but it does not use quotation marks, italics, underlining, or boldface font. The name of the author appears on the next line. Because APA is designed for publication by professionals in psychology and other fields, the institution where the writer is employed appears as the third line of the endorsement. For a class, you may be asked to include the name of the class, the date, or other information. Ask your instructor to be sure you know exactly what information he or she wants.

1 Benefits of Breastfeeding   1

2 Running head: BREASTFEEDING BENEFITS MOTHERS

3 The Benefits of Breastfeeding for Mothers

Melissa Lofts

Megacity Community College

4 The word *Abstract* is centered at the top of the second page.

5 The abstract—a short, descriptive summary of the content of the paper—is provided in block paragraph format (no indentation). In APA the abstract is limited to 120 words.

4 Abstract

5 In addition to the well-documented benefits to infants who are breastfed, there is evidence that nursing has a positive impact on the mother's health as well. Lactating provides immediate benefits while women are recovering from childbearing. Furthermore, many experts agree that breastfeeding decreases the likelihood of acquiring some of the most serious health risks to women: cancer, osteoporosis, and heart disease.

6   The title is centered on the first line of the third page.

7   The introduction draws on three reputable agencies to establish the importance of breastfeeding. Each reference to these corporate authors is followed by the date of publication.

8   To establish the need to encourage mothers to breastfeed longer, this paragraph draws on a survey conducted by the CDC and posted online. Because the information appears online, no page numbers are available for the parenthetical citations.

9   This paragraph makes the transition to the main focus of the paper—the benefits to mothers.

6 The Benefits of Breastfeeding for Mothers

7 Human milk is widely known to be the best form of nutrition for babies, as it is produced specifically for human infants and adjusts to meet their changing needs. The American Academy of Family Physicians (2001) and American Academy of Pediatrics (2005) agree that breastfeeding should be done exclusively for the first six months of life and be continued for at least the first year and as long as mutually desired by mother and child. The World Health Organization (2003) has also recognized the importance of breastfeeding, especially during the first six months of a child's life, and has made it a priority in its attempts to address nutrition worldwide.

8 Although the majority of mothers breastfeed their newborns immediately after birth, many of them do not continue for as long as these organizations recommend. A survey conducted by the Centers for Disease Control and Prevention (2007) found that mothers of 73.8% of the children born in 2004 initially breastfed their children. By the time infants reached the six-month mark, however, the number dropped to 42.5%, and only 20.9% of mothers were still nursing by the baby's first birthday. These numbers reflect only the percentage of babies receiving *some* breast milk with supplementation such as formula. This same study found that only 30.5% were *exclusively* breastfed at three months, with a mere 11.3% receiving only their mother's milk at six months.

9 The benefits infants receive from breastfeeding are well documented, and they provide compelling reasons for urging women to follow the recommendations of these organizations whenever possible. In addition, there is evidence that nursing also has a positive impact on the mother's health as well. Lactating provides immediate benefits to the health and well-being of women in helping them recover from childbearing. Furthermore, many experts agree that breastfeeding decreases the likelihood of acquiring some of the most serious health risks to women: cancer, osteoporosis, and heart disease.

After giving birth, many women wonder if their pre-baby bodies will ever return. Breastfeeding will help them get back to their pre-pregnancy size sooner. Most notably, breastfeeding burns calories. Producing milk uses between 200 and 500 calories per day, which is equal to the amount of calories burnt swimming

10 Two sources providing essentially the same information are combined in a single parenthetical citation. Note that both sources are paginated, so numbers can be provided to direct readers to specific information.

11 The names of the joint authors appear in the body of the text and are joined with the word *and* rather than an ampersand. Note that the paraphrased information can be located on a specific page in the source, so a page number is provided.

12 The two sources by Dermer are easily distinguished by the date of publication. A page number is provided for the specific information taken from the print source.

13 Sources providing the same information are combined in a parenthetical reference.

14 The ellipsis indicates that words have been omitted from the quotation; the word in square brackets has been added to the quotation.

15 Note the placement of the page reference following the end of the quotation. APA style would also allow the writer to combine the page number with the year in a single parenthesis, like this:

Sears and Sears (2000, p. 11) note a reduction in the risk of breast cancer "by as much as 25% . . . ."

30 laps or biking uphill for one hour daily (Dermer 2001). The baby's suckling itself can be credited with a

smaller waistline. Nursing stimulates the release of the hormone oxytocin, which not only triggers a

mother's milk ejection reflex but causes the uterus to contract and shrink back to the nonpregnant

10,11 condition (American Academy of Pediatrics, 2005, p. 496; Heinig & Dewey, 1997, p. 38). Sears and Sears

(2000) refer to a study that indicates new mothers who nurse have more fat loss and a larger decrease in

hip circumference than their formula-feeding counterparts (p. 10).

The contractions caused by oxytocin also lessen uterine bleeding following childbirth, significantly

12 reducing the risk of post-partum hemorrhage (Dermer, 2001). This hormone is produced at every feeding

(Dermer, 1998, p. 428), so continuing to breastfeed will sustain the production of oxytocin. Its continuing

presence has several implications for the woman's health, including a delay in the return of menstruation.

This delay—known as lactational amenorrhea—can benefit the mother in several ways. For one thing,

nursing mothers have a decreased risk of iron-deficiency anemia because milk production uses less iron

13 than menstrual bleeding (American Academy of Family Physicians, 2001; Dermer, 2001). Perhaps the most

obvious result of delayed menstruation is the increased spacing between children, which allows time for

optimal physical recovery of a mother before another child is born (Dermer, 1998, p. 428; Labbok, 2001).

Lactational amenorrhea has important long-term health implications for women as well. Delayed

menstruation is far more than a convenience; it appears to help prevent some of the most life-threatening

cancers afflicting women today. A number of studies suggest that nursing may lower the risk of

pre-menopausal breast cancer, uterine cancer, and ovarian cancer. *The Womanly Art of Breastfeeding*

suggests that "extended periods of lactational amenorrhea may help to explain the lower rates of ovarian,

14 endometrial, and breast cancer . . . [because] the absence of the repeated hormonal ups and downs of

regular menstrual cycles may leave the breasts and reproductive organs less vulnerable to cancer" (La Leche

League, 2004, p. 379).

Additionally, the reduction in cancer rates appears to be greater the longer a woman breastfeeds. Sears

and Sears (2000) note a reduction in the risk of breast cancer "by as much as 25%, depending on how much

15 time the woman spends breastfeeding during her lifetime" (p. 11). Reviewing studies of the correlations

between breastfeeding and reduced incidence of breast cancer, Labbok (2001) concluded that a "a clear and

16 The ellipsis signals that the quotation is an incomplete sentence (as quoted, it appears to be a full sentence).

17 Two types of benefits—effects on blood sugar and cholesterol—are combined as heart health.

18 When the names of the joint authors appear inside the parentheses, they are joined with an ampersand rather than the word *and.*

19 For citing an indirect source in APA, give the author and date of the information you wish to cite (in this case, the study by Altemus et al.) and provide a parenthetical citation for the source you actually use, preceded by the words *as cited in.* The reference list should include only the source you actually used (Dermer, 2001).

consistent protective effect is reflected in nearly all of the analyses of extant data sets." Labbok reached a similar conclusion in reviewing studies of the link between breastfeeding and the reduction of risk for ovarian cancer, noting that the average protective level was 20%.

Other likely health advantages include a decreased risk of osteoporosis. It now appears that, like *drinking* milk, *giving* milk builds stronger bones. Because women lose calcium during lactation, there was a misconception in the medical community that women put themselves at increased risk of osteoporosis (Dermer, 2001). However, according to the American Academy of Family Physicians (2001), "lactation

16 affects calcium metabolism, with increased bone density after weaning . . . ." Benefits appear to extend beyond childbearing years. Sears and Sears (2000) point out that the likelihood of suffering postmenopausal hip fractures and developing osteoporosis is four times greater in women who do not breastfeed (pp. 11-12). There is now a general consensus among healthcare professionals that nursing can actually result in stronger bones and reduced risk of osteoporosis.

Additionally, breastfeeding is shown to lower blood sugar. As a result, women with diabetes typically need less insulin during the time that they nurse. The lower blood sugar coupled with optimal weight loss, therefore, may decrease the risk of diabetes later in life (Dermer, 2001). To those benefits can be added a high level of HDL cholesterol, the good cholesterol, in lactating women. This factor, together with the

17 others, suggests that breastfeeding "may ultimately pay off with a lower risk of heart problems" (Dermer, 2001). While further research is needed into the impact of breastfeeding on diabetes and heart health, there likely is *some* added protection for women.

Finally, the physiological effects of breastfeeding include at least one psychological benefit. The stress, fears, and lack of sleep experienced by a new mother can be overwhelming physically, emotionally and psychologically. Luckily, prolactin, one of the hormones that contributes to milk production, "is known

18 to be one of the body's stress-fighting hormones" (Sears & Sears, 2000, p. 11). Together with oxytocin, the hormone that stimulates the milk-ejection reflex, prolactin "may help to produce the feeling of relaxation that mothers come to associate with nursing sessions" (La Leche League, 2004, p. 375). According to one

19 study, mothers who are nursing have a less intense response to adrenaline (Altemus et al., 1995, as cited in Dermer, 2001).

20 A brief conclusion restates the main point of the paper, stressing the practical application of the ideas discussed.

20   Breastfeeding, then, provides psychological as well as physical benefits to the mother. While the benefits to baby are fairly well known, many people do not realize the extent to which it is advantageous to mothers as well. By carrying out nature's plan, women give their bodies the capability to better ward off many debilitating and, sometimes, fatal diseases. The risks of *not* breastfeeding are too great to overlook. Women should be educated about nursing infants and encouraged to follow the feeding recommendations of reputable health agencies.

21 On a new page, center the word *References* on the first line, then alphabetize the references according to the first word. For more than one entry by the same author or group of authors, arrange the entries chronologically, beginning with the earliest (see the Dermer entries for an illustration).

22 Corporate author; online document; no retrieval date needed for final version of document; URL divided after slash

23 Corporate author; article from journal with continuous pagination; DOI assigned

24 Corporate author; online document; no retrieval date needed for final version of report; URL divided after slash

25 Government report; online document; retrieval date provided because page appears to be subject to change; URL divided after slash

26 Article from journal with continuous pagination; first of two entries by same author, arranged chronologically

27 Article from journal with separate pagination for each issue; online version; second entry by same author, arranged chronologically; no retrieval date provided for final version of article

28 Article from journal with continuous pagination

29 Article from journal with continuous pagination; no retrieval date provided for final version of article; URL provided for home page of journal in which content is available only to subscribers

30 Corporate author; book; edition other than first

31 Two authors; book

32 Corporate author; online document; no retrieval date provided for final version of document; URL divided after slash

21 References

22   American Academy of Family Physicians (2001). Breastfeeding (position paper). Retrieved from http://
www.aafp.org/online/en/home/policy/policies/b/breastfeedingpositionpaper.html

23   American Academy of Pediatrics (2005). Policy statement: Breastfeeding and the use of human milk.
Pediatrics 115, 496-506. doi:10.1542/peds.2004-2491

24   Centers for Disease Control and Prevention (2007). Breastfeeding practices: Results from the National
Immunization Survey. Retrieved from http://www.cdc.gov/breastfeeding/data/NIS_data/
data_2004.htm

25   Department of Health and Human Services, National Women's Health Information Center (2005). Benefits
of breastfeeding. Retrieved November 12, 2007, from http://www.4woman.gov/Breastfeeding/
index.cfm?page=227

26   Dermer, A. (1998). Breastfeeding and women's health. *Journal of Women's Health 7,* 427-434.

27   Dermer, A. (2001). A well-kept secret: Breastfeeding's benefits to mothers. *New Beginnings 18*(4),
124-127. Retrieved from www.lalecheleague.org/NB/NBJulAug01p124.html

28   Heinig, M. J., & Dewey, K. G. (1997). Health effects of breast feeding for mothers: A critical review.
Nutrition Research Reviews 10, 35-56.

29   Labbok, M. H. (2001). Effects of breastfeeding on the mother. *Pediatric Clinics of North America, 48,*
143-158. Retrieved from http://www.pediatric.theclinics.com/

30   La Leche League International (2004). *The womanly art of breastfeeding* (7th ed.). New York: Plume.

31   Sears, M., & Sears, W. (2000). *The breastfeeding book: Everything you need to know about nursing your
child from birth through weaning.* New York: Little Brown and Company.

32   World Health Organization (2003). *Global strategy for infant and young child feeding.* Geneva,
Switzerland: Author. Retrieved from http://www.who.int/nutrition/publications/
gs_infant_feeding_text_eng.pdf

Checklist for Documenting a Paper APA Style

✔ I can identify the category of every work that I will cite—such as whether it is a book, a journal with continuous pagination, an online newspaper, and so on.

✔ I know how to locate each kind of source within this chapter.

✔ I can explain each element of the citation forms I have used—such as author, title, volume number, issue number, publication date, access date, and so on.

✔ I have verified that every piece of borrowed information has a parenthetical citation identifying the source.

✔ I have not repeated any information from my text unnecessarily in the parenthetical citations.

✔ I have verified that every parenthetical citation has a corresponding entry on the References page.

Appendix

Abbreviations and Basic Terms

In the documentation and occasionally in the text of a paper, abbreviations and reference words are acceptable. None should be used that do not save space and the reader's time.

Scholarly Forms

Many Latin forms have virtually disappeared from scholarly writing, but a number of them are included here because you may encounter them in your reading. Latin terms such as *et al.* and *sic* are used so often that they have been assimilated into English and usually are not italicized. A less common term such as *aetatis* should be italicized. Learn and follow the preference of your instructor. Usage varies, but common practice with an abbreviation consisting of all capital letters is not to space between the letters and not to follow the letters with periods (U.S. is an exception). An abbreviation containing lowercase letters is followed by a period. Latin words are italicized in the listing below, but Latin abbreviations are not.

abbr. abbreviated, abbreviation
abr. abridged, abridgement
AD *anno Domini*, in the year of the Lord (precedes numerals: AD 2000); see CE
adapt. adapted by, adaptation
aet. *aetatis*, at the age of
ALS autographed letter signed
anon. anonymous
ante before
app. appendix
approx. approximate, approximately
art., arts. article, articles
assoc. association
attrib. attributed to
b. born
BC before Christ (follows numerals: 460 BC); see BCE

BCE before the common era (increasingly used instead of BC)
bibliog. bibliographer, bibliography
biog. biographer, biography
bk. book
bull. bulletin
© copyright (followed by a year)
c., ca. *circa*, about (used with approximate dates: c. 1340)
CE Common Era (increasingly used instead of AD)
cf. confer, compare (used chiefly in reference notes to acknowledge a contradictory or contrasting opinion)
ch., chs. chapter, chapters
col., cols. column, columns
comp. compiler, compiled by
cp. compare

227

d. died

diss. dissertation

doc., docs. document, documents

ed., eds. editor, edition, edited by; editors, editions

e.g. *exempli gratia*, for example (ordinarily preceded and followed by a comma; not to be confused with *i.e.*)

enl. enlarged

esp. especially (as in "see Mason, esp. ch. 3")

et al. *et alii*, and others (Used for more than three authors in MLA style and for more than five in APA style: Tyler et al. Note that *et* is a word and is not followed by a period.)

etc. *et cetera*, and others, and so forth

et seq. *et sequens*, and the following

f., ff. and the following page, pages (Use after a page number, but 31–38 is more meaningful than 31ff.)

fig., figs. figure, figures

fl. *floruit*, flourished, lived (Use when dates of birth and death are unknown: fl. 1182–1201.)

front. frontispiece

fwd. foreword by, foreword

ibid. *ibidem*, in the same place (used only in documentation; never used in MLA style and seldom in any other)

idem the same as previously mentioned

i.e. *id est*, that is (ordinarily preceded and followed by commas; not to be confused with *e.g.*)

illus. illustrated by, illustrator, illustration

infra below

introd. introduced by, introduction

jour. journal

l., ll. line, lines (Spell out if there could be confusion with the numbers one or eleven.)

loc. cit. *loco citato*, in the place cited (another virtually obsolete Latin term; used in the text to refer to a passage previously cited)

mag. magazine

misc. miscellaneous

ms., mss. manuscript, manuscripts (sometimes written in full capitals with no periods)

n., nn. note, notes ("142n." means a note on page 142.)

narr. narrator, narrated by, narrative

NB *nota bene*, mark well, take careful note

n.d. no date

no. number

n.p. no place of publication (when used before the colon in a bibliographical listing)

n. pag. no pagination

n.s. new series (used for periodicals published in more than one series of volumes)

NS New Style (used when necessary for a date after 1752 reckoned by the Gregorian calendar)

obs. obsolete

op cit. *opere citato*, the work cited (used after an author's name in a secondary citation; never used in MLA style; virtually obsolete, like *ibid.*)

orch. orchestrated by, orchestra

o.s. old series, original series (used with periodicals; cf. *n.s.*)

OS Old Style (used when necessary for a date before 1752 reckoned by the Julian calendar)

p., pp. page, pages (not used before page numbers in MLA style)

passim here and there (used for scattered references: "Ch. 6 passim" or "152–56 et passim")

perf. performer, performed by

per se in or of itself (Avoid using if possible.)

post after

pref. preface

proc. proceedings

prod. producer, produced by

pseud. pseudonym

pt., pts. part, parts

qtd. quoted

quot. quotation

q.v. *quod vide*, which see (used for a cross-reference)

rev. reviewed by, review; revised by, revision (Spell out if ambiguous.)

rpt. reprint, reprinted

sc., scs. scene, scenes

scil. *scilicet*, namely

ser. series

sic thus (written in brackets after an obvious error [sic] in a quotation)

soc. society

st., sts. stanza, stanzas

sup. *supra*, above

supp. supplement

s.v. *sub verbo*, under the word (used to refer to an item in an alphabetized list)

TLS typewritten letter signed

trans. translator, translated by, translation

v., vid. *vide*, see

v., vs. *versus*, against

var. variant

viz. *videlicit*, namely, that is

vol., vols. volume, volumes

writ. writer, written by

Library Terms and Abbreviations

Like all professionals, librarians have their own specialized vocabulary. Some of the more common terms and abbreviations are defined here.

abstract a summary of the substance of a book or an article; useful for evaluating the relevance of a source before looking for the original

ALA American Library Association

analytical entry a catalog card for a portion of a work; e.g., a play in an anthology

annotated bibliography a listing of sources with a brief evaluation and identification of each; also called a *critical bibliography*

BIP *Books In Print*, annual author, title, and subject indexes of books currently available from publishers.

CBEL *Cambridge Bibliography of English Literature* (**NCBEL** designates the revised edition.)

CBI *Cumulative Book Index*, a monthly author, title, and subject listing of books published in English; annual and biennial cumulations

CIS Congressional Information Service, publishers of indexes and abstracts of government publications

Congr. Rec. *Congressional Record*

cumulation the recombination of entries from several issues of an index into a single alphabetical arrangement

DAB *Dictionary of American Biography*

DAE *Dictionary of American English*

descriptor a reference word keyed to an entry in an index; also called *search term, key word, primary term,* or *permuterm*; essential to the retrieval of computerized data

dictionary catalog a card catalog in which all cards are filed in a single alphabetization

divided catalog a card catalog in which author, title, and subject cards are filed in separate alphabetizations

DNB *Dictionary of National Biography*

edition bound copies of a book printed from a single setting of type

ERIC Educational Resources Information Center

f. folio, a book more than fifteen inches high; probably shelved with oversized books rather than according to its call number

Festschrift a collection of essays by several authors in a commemorative volume to honor an event or a person

GPO Government Printing Office

incunabula books printed from movable type before 1501

journal a publication such as a newspaper or a news magazine; also a periodical intended for specialists, often called a *scholarly journal* (e.g., *Journal of Political Economy*)

LC Library of Congress

LHUS *Literary History of the United States*

magazine a periodical of general interest, usually published weekly or monthly

OED *Oxford English Dictionary*

per. periodical; on a catalog card an indication that a journal is shelved in the periodical room

periodical a publication that appears at regular intervals; generally used for magazines and journals, sometimes for newspapers

q. quarto, a book eleven to fifteen inches high (cf. *f.* above)

quarterly a scholarly journal published four times a year (e.g., *Film Literature Quarterly*)

recto the front of a printed page; the right-hand page of an opened book; always odd-numbered (cf. *verso*)

ref. reference; "Ref." on a catalog card indicates that a work is shelved in the Reference Room.

review generally a journal that emphasizes critical articles and book reviews (e.g., *American Political Science Review*)

see a cross-reference from a heading that is not used to one that is used (viable)

see also a cross-reference from one viable heading to another viable heading; often abbreviated "sa"

serial a general term for any publication issued in a consecutive sequence (e.g., periodicals, newspapers, yearbooks, installments of a work published in successive issues of a magazine)

shelf list a library's holdings listed by call numbers, often in the form of a computer printout

TLS (London) *Times Literary Supplement*

tracing descriptors on a library card indicating other headings under which a work is listed; also called *added entries*

ULS *Union List of Serials*, a useful, though out-of-date, listing of U.S. magazines, their publishing history, and libraries where they can be found

UMI University Microfilms International

union catalog an online or card catalog listing the holdings of a group of cooperating libraries

verso the back of a printed page; the left-hand page of an opened book; always even-numbered (cf. *recto*)

vertical file pamphlets, clippings, and similar material not listed in the catalog but filed in folders

Publishers' Names

MLA style uses shortened forms of publishers' names in Works Cited. If a name is usually abbreviated, the abbreviation is acceptable: e.g., GPO (Government Printing Office), MLA (Modern Language Association), UMI (University Microfilms International). The words *University Press* are abbreviated U and P without periods and are placed where they occur in the name of the press:

Vanderbilt UP
U of Arizona P
UP of Mississippi

To shorten the name in other cases, use the following pattern. If the name of the publisher is the name of a person (e.g., Harry N. Abrams), use the last name (Abrams); if it is a compound name (e.g., Harcourt Brace Jovanovich, Inc.), use only the first name (Harcourt). To illustrate, the MLA shortened versions for a few publishers' names are listed below.

ALA American Library Association
Appleton Appleton-Century-Crofts
Barnes Barnes and Noble Books
Beacon Beacon Press, Inc.
Bobbs The Bobbs-Merrill Co., Inc.
Dodd Dodd, Mead and Co.

Doubleday Doubleday and Co. Inc.
Dutton E. P. Dutton, Inc.
Farrar Farrar, Straus, and Giroux, Inc.
Gale Gale Research, Inc.
Harper Harper and Row, Inc.; HarperCollins Publishers, Inc.

Knopf Alfred A. Knopf, Inc.
Lippincott J. B. Lippincott Co.
Little Little, Brown and Company, Inc.
McGraw McGraw-Hill, Inc.
MLA Modern Language Association of America
Norton W. W. Norton and Co., Inc.
Pocket Pocket Books

Prentice Prentice-Hall, Inc.
Putnam G. P. Putnam's Sons
Rand Rand McNally and Co.
Random Random House, Inc.
Scribner's Charles Scribner's Sons
Viking The Viking Press, Inc.

Months and States

Months of more than four letters are abbreviated in a citation but are written out in the text of a paper.

Jan.	May	Sept.
Feb.	June	Oct.
Mar.	July	Nov.
Apr.	Aug.	Dec.

A state name is abbreviated after the name of a city in an address, but in the name of a university press and in most other instances, it should be written out. State names are not included in MLA citations. Conventional abbreviations for states with names of more than four letters are listed on the left; two-letter postal forms (written without periods), which are generally acceptable, are listed on the right.

Ala.	AL	Ky.	KY	N. Dak.	ND
Alas.	AK	La.	LA	Ohio	OH
Ariz.	AZ	Me.	ME	Okla.	OK
Ark.	AR	Md.	MD	Oreg.	OR
Calif.	CA	Mass.	MA	Pa.	PA
Colo.	CO	Mich.	MI	R.I.	RI
Conn.	CT	Minn.	MN	S.C.	SC
Del.	DE	Miss.	MS	S. Dak.	SD
D.C.	DC	Mo.	MO	Tenn.	TN
Fla.	FL	Mont.	MT	Tex.	TX
Ga.	GA	Nebr.	NE	Utah	UT
Haw.	HI	Nev.	NV	Vt.	VT
Ida.	ID	N.H.	NH	Va.	VA
Ill.	IL	N.J.	NJ	Wash.	WA
Ind.	IN	N. Mex.	NM	W. Va.	WV
Iowa	IA	N.Y.	NY	Wisc.	WI
Kans.	KS	N.C.	NC	Wyo.	WY

Chicago Manual of Style (CMS)

The *Chicago Manual of Style*, 15th ed. (Chicago: U of Chicago P, 2003) is recommended in a number of fields and is so widely used that you are likely to encounter it in the course of your research. This appendix is meant to introduce you to some basic conventions of this style of documentation. Because CMS is intended for professional authors and editors, the amount of detail may be overwhelming for many student writers. A more manageable version of Chicago style is Kate L. Turabian, *A Manual of Style for Writers of Term Papers, Theses, and Dissertations*, 7th ed. (Chicago: U of Chicago P, 2007), a book known to generations of students (and their teachers) simply as *Turabian*.

CMS includes two styles of documentation—notes (sometimes used in conjunction with bibliographies) and parenthetical author-date citations used with a reference list. The latter is similar to APA style (Chapter 10). CMS notes may be either footnotes or endnotes. Because these notes contain complete bibliographical information, a separate bibliography is generally not included; for a class, however, you may be asked to provide both. CMS offers alternative ways of providing information, so be sure to employ forms consistently.

Four features of CMS style might be noted as a starting point.

1. In the CMS style using notes, notes are presented essentially as a single sentence, ending with a period and indented like a paragraph.
2. Chicago style does not abbreviate dates.
3. The *Chicago Manual of Style* does not shorten publishers' names to the extent that MLA does.
4. When the city of publication may not be well known, Chicago style adds the state (using the standard two-letter postal code).

The following sample notes illustrate citations for a book (notes 1 and 2), a selection in an anthology (3), a journal article (4), a magazine article (5), an online book (6), an online periodical article (7), a Web site (8 and 9), and a government document (10).

Book

1. Deborah Kennedy, *Helen Maria Williams and the Age of Revolution* (Lewisburg, PA: Bucknell University Press, 2002), 12.

Book

2. Jack Shadoian, *Dreams and Dead Ends: The American Gangster Film,* 2nd ed. (New York: Oxford University Press, 2003), 119.

Anthology

3. Colin Lucas, "Nobles, Bourgeois, and the Origins of the French Revolution," in *The French Revolution: Recent Debates and New Controversies,* ed. Gary Kates, 62 (New York: Routledge, 2002).

Periodical (Journal)

4. Rebecca L. Spang, "Paradigms and Paranoia: How Modern Is the French Revolution?" *American Historical Review* 108, No. 1 (2003): 122.

Periodical (Magazine)

5. Martin Smith, "History and the Media: Are You Being Hoodwinked?" *History Today,* March 2003, 29.

Online Book

6. G. H. Smith and G. J. McLelland, *On the Shoulders of Giants: A Course in Single Variable Calculus* (Sydney: University of New South Wales, 2003), NetLibrary e-book.

Online Periodical

7. Jay Edwards, "Structural Analysis of the Afro-American Trickster Tale," *Black American Literature Forum* 15, no. 4 (1981): 157, http://links.jstor.org/ (accessed January 30, 2008).

Web Site

8. Peter Hughes, "William Gaskell," Dictionary of Unitarian and Universalist Biography, http://www.uua.org/uuhs/duub/articles/williamgaskell.html (accessed January 30, 2008).

Web Site

9. National Council of Teachers of English, "Resolution on the Reading First Initiative," http://www.ncte.org/positions/statements/readingfirst (accessed February 14, 2009).

Government Document

10. Senate Subcommittee of the Committee on Appropriations, *Anthrax Decontamination: Hearing before a Subcommittee of the Committee on Appropriations,* 107th Cong., 1st sess., November 28, 2001, 13.

The preceding notes would take the following form if a separate listing of references were required.

Online Periodical

Edwards, Jay. "Structural Analysis of the Afro-American Trickster Tale." *Black American Literature Forum* 15, no. 4 (1981): 155–64. http://links.jstor.org/ (accessed January 30, 2008).

Web Site

Hughes, Peter. "William Gaskell." Dictionary of Unitarian and Universalist Biography, http://www.uua.org/

uuhs/duub/articles/williamgaskell.html (accessed January 30, 2008).

Book

Kennedy, Deborah. *Helen Maria Williams and the Age of Revolution*. Lewisburg, PA: Bucknell University

Press, 2002.

Anthology

Lucas, Colin. "Nobles, Bourgeois, and the Origins of the French Revolution." In *The French Revolution:*

Recent Debates and New Controversies, ed. Gary Kates, 44–67. New York: Routledge, 2002.

Web Site

National Council of Teachers of English. "Resolution on the Reading First Initiative," http://www.ncte.org/

positions/statements/readingfirst (accessed February 14, 2009).

Book

Shadoian, Jack. *Dreams and Dead Ends: The American Gangster Film*. 2nd ed. New York: Oxford University

Press, 2003.

Online Book

Smith, G. H., and G. J. McLelland. *On the Shoulders of Giants: A Course in Single Variable Calculus*. Sydney:

University of New South Wales, 2003. NetLibrary e-book.

Periodical (Magazine)

Smith, Martin. "History and the Media: Are You Being Hoodwinked?" *History Today,* March 2003, 28–30.

Periodical (Journal)

Spang, Rebecca L. "Paradigms and Paranoia: How Modern Is the French Revolution?" *American Historical*

Review 108, No. 1 (2003): 119–47.

Government Document

U. S. Congress. Senate. Subcommittee of the Committee on Appropriations. *Anthrax Decontamination:*

Hearing before a Subcommittee of the Committee on Appropriations, 107th Cong., 1st sess.,

November 28, 2001.

After you have given the complete information in a note citation, it is not necessary to repeat the full data when you cite the source again. CMS uses the name of the author and a
shortened form of the title along with the page number. When consecutive notes refer to the
same single source, CMS uses the abbreviation *ibid.* (*ibidem,* "in the same place") to replace the
name of the author and title as well as the page number if it does not change. The abbreviation is not italicized. The following set of notes illustrates a typical combination of first and
subsequent references.

1. Deborah Kennedy, *Helen Maria Williams and the Age of Revolution* (Lewisburg, PA: Bucknell University Press, 2002), 12.

2. Colin Lucas, "Nobles, Bourgeois, and the Origins of the French Revolution," in *The French Revolution: Recent Debates and New Controversies,* ed. Gary Kates (New York: Routledge, 2002), 62.

3. Ibid.

4. Ibid., 63.

5. Kennedy, *Helen Maria Williams,* 14–15.

The CMS author-date system, like MLA and APA in-text citations, provides an alphabetical list of references at the end of the paper and parenthetical references in the body of the paper. In author-date style, the list of references cited previously would take the following form.

Edwards, Jay. 1981. Structural analysis of the Afro-American trickster tale. *Black American Literature Forum* 15, no. 4: 155–64. http://links.jstor.org/ (accessed January 30, 2008).

Hughes, Peter. William Gaskell. Dictionary of Unitarian and Universalist Biography, http://www.uua.org/ uuhs/duub/articles/williamgaskell.html (accessed January 30, 2008).

Kennedy, Deborah. 2002. *Helen Maria Williams and the Age of Revolution.* Lewisburg, PA: Bucknell University Press.

Lucas, Colin. 2002. Nobles, bourgeois, and the origins of the French Revolution. In *The French Revolution: Recent debates and new controversies,* ed. Gary Kates, 44–67. New York: Routledge.

National Council of Teachers of English. 2002. Resolution on the Reading First Initiative. http://www.ncte.org/about/over/positions/category/read/107475.htm (accessed January 30, 2008).

Shadoian, Jack. 2003. *Dreams and dead ends: The American gangster film.* 2nd ed. New York: Oxford University Press.

Smith, G. H., and G. J. McLelland. 2003. *On the shoulders of giants: A course in single variable calculus.* Sydney: University of New South Wales. NetLibrary e-book.

Smith, Martin. 2003. History and the media: Are you being hoodwinked? *History Today,* March, 28–30.

Spang, Rebecca L. 2003. Paradigms and paranoia: How modern is the French Revolution? *American Historical Review* 108, no. 1: 119–47.

U. S. Congress. Senate. Subcommittee of the Committee on Appropriations. 2001. *Anthrax decontamination: Hearing before a Subcommittee of the Committee on Appropriations,* 107th Cong., 1st sess., November 28.

The parenthetical in-text citation would consist of the name(s) of the author(s), the date, and (if appropriate) the page number: (Kennedy 2002, 12), (Smith and McLelland 2003), (U. S. Senate Subcommittee 2001, 13), and so on.

Credits

7: Tufts Center For Animals and Public Policy

8: Courtesy AnimalConcerns.org

26: Reprinted by permission of Wright State University Libraries

27: Reprinted by permission of Wright State University Libraries

28: Reprinted by permission of Wright State University Libraries

33: Courtesy of Librarians' Internet Index

35: © 2008, EBSCO Publishing, Inc. All rights reserved. Used by permission.

36: © 2008, EBSCO Publishing, Inc. All rights reserved. Used by permission.

38: Copyright © 2009 LexisNexis, a division of Reed Elsevier Inc. All Rights Reserved. LexisNexis and the Knowledge Burst logo are registered trademarks of Reed Elsevier Properties Inc. and are used with the permission of LexisNexis.

39: © 2008, EBSCO Publishing, Inc. All rights reserved. Used by permission.

48: Books In Print® © 2009. R.R. Bowker LLC. Used with permission

49: Books In Print® © 2009. R.R. Bowker LLC. Used with permission

50: Reprinted with permission from Reader's Guide to Periodical Literature published by The H. W. Wilson Company.

51: © 2008, EBSCO Publishing, Inc. All rights reserved. Used by permission.

52: © 2008, EBSCO Publishing, Inc. All rights reserved. Used by permission.

54: © 2008, EBSCO Publishing, Inc. All rights reserved. Used by permission.

55: Courtesy of Thomson Reuters (Scientific) Inc. Source: Web of Science®

56: Courtesy of Thomson Reuters (Scientific) Inc. Source: Web of Science®

57: From BOOK REVIEW INDEX, Vol. 44, No. 1 2008. © 2008 Gale, a part of Cengage Learning, Inc. Reproduced by permission. www.cengage.com/permissions.

115: Paragraph from Sasha Frere-Jones, "Living Pains: Mary J. Blige's Chronic Brilliance," *The New Yorker,* 11 February 2008. Reprinted by permission of the author.

133: From Rawlins, THE WRITER'S WAY, 7E. © 2009 Heinle/Arts & Sciences, a part of Cengage Learning, Inc. Reproduced by permission. www.cengage.com/permissions

143: Sample title page of academic journal LEVIATHAN. Used by permission of Blackwell Publishing Ltd.

Index